MABEL DODGE LUHAN

Edge of Taos Desert

AN ESCAPE TO REALITY

VOLUME FOUR OF

INTIMATE MEMORIES

HARCOURT, BRACE AND COMPANY

NEW YORK

EDGE OF TAOS DESERT

TONY   *by Sally Flavin*

*He who loves with passion lives
on the edge of the desert.*

EAST INDIAN PROVERB

Illustrations

ILLUSTRATIONS

EDGE OF TAOS DESERT

Chapter One

THE LAST evening I spent at 23 Fifth Avenue is still vivid in my memory. The large living room was softly lighted at each end, and dinner was served before the oakwood fire.

We left that room, with the fire glowing and the lights burning upon the patient household gods that had moved around with me, as though I were just going to pay a visit next door.

I went out of there intending to return. I was going to the Southwest, a little known neighborhood, for perhaps a fortnight, because I wanted to see what Maurice was doing, for his letters had intrigued me. I had always heard of people going to Florida or California, and more occasionally to the West, but no one ever went to the Southwest. Hardly anyone had ever even heard of Santa Fe.

I armed myself with letters of introduction to several individuals who stood out in that unknown and unexplored land. Among them, one was to Ford Harvey and another to Lorenzo Hubbell. These letters were both given me, after some effort to find people who had been to New Mexico, by a priest named Father Douglas who had lived near a tribe named Hopi. He was a friend of Sister Beatrix's, and he had told me strange, wonderful stories about those people.

Ridgely Torrence, too. He and Olivia came to dinner one evening before I left. Leo Stein was also there, I believe. I think it was he who brought me a tome with many reproductions of Aztec and Mayan deities, and I pored over these. As people's minds begin to churn and bring up bits of relevant oddities for the benefit of a friend traveling out of the familiar radius, so Ridgely, his eyes widened to their utmost, related tales of Indian magic told him by a friend who had "been there."

One story was of a white man who had been taken into a tribe because the Indians liked him and to a certain extent trusted him. That is, they trusted him to the extent of allowing him to be present at some of their ceremonies blindfolded! Evidently they were right, for he told all he *could* tell. One of the things he told was that he knew the Indians had the power of levitation, but he didn't know how they did it. People went on journeys in the air, he said, went on errands to a distant spot and returned in a short time. Once they took him down into a hole in the ground. It was a round, underground chamber with a roof made of seven portions, by tree trunks joined and fitted together, with heavy dirt on the top. In the center of this roof, a round opening to the sky, and below it, resting on the earth, lay a great round stone. There was a stout thong made of hide tied about the stone with its end lying on the ground. The Indians sat in a circle on their haunches, their backs against the earthen wall. But first they blindfolded the white man.

Then they began a low chanting over and over again like a mantra. The man said they kept this up for a while and presently he felt a change in the atmosphere, as though someone moved, or broke the circle, and after that a low humming was added to the chant, and at regular intervals a wind passed against his cheeks as though the air was heavily displaced before him. Round and round him something moved, each time faster while the humming sound grew higher pitched. Something rose on the solid body of the chant—rose in the room, fanning him briskly, higher and higher until he no longer felt the air moving on his face and it stirred his hair no more, but the great whine of an enormous rotary motor filled the hollow chamber of earth above him. For a few seconds only, and then, apparently, it passed out through the roof and soared away. The man heard it humming farther and farther off, then growing so dim that he couldn't hear it any more. The Indians continued their chanting, and they sat there and sat there—he didn't know how long. Finally he heard *it* coming back. He distinguished that low, far-away humming. It came nearer until it was a roaring overhead, and then it was inside the chamber with him. Once more he felt the air stir across his face as the thing passed and repassed him. It slowed down and its whine, too, sank to a low, deep sound. It came to rest in the center, and the men stopped chanting and began talking in Indian. One among them told a tale. He was narrating something. Others questioned him and he answered. When they ended, they unfolded the cloth from the white man's eyes —and everything looked exactly as it had before. The light was faded a little from the room, that was all. Maybe two hours had passed. The circle of Indians was complete, as it had been, the stone was in the same place. . . .

Ridgely's story touched the love of power that is latent in us all. We felt the secret tincture stir and mingle with our blood, and reborn again for the thousand thousandth time was the desire to know How.

"We have still to discover how the stones of the Pyramids were raised," said Leo. "It is only conjecture that attributes it to slave labor. And I doubt very much whether the great stones of these Mayan temples were raised by hand," he went on, turning over the leaves of his book. "Possibly they had hold of some law we have replaced by mechanical invention."

I took up the *Story of Atlantis* by Ignatius Donnelly from

the table: "They say the Atlanteans had a great many powers they lost because they abused them," I murmured a little coldly, because I was afraid someone would jeer at me. One could speak of Atlantis all right to Ridgely, but not to Leo or Olivia.

Just as I feared, Leo looked smilingly contemptuous and replied, "Oh, I do not think it is necessary to go as far as the myths of Atlantis," he said kindly; and his mouth turned down at the corners.

"How *far* people will or will not go determines their sense of superiority over others," I thought, "and here I am going to the *Southwest* where none of them has gone! But I might be going to Atlantis, for all they know! For Leo, though, it would not be Atlantis, while for me it would. Leo would call it by a safer name and feel superior—just as I would call it by a far-away, magical name and feel superior myself!"

When I left, on the last night, I only took along a suitcase and a small trunk.

"Well, I want a vacation," I said to myself. "I've had a horrid time lately. I feel like a Change."

I got it. My life broke in two right then, and I entered into the second half, a new world that replaced all the ways I had known with others, more strange and terrible and sweet than any I had ever been able to imagine.

Whether it was to Atlantis I went or not I do not know, nor have I ever been interested in conjecturing about it. I suppose when one gets to heaven one does not speculate about it any more. And the same must be true of hell. Anyway, I was through with reading books about Atlantis, Rosicrucianism, the Seven Worlds of Theosophy, or about any other mythical things. I entered into a new life that they were concerned with and I was done with reading any books for a long time.

Chapter Two

THE TRAIN was crowded with Christmas holiday young people and the journey seemed interminable to me. I had telegraphed John, who was spending the winter with the Rumseys at Cody, to meet me in Santa Fe for his vacation. I hadn't seen him for months, for he had gone out there after he left the Morristown School in the spring, and when Maurice appeared in their midst upon his solitary honeymoon, this had so horrified John that he had begged to stay through the winter.

Bob Rumsey, the hero of Rumsey's Pond, the hero of so many young hearts, married now to a woman his mother's age, had undertaken to console my son for a mother's inconsiderateness. He was tutoring John himself—preparing him for Yale, which he had influenced the boy to choose. I myself would have preferred him to go to Harvard. Yale seemed to me smug and self-righteous and to my mind produced blue-eyed boys who were not on to themselves.

I had a mental picture of John and Maurice on the station platform at Lamy, where my train appeared, from the time-table, to let me out at some distance from Santa Fe. They would be standing there with eager faces and a large, closed car to drive me to the house Maurice had rented. This house, like houses in general, presented itself to me in a blur of warmth, light, and color—with cushions, flowers, white enamel, shining metal, and a table set ready for a delicious meal. That is what a house suggested of its own accord.

7

Not accustomed to traveling by myself, I got on all the wrong trains, and the final one was the kind that is full of children eating bananas and apples, and that stops at every station, and as the last afternoon dragged on, I could hardly endure it. My heart was pounding with impatience, for in spirit I had already arrived and only my body was left behind on the smelly train. Every time we stopped I went to the door and sniffed the clean air that was so good after New York.

Finally about five o'clock, we stopped at a little place for quite a while. From the window I saw two girls in big hats and riding clothes waiting on their horses beside the station platform. There were two or three old cars standing there too. The station-house was of ancient gray wood, and the open space behind it was worn and dusty, but there was the loveliest light all over everything and an empty road leading away, and beyond, just beyond, the bluest mountains I had ever seen. In an instant I rejected that train and ran out to where the automobiles stood. No drivers were about, so I blew a blast on one of the horns and this summoned a long, slow boy from somewhere.

"Listen! This train is supposed to reach Lamy by eleven o'clock. Can't you motor me to Santa Fe quicker than that? Isn't there a road?"

"Guess I can," answered the boy, without much interest.

"Well, wait till I get my bag." I was breathless and excited. Out in the still air everything sounded so strange. My own voice sounded out of key in my ears. "Why does it feel like church?" I wondered.

Against the windows of the train were glued the pale faces of passengers who were watching me with dreary attention (as they had been doing all day). The more they watched, the greater grew the distance between us, or so I had felt. What possible connection had I with them? (Dreary, drab people—I wish I could cut myself off from you forever, I thought to myself.)

I rushed into the train and secured my bag and my fur coat, and left behind on the seat *The New Republic,* the *Atlantic Monthly,* and the *Mercure de France.* And I left behind the staleness and the dull, enduring humans all dressed in browns and blacks, with their grimy handkerchiefs in pockets gritty with the deposit of their dull lives!

I ran into the station and telegraphed Maurice:

AM MOTORING TO SANTA FE WILL MEET YOU AT YOUR
HOUSE LOVE   MABEL

And then I hurled myself at the big boy who stood dazed beside the waiting automobiles.

"Now we must hurry!" I cried. "I want to beat that train."

"This hyah is my car, lady," said the boy, leading me to the end one. It was the most dilapidated vehicle I had ever seen. It had no top and its black, shiny leather seats were ripped and gray. Horsehair bulged through the rents. I didn't care. I hastened into the back seat, my bag in front with the driver, and he started to crank the engine. Nothing happened, and after he yanked it round and round, he stood up and smiled with some embarrassment at the small crowd that now surrounded us. One of the girls on horse-back called out:

"Where you think you're goin' in that car, 'Lisha?"

He didn't answer her or look at her, and finally the motor gave a start as though awaking from a trance, and began to throb violently. 'Lisha wiped his face with a red handkerchief and slowly lowered himself into the ancient seat. From

2

where I sat, only his huge hat appeared before me, and in that bright winter evening light we started off down the alluring road towards the mountains. I heaved a great sigh of relief. How good it felt! How *good* this fresh air, this clear simplicity.

But all too soon I began to notice a painful jarring under me.

"Wait a moment. What *is* this bumping, anyway?" I tapped him on the shoulder. He turned his face towards me and called:

"Oh—them back springs is busted. I guess we'll make it though. If these two cylinders hold out. . . ."

A horse poked his head through the wayside thicket and started to cross the road slowly. 'Lisha hastily leaned forward and squeezed a rubber bulb. No sound whatever.

"Horn's gone," he announced cheerfully.

"What kind of a car is this anyway?" I asked angrily.

"Dodge," said he.

The wind was whistling past us now and I could scarcely hear him above the rattle and wheeze of the straining machine and its antique body.

"How much is this trip going to cost?" I cried.

"Oh, 'bout sixteen dollars if we make it," he returned.

He was leaning forward now, in the crouching attitude of a racer. He had a cigarette hanging from the corner of his mouth and his ashes blew black into my eyes every time he turned towards me, so I stopped talking to him. Holding myself as firmly as I could in the hopping motion of the back end, I began to watch the country we were careening through. I thought I had never seen a landscape reduced to such simple elements.

There was the long dirt road stretching out straight ahead and becoming a thin line in the distance, and on either side a desert, flat, dark green, and soft-looking, that rolled away for miles and miles, empty, smooth, and uninterrupted until it reached the mountains on the west side—just the sky horizon on the other. The sun was sinking behind the range. Its rays came over to strike us sideways, warming us on the left hand while from the right a coldness rested upon my cheek. The mountains were a long blue-black wavering line along the western sky—the sun sank heavily below them all of a sudden, which made them appear thin and flat. The sky changed rapidly from rose to green, and the evening air grew cold and thin and flat like ice. The desert on either side of the road changed to black velvet, unfathomably soft and wide, and suddenly it was night.

"Gee! We got no lights," suddenly said 'Lisha.

"No *lights?* Well, how do you think we can travel until ten o'clock or eleven without *lights?*" I cried. I was beginning to get mad.

"Dunno. P'rhaps we can make Wagon Mound."

(*Wagon Mound!* What a name! I thought, incensed.)

"How far is that?"

"Oh, 'bout fifty, I guess."

"And how far is that from Santa Fe?"

"Wal, I never been there. I don't rightly know how fur *that* is. But I guess we kin make it. If these cylinders hold out, we kin."

As the road grew darker, he began to run into ruts and bump more and more.

"This is pleasant," I said to myself. "Out in the middle of a desert with a half-wit boy and no lights." I began to get hungry, too.

"Can we eat in Wagon Mound?"

"Wal, I guess we can find sumpin'," he said, hopefully.

Suddenly there was the most wonderful smell in the darkness. It made one's heart jump.

"What *is* that smell?"

"Sage. I guess thar's some cattle along in there," he answered, pointing into the night.

Never mind. I couldn't stay irritated. I was cold and tired from the jolts and bumps, and hungry, too, but everything above and below that personal discomfort was all right. It was a fresh, beautiful world that surrounded me on all sides. I had a sense of renewal and a new awareness.

We fumbled on and on through the darkness. 'Lisha must have kept on the road by instinct, for I am sure he couldn't see it. I lost all track of time and place. I was an unidentified atom pressing forward in space, a wide, perfumed space, that was dotted with white stars liquid and bright as dew. I felt humble from a kind of unfamiliar richness and savor the universe possessed and as my body grew numb, my heart grew clear. After ages of time passed, I saw a little group of yellow lights ahead.

"Look! What lights are those?" I exclaimed, tapping 'Lisha.

"Guess that's Wagon Mound," said he. We bumped into it. There was a station beside a railway track, dimly lighted by oil lamps, and I suddenly longed for a train!

"When does a train go through here for Santa Fe?" I asked the old man in the ticket office.

"Tonight's train goes through in 'bout twenty-five minutes," he told me. "You kin get on her then."

I hastily sent another telegram to Maurice, saying:

COMING BY TRAIN AFTER ALL LOVE

And then I asked the man:

"Is there any place to eat here?"

"Wal, I reckon you kin git a bite over at Mis' Perkins'. She gen'ally serves supper at six-thirty but mebby you kin git a bite." He pointed down a road. A lamp shone in a window and I hurried out to 'Lisha.

"Over there," I pointed. "Hurry up. I'm going to catch this train when it comes in. But we can eat first."

He tried to hurry but he couldn't. The car, having stopped, refused to start again. Impatiently I picked up my skirts and ran down the dusty road to the lighted window.

I entered a room that had a long table in it. There was a stained white table-cloth on it, and in the center a cruet containing two bottles, and next to these, tomato catsup and Worcestershire sauce were grouped with salt and pepper-pots. A hanging oil lamp blazed down and lighted up a couple of men in shirt sleeves who sat leaning back on two legs of their chairs. They were smoking pipes. I grew dignified and wondered if it was dangerous here. I said, coldly:

"Could I get something to eat? I'm going to take a train in a few moments."

"Mis' Perkins!" called one of them.

An old woman appeared at the door at the end of the room. She had on a blue and white calico dress and a gray apron.

"Lady wants to eat," said the man, laconically, waving at me with his pipe. 'Lisha stepped into the light from behind me. He wanted to eat, too.

"Wal, I kin give you some beans and a coupla' fried eggs, I guess," she said.

"Well, I have to leave awfully soon. I don't think I'll wait for the eggs."

She disappeared and returned with a plate of sliced bread. I took a piece and it tasted like sawdust. 'Lisha sat down beside

2 ★

me and removed his hat and wiped his face with his red handkerchief.

"Some ride," he said.

"How much do I owe you so far?"

"Wal, I guess about five dollars. I got to go back," he replied.

The old woman brought in a dish of beans. They were *wonderful*. I ate all I dared, paid, and left as rapidly as I could without seeming undignified. I felt those men were trying to size me up. Perhaps they were and again perhaps they weren't. Anyway, I always felt guilty and slightly apologetic whenever I was alone in a strange place.

Outside the door, I ran with all my might to the station, for I saw the train in the distance. I just had time to buy a ticket and hasten into the lighted car. A familiar atmosphere greeted my nose! Good heavens! There were those same dreary passengers that I had left behind me forever! There *The New Republic!* There the old *Atlantic!* All the blank, pale, inquisitive faces turned towards me as I sank breathless into the seat I had left.

"Well," I thought, "I had some fresh air, anyway!"

When we pulled into the Lamy station, I looked for Maurice and John, but no one was there. A delicious odor of incense struck me vividly. It was nearly the best smell I had ever had in my life. "These smells are *alive*," I said to myself. "One could live in this country just for them!"

"What *is* that smell?" I asked the conductor, who was trying to help me off the train.

"Oh, they're burning *piñon* wood to make charcoal down the line there," he answered, and went on, "The Santa Fe train is right over there on that track."

I began to feel neglected. Here I was all alone in the middle

of the night going to a perfectly strange town! I had never
before been in such a situation. I managed to get on the new
train. It was tiny, and lighted at each end by a kerosene lamp.
Another man got on and sat across from me and looked at me
from under his hat brim, so I thought he looked sinister and
I composed my face into a cold, aloof expression. An old,
foreign-looking porter got on the train and shut the door
and it started with a lurch.

I peered out the window and I don't know how long it was
before I saw the lights of a town. It looked about as large as
Yonkers! The little train paddled into the station and there
was Maurice on the platform.

I got out and he seized me timidly by the arm, his face
a conflict of ruefulness and pleasure, for he never was un-
mitigatedly glad to see me. But then, I wasn't glad at all
to see him.

"Dar-r-r-ling! What *have* you been doing, jumping on and
off that train?"

"Oh, I got tired of it and got off. And got on again," I
answered, uncommunicatively. "Where is John?"

"Oh, he's staying with some people here. The Parsonses."

We were hurrying along now towards the outside of the
station.

"You know, darling, you didn't send him any money and
those Rumseys didn't provide him with any—and he arrived
without a *cent!* I was away at a dance myself. Here's the
stage. It will take us up to town."

"Maurice! No *car?*"

"Well, darling, I thought we'd go up in this. There are
very *few* cars here."

"Well, where's John now?"

"Well, he met this Sara Parsons. *I* introduced them. She's

a ve-r-r-r-y attractive girl. And they invited him to stay there. My little place is very small. . . ."

"Oh, Maurice!" My heart was sinking. "What about this girl?"

"John seems quite smitten! I am myself! A little. She has a pair of very fast horses she drives around. Very jolly."

The stage rolled from side to side and bowled us into town through the silent streets that were lined with leafless trees. There were very few street lamps. It seemed a sleepy little place. We drove into a large, empty plaza that looked European, and stopped there. The other passenger got out and reached a quarter up to the driver. "Thanks, José," he said and walked away. Then we drove up a hilly, narrow street past a convent or something. Maurice said:

"That's the College. St. Michael's. For boys." He acted like one who had lived there for some time. I resented that. It made me feel so inadequate and dependent. I saw a great many little low cottages of mud along this street and I began to wonder where Maurice's house was. Presently he stopped the stage at one of these mud huts.

"This is it," he said, and helped me out. My thoughts were all in a turmoil at the unexpectedness of everything. To reach this distant city finally, and to find both John and Sterne more or less *in love* (yes, they are—they're *in love*) with the same girl—and to be left standing on a dark street in front of a mud hovel that I had to enter and *sleep* in. I could hardly believe it was true. So *this* was the Southwest! *Well!*

Chapter Three

THE FOLLOWING morning Maurice's house shone in the deep yellow sunshine which flooded the three little rooms and made one ashamed of ill humor. From the very first day I found out that the sunshine in New Mexico could do almost anything with one: make one well if one felt ill, or change a dark mood and lighten it. It entered into one's deepest places and melted the thick, slow densities. It made one feel *good*. That is, alive.

The little house was white-washed inside and it had no furniture of any kind I was used to. A couple of unpainted, low, wooden couches served for beds; there were two or three pine tables and chairs and the chairs were hand-made and looked like the peasant chairs of Europe. Maurice's painting things were all about and he had several very bright-colored, striped woolen blankets thrown on the beds and on the blue-painted floor. His clothes hung in recesses that were cut into the thick adobe walls and these, too, had bright rugs hanging across them. Maurice called them "serapes."

He made a fire in a little arched fireplace and then he made breakfast on a blue kerosene oil stove, and we ate it in the sunshine. It was very different from anything I had ever done before. Through the window, one saw dark, rich mountains behind the house and the doors were open and the air was crisp and cold and sweet-smelling; and yet one was warm from the sunshine and the little snapping fire.

Maurice looked changed. He had on a gray flannel shirt,

open at the throat, riding trousers, and high, black riding boots. He looked really Russian now. This life and this place suited him. When we had eaten, he said:

"Go outside and sit in the sunshine. I'll wash up."

Behind the house, the land sloped upwards. It was hard and stony and dotted all over with small evergreen trees. He told me they were cedars. I broke off a twig and smelled it —and then tasted it. Bitter, pungent, strong taste of cedar! It entered and took possession right then forever.

I climbed the hill until I could look down over the town and saw that it lay in a large hollow with the snow-topped mountains all around it except where the long stretches of desert country sloped away southwards in vast, shimmering, gray-green masses that pulsated in the clear light. Everything was in such a high key that one couldn't tell whether it was light or dark, and the town, though it looked very still as it lay pale and flat on the ground, seemed to vibrate and to breathe. It was a living thing.

Out of the crouching buildings a pale yellow church lifted two square towers from which deep bells were ringing with a full, gay sound. It was curious how round and complete all sounds came to one's ears. Sitting there on that stern hillside, that had nothing soft and comfortable about it like other hills in milder places, I had a complete realization of the fullness of Nature here and how everything was intensified for one—sight, sound, and taste—and I felt that perhaps I was more awake and more aware than I had ever been before. It was a new enchantment and I gave myself up to it without resistance.

Then John came calling "Mother!" and I went down to meet him. He looked excited and happy. His hair was untidy and his finger-nails, I noticed, were terrible. But he had a yellow silk handkerchief knotted around his neck and spurs on his boots.

"This is a *swell* place, mother!" he told me at once. "You'll love it!"

Soon we walked down to the plaza. There were a lot of bare-limbed trees planted around the square, edging the padded-down, earthen paths that crossed it, and a Soldiers' Monument with the ugliness of the last century was there in the middle of it.

Santa Fe was the strangest American town I had ever seen. In that bright December sunshine the plaza was a queer mixture of oddities. There were wood-carts drawn by burros, with the short lengths of piñon wood made into square piles and set in sort of high cages, and these were led by dark Mexicans. The Americans outside the shops were all in riding clothes, with great-brimmed hats and silk scarves. They tied their horses to hitching posts when they were not riding around.

The first Indians I had ever seen, except at the circus, were there in the plaza that first morning. They had black, glossy hair, worn in a Dutch cut with brilliant, folded silk fillets tied around their bangs. With their straight features, medieval-looking blouses and all the rest, they were just like Maxfield Parrish illustrations.

I saw only two or three automobiles. People rode horseback or drove two-seated buggies, as Sara Parsons did; she appeared shortly, and made John and Maurice look bright. She was a small girl with green eyes and freckles. She, too, had on riding trousers and a leather coat. The only Americans I saw who looked like people I was accustomed to, were the shopkeepers in the few stores I went into. The plaza was mostly taken up by the old Governors' Palace, a long, low building with wooden posts that supported a roof over the sidewalk, a couple of dry-goods stores, two drug stores, several groceries, and some little cafés.

There was a curio shop run by a man named Collins. He had some wonderful serapes and I wanted to buy one right away, but Maurice said to wait—one could get them so cheap from the Mexicans.

Down a street, leading out of the plaza, was another curio shop, very crowded and dusty and full of atmosphere. It had a great jumble of antiquities in it, and on the roof there was an old ox cart with solid wooden wheels. A man named Candelario owned it. He had a dark, clever face, very observant and watchful. Wandering around the musty interior I started talking to him and told him I wanted to know the Indians. "No one can know an Indian except an Indian," he replied curtly.

The air of the whole town was perfumed by the piñon wood people burned in their houses, for piñon wood heated the city.

It was one of those neighborhoods where everyone knew everyone else, and already John and Maurice seemed to be part of it. They said hello to everybody they met, and kept stopping to introduce me to people. This made me ill at ease and my spirit turned back inward. These Americans seemed to me too eager and cordial. Why should they be so glad to see me?

Maurice bought some things for lunch and we walked back up the hill.

"Well, how do you like it?" asked John.

"I like the place—I don't care much for these *people*, though. Why are they so jolly and so oncoming?"

"Oh, they're all right! I guess most of them are lonesome because they're here because they *have* to be!"

"Why have to be?"

"Well, it's a cheap T.B. climate. That's why most of them come here."

"Yes, they come to get well and remain to paint," Maurice remarked sarcastically. "There are some of the worst painters here I've ever seen anywhere. I guess I'll take to sculpture!"

"How about your friends the Burlins?" I asked. "They're painters, aren't they? Where do *they* live?"

"Oh, they! They're more like pioneers. Paul really *sees* the material here. And Natalie Curtis collects Indian music, you know. They live right across from us. They asked me to bring you in there to tea today."

This made me stiff-necked right away. I couldn't see myself in that position at all and it made me feel sore all over even while I fought against my touchy egotism. I did manage to keep my mouth shut, however.

Maurice and John cooked a lunch together; they seemed to get along better than before. We had beefsteaks that were very tough, but they tasted marvelous, and fried potatoes. In fact, everything seemed to be fried. Then we had black coffee and some yellow cheese and crackers. I felt awfully sleepy right after lunch.

"That's the altitude," Maurice said. This was the first time I ever heard of altitude and I have been hearing about it ever since. "You see, we're nearly eight thousand feet high. You'd better lie down and rest."

I lay down and read a magazine and Maurice lighted one of those cigars of his and fussed around among his paints. John had secured some money from me and went off to pay his debts.

That after-lunch feeling in New Mexico has always persisted, as though one slowed down oneself while all around one the quick bright life went humming on.

Going across to tea at the Burlins, later, was the first really tiresome thing that happened. Their little adobe house was like Maurice's, only with more things done to the inside of it. These houses didn't seem to have real bedrooms. Any room might be a bedroom or a living room. The couches were so low that people slept only a foot or so above the floor, and they were called day-beds.

There was a good deal of bright paint about—yellow and blue—and Paul Burlin's modernist paintings here and there on the walls. Natalie Curtis, his wife, was a little old doll that had been left out in the sun and the rain. She had faded yellow hair, cut in a Buster Brown bob, and faded blue eyes. Paul was much younger and looked fresher. He had curly red hair above a round forehead, and the absent, speculative thoughtful look of an intelligent Jew.

A small woman sat on one of the day-beds knitting a khaki-colored sweater. She was presented: Mrs. Henderson. She smiled, they all smiled. Maurice smiled. I tried to and couldn't. I felt dead. We had tea and Mrs. Henderson began to talk about Harriet Monroe. Did I know her? I did. She framed words that showed me she and Harriet were co-editors of the *Poetry Magazine*. I didn't care. She told me how many sweaters she had knitted for their Red Cross. I didn't care about that, either. I generally forgot about the war when Maurice let me.

The others were talking about an Indian dance on Christmas Day at Santo Domingo—making plans to go the night before and see the mass at the church at midnight.

"We can sleep at the School House. I know the teacher,"

Mrs. Burlin was saying. There was a lot of talk about securing a car from someone—it must be a good one. The road was terrible from the sand that constantly blew across and covered it. . . .

Quite soon I got up to go and Mrs. Henderson asked me to come to tea at her house the next day. To get out of this —I certainly didn't want to begin going to tea parties out here!—I said, "Well, I think we'll motor up to a place called Taos tomorrow."

"*Taos?* Why?"

"Oh, a friend in New York told me to be sure and see it," I said, airily. Someone had—I couldn't remember who, though.

"But, *darling,* it's quite hard to go up there, I've heard," began Maurice, plaintively.

"And doesn't amount to anything," went on Paul Burlin. Sara Parsons came in.

"Hello!" she said, smiling, and blinking her green eyes.

"Mrs. Sterne is just talking about going up to Taos!" exclaimed Mrs. Henderson, with a kind, amused, round-cheeked smile.

"Taos? Heavens!" laughed Sara Parsons.

This all made me more and more determined to go.

"Why, there's nothing to Taos! It's just a little plaza where every other door is the entrance to a saloon!"

"Well, I'm going up to see it, anyway," I replied, getting up. They all got up. Maurice looked around at them apologetically behind my back, and then followed me out and across the street.

"Now, look here, Maurice. I don't like it here. All these people! I want to get *away* somewhere. I don't like living on this *street* and going to *tea parties!* You know you'll never work, living like this. I'm going to see what that Taos is like and rent a house there if it's nice. I'm going to find a car and motor up. You needn't go along if you don't want to, but I'm going. Tomorrow."

"Well, if you're determined, darling, I don't think you should go alone. Of course I'll go with you. There's a man—Mr. Craft—who has a little Ford car. Maybe he would drive us."

"Oh, do go and see. How far is it?"

"Well, it's a long day's drive. A very bad road, judging from the road out to Tesuque Pueblo! That takes over an hour and it's only a few miles."

"Are there Indians up there in Taos?"

"I guess so. There are Indians all over this country. But *why* go so far?"

"To get away from these *people*," I answered, irritably.

Chapter Four

AFTER the sunset, a fast wind came tearing over the town from the north. It penetrated through every chink in the house, under window-sills and door-frames. The fire blew perfumed blue smoke out into the room and seemed to lose its heat. It was bitter cold and we went to bed early to keep warm, heaping the serapes from the floor upon us. I could not believe I had sat out upon the ground only that morning toasted by the sun.

Maurice grew tender and protective when he saw me lying there bundled up to my nose in the yellow lamplight. He was always more comfortable, anyway, when I was lying down. He laughed and climbed in beside me.

"Darling Mabel! You look like a little girl! I'm afraid I'm very fond of you, rea-ally!" I liked him, too, that night; *liked* him, without any pain or urgency or need to analyze him.

"Let us try and make a nice life out here, Maurice. It seems to me we could if we would be more *alone* and you would work. There is something so real about this country. It makes people seem trivial and false. We've *always* had too many people around."

"But, dearest! You can't get along without them! Don't you remember how lonely you were on Monhegan Island?"

"But that was different. You were so queer there. And I had nothing to *do*. Here, it seems to me, the climate in itself is a career. I'd like to learn to cook and do things like that—with just you and John and me, together. Don't you think we could?"

"Well—we'll see. . . ."

"I have a feeling Taos is going to be just right for us," I murmured drowsily, and, sticking my nose down against his arm to avoid the flickering firelight in my eyes, I fell asleep.

We left the house soon after breakfast the next morning in Mr. Craft's Ford car. The sun was warmer than ever after the wild wind. Not a branch stirred in the bare trees. Everything was still. There was a smile in the sunlight over the quiet town and it had a Holy Sunday morning look.

"It looks like Sunday," said I.

"Well, it *is* Sunday," replied Mr. Craft. He was a small, hard-looking man with a rather experienced face and a weather-beaten skin. He owned one of the hotels in Santa Fe. When we drove through the plaza and up a street, he pointed out a large, square, yellow house back under some trees.

"That's where we live," he told me. "If you ever need rooms when you're in town, we can accommodate you. No meals, though."

It was a comfortable-looking house and looked more like Buffalo than most of the others I had seen. But now, as I looked, I saw that nearly all the houses in this part of town were more like the American houses I was used to. Red brick houses with wooden verandas, substantial frame houses of divers colors, set back in withered lawns with trees beside them that must have shaded them in the summer-time. Trees lined the concrete sidewalks on both sides of the street, too. It was really just like Buffalo except for the clear, yellow light that beamed over everything. I was glad when all of a sudden we were out of town. It happened very quickly without the gradual diminution in the neighborhood from luxurious homes to more modest ones and then on into poverty and slums. There was no outskirting sordidness. These large, pleasant houses stopped just before we crossed a bridge and there we were climbing a hill in country as empty of human life as one could desire.

The road was narrow and full of frozen ruts and we shook and joggled from one side of the car to the other. The sky was a burning, deep blue over us and my heart rose higher and higher until I was thrilling all over. It seemed to me I had never been happy before, just from being in good air and sunshine. Really, it seemed to me, I had never been happy before at all. I felt myself gathered altogether right there with nothing left behind in New York or anywhere else in the world.

"I am Here," I thought, with exultant surprise, and I looked at my hands and rubbed them together, feeling them both cold and warm from winter air and a hurrying heartbeat.

"I guess you folks must miss the Big City," remarked Mr. Craft out of the side of his face.

"Oh, no! *I* don't," I cried. "This is much nicer."

"Well, it's the capital of the state," he answered, looking at the little cedar trees climbing the hillside. "But except for them politicians, they's not much life goin' on here. I'd like to get to go to New York again, onct. Shows and things."

"Why, you have your own shows here! Those beautiful Indian dances," said Maurice in a sententious voice.

"Oh, them!" Mr. Craft sniffed. "Well, I guess they're all right for those fellers, but I don't take much stock in 'em. Feathers don't mean a thing in *my* life."

"How often do they dance?" I inquired eagerly.

"Oh, just when they feel like it, I guess. They're like the

rest of us. When they feel like dancin', they dance; and when they feel like drinkin', they get drunk."

"I haven't seen any Indians drunk since I've been here," Maurice said in an injured voice.

"Oh, well, perhaps *you* haven't. But I've heard it said they have high old times among themselves. People going by their villages tell of how they heard 'em singin' and yellin' till all hours of the morning. We don't mix into it, though. They keep to themselves and we keep to ourselves. No use tryin' to get into that."

I wondered just what "that" really was.

We had slowly climbed the big hill and now we were winding down the other side of it. Santa Fe was behind on the other side, warm in its hollow bowl. The mountains over to our right were huge, black, tumbled forms with snow capping their peaks. The masses of snow against the sky cut clear into the thick blue and made it darker. Three men, muffled to their ears, came up the road, driving a string of tiny burros and each of these staggered under a load of cut wood that was roped over the back and around the two sides.

"A day late!" remarked Mr. Craft. "Too much mañana!"

"*What?*" I queried.

"I reckon they were trying to get to sell that wood in town yesterday. They gen'ally come in Saturdays. They bring it in most days but more come in on Saturdays."

"Does everybody burn wood in Santa Fe?" I asked. I couldn't see how they ever got enough to keep the town supplied.

"Yes-sir. Nearly everybody burns wood from these hills. You don't see any coal smoke over our town except coming out of the Pen'. If you couldn't make a livin' any other way, you could chop wood! That's how most of these Mex's support themselves."

We passed through a dip at the bottom of the hill with a few adobe houses, some set alongside the curving road, and some back in the fields with old orchards beside them. I liked these long, low adobe houses out here in the country better than the ones on College Street, where Maurice lived. They seemed to grow right out of the earth. They all had pale blue smoke coming straight up out of their squat chimneys, and there were bright geraniums in their small-paned windows. Home-like.

"This is called Tesuque," Mr. Craft explained, waving his hand vaguely around. "There's one of them pee-eblos along ahead named for it."

"Yes, I've been in there. It's very interesting," Maurice broke in. I could see he was getting tired of Mr. Craft. So was I.

"Oh, can't we stop and see it?" I cried.

"Well, we better keep goin', I think. Can't ever tell what may happen. We've got to make Taos tonight and this road up there is something awful."

"But it's only seventy-five miles, isn't it?"

"I guess you ain't used to the *kind* of miles we have out here," chuckled Mr. Craft. "Do you know we've only come seven *now?*"

We *had* been moving for quite a while, I thought. Well, we kept going and going and after a while we climbed another hill and looked down over the strangest landscape I had ever faced. Great stretches of pink and yellow hills only occasionally dotted with a few small evergreens here and there —miles and miles billowing away on all sides with our tiny road meandering through it.

On our right, vastly distant, a group of round and square structures showed ruined battlements and great buttresses like the hill towns in Italy seen from afar, or perhaps like monas-

3 ★

teries in the high deserts of Tibet. Jagged pink peaks pierced
the sky to one side, forming a climbing canyon. Looking down
upon these miles was like seeing a relief map of some unknown and unexplored country.

"Why, it looks *mythical,* Maurice! Look, it seems to heave
up and down! Isn't that *queer?* There should be camels and
elephants in it. . . ."

"They do say an old-timer saw two camels pass across here
onct going east," Mr. Craft volunteered. "Escaped from a circus, I s'pose."

"*Circus!*" I exclaimed. "A circus from Mars, then!"

"Well, we had Ringling out here a couple of years ago."
His voice was injured, now.

The going was hard across those featureless sands. We
struggled over a road that was half buried in some places and
where Mr. Craft had to dig his way through and Maurice
had to help him lift the car out of the holes it plowed itself
into; but finally we reached a harder bottom and then climbed
out onto a mountain on the other side. It had been, like a
passage through a pink and yellow dream, surrounded on
all sides with that dry, unmagnetic sand—blue sky staring
down and the bright air making everything seem to waver and
vibrate around us.

We reached a village called Santa Cruz, with a big church
in a little plaza, and here we stopped to drink water, for
we were tired and the men were dry and the car was boiling.

"We got to hurry to make Embudo for lunch," exclaimed
Mr. Craft, looking at his watch.

I cannot describe every step of the journey—it would take too
long. But by noon, after passing several hamlets and crossing
another desert, we reached the opening of a canyon where

the Rio Grande ran narrowly between the walls of mountains. The noonday sun shone down upon the fast green river; it had great, black chunks of lava with soft-looking edges piled along the shores, fallen there from the sides of the steep slopes on either side. This lava lined the canyon, making it unutterably dark in an unnatural kind of sunny way. I had never been in the midst of lava before, and I stared, fascinated by it. Beside the river, where the water had washed it for centuries, it was smooth and shone with a dark, lustrous polish that had something reptilian in it. While I looked at those great cubes and squares tossed together upon each other, I saw them all move, swaying together, swinging. The mountainside moved gently, too. Nothing was rigid and fixed in its place. I rubbed my eyes, not believing what I saw. But I had not made a mistake. Ever since that day, I have seen the mountains and the hills move from time to time. The rocks vibrate and sway, dancing together. In this country everything lives and moves and has its being.

Soon after twelve, we crossed the river on an insecure and casual bridge, and drew up at a small, bleak, repellent-looking building. This was Embudo, where the little train of the Denver and Rio Grande Railroad stopped between Taos Junction and Santa Fe, and where the conductor and passengers got out for lunch.

We went into the solitary house and a blast of hot, fetid air struck upon us from the stove in the end of the room. The smell was horrible, made up of old cigar smoke, boiled meat, and men. A long table, with a grayish white cloth, stood in the middle of the room and several men lounged there, picking their teeth. In this country it seemed as though people's living and all their ways showed up much more unattractively than in other places. There was the bright, immaculate outside life going on, in a high, happy vibration of its own, but wherever people landed and attempted to dig into it and live, they seemed to be in a strong and unbearable contrast to it. The shining ether that brought out every height and depth of tone and color in the natural world and enhanced them beyond the ordinary, made mankind appear dingy and alien to the environment. Nowhere in the world were those words so true: *"L'homme est un animal imprévu sur la terre. . . ."* Yes, that was how these people seemed, for the most part: "unexpected" and uncomfortable.

A woman brought us something to eat. She had a discontented, put-upon expression, and her dinner was ignoble. I got outside again as quickly as I could and sat in the car waiting for the others. It was intensely silent out there without a stirring of anything; and yet I seemed to hear, inside the silence, a high, continuous humming, like a song; and it made me happy. For the first time in my life I heard the world singing in the same key in which my own life inside me had sometimes lifted and poured itself out. But that had always been a solitary thrill before this. Now the world and I were met together in the happiest conjunction. Never had I felt so befriended.

I looked up at the hills that rose on either side of me. They were dotted with dark, deep, green cedars and the pinkish earth showed between. Along the canyon the branches of cottonwood trees were a film of gray lace, tinged with lavender: the most wintry trees I had ever seen. The river moved slowly here, profound and silent. Clumps of red willows melted into the shore line, and some way up ahead, yellow spires of sandstone suddenly thrust their peaks into the Ionian blue of the sky.

"Holy! Holy! Holy!" I exclaimed to myself. "Lord God

Almighty!" I felt a sudden recognition of the reality of natural life that was so strong and so unfamiliar that it made me feel unreal. I caught a fleeting glimpse of my own spoiled and distorted nature, seen against the purity and freshness of these undomesticated surroundings. " 'Tis the beauty, not the strangeness, turns the traveler's heart to stone!"

My courage diminished a little and I felt somehow unequal to the power that rose all about me. Surely no one had ever been able to dominate and overcome this country where life flowed unhampered in wave upon wave of happiness and delight in being. Everything had its being—the water, the trees, the earth and sky. "It lives and moves and has its *Being!*" I thought again. "Much more than other places." How faint the life of Italian earth seemed to me as I recalled it; how faint and dim and dying out. And New York! Why, when I remembered that clamor and movement out here beside this river, listening to the inner sound of these mountains and this flow, the rumble of New York came back to me like the impotent and despairing protest of a race that has gone wrong and is caught in a trap. How unhappy, how horribly unhappy, the memory of the sound of New York was in my ears! I felt scared. Could I hook on here and mingle with it, or was it too late? I recognized that it was mine for the recognition, but had I stayed away too long?

Maurice and Mr. Craft came out and broke up my reverie. . . .

We wound our way up the canyon. Sometimes it was narrow and the dark green trees climbed above us on both sides; and sometimes it widened out into valleys where fruit orchards lay dreaming. At several places Mexican adobe houses nestled cozily under great cottonwood trees beside the river. I have always hated that word "nestle," but that is what they did.

Wherever Mexicans lived in houses, they seemed to fit into the land better than the Americans. We occasionally saw them outside their homes, and both the people and their little houses looked homogeneous and connected; and their faces, although they were often haggard and worn and twisted, fitted into the landscape. It was as if they had been marked by struggles that were more fitting than the Anglo-Saxon fight for life out here. They had had to fight the elements to secure a living from them, and their constant touch was with fire, water, and the earth. Something of this contact was graven on their gnarled and twisted features and in their spare, distorted frames. A fire burned in those dark and often sunken eyes, and a glow passed in a smile over the darkened skin. They were worn down by struggle, but they were not hard-boiled nor deprived of their essence, as seemed the few lower-class Americans I had seen. The faces of *these* were often depraved and dead: it did not seem to agree with them to live in this wide state.

We moved along beside the twisting river as best we could over the rutted road. The shadows grew long before we reached the foot of the mountainside where we must turn from the river and climb to reach the table-land of Taos Valley, whose long, level rim was so far above.

Down in the canyon it had grown somber, but we saw sunlight, golden upon the tops of trees on the upper rim of land.

Mr. Craft stopped the car before he attempted the long climb and we got out and stretched ourselves while he filled the radiator from a bottle that he carried. We were in the wildest spot imaginable, climbing northwards through a narrow pass. Here in these depths of the mountains, a steep road mounted alongside the high slope on the opposite side, and it was rutted and washed narrow. We could look down into the black chasm we had left, and it was to be hoped we would not meet anyone coming towards us!

We were away from river life now, working our path upward to the Taos table-land.

Mr. Craft sighed as he struggled along. Now we were really headed away from civilization. Now indeed we left the world behind. The Rio Grande Canyon was a part of the world he knew; it had a railroad station in it, down below, and the familiar river that flowed near Santa Fe had kept us company all day. Now we were going into isolation.

The road mounted steadily, cut out of the mountainside and sometimes it was not much wider than the car, and without anything to keep us from rolling down. Had the steering gear broken, or the engine failed us on that steep incline, we would have been in terrible danger. Mr. Craft leaned forward over his wheel and Maurice giggled nervously. He put his hand on my arm and murmured, "Where *are* you taking me to, dar-r-r-ling?"

As we climbed out of the shadowy depths, and descended again, and climbed again and wended our blind way through the dark trees, the light grew more golden and more fair, until suddenly we reached the top and swung around a curve onto level land: and there we were in a great blaze of sunlight, so mellow and so enveloping that we could see nothing for a moment.

The sun, with a great smile radiating from it, was just at the rim of the faraway horizon, level with our eyes where we paused to look about us. Its rays came to our faces straight and unobstructed across the gulf of the black Rio Grande Canyon over westward. The interminable desert beyond stretched between it and us like a soft, darkened carpet. The

little canyon we had come through had spewed us up out
of its depths and we stood breathless in awe at the scene that
stretched before us that was revealed only for the short time
it takes a sun to sink below the edge of the earth when it
is many miles distant.

Over towards the north, a crescent-shaped mountain range
curved like an arm around the smooth valley. At its loftiest
portion, a mountain shaped along the snowy heights like an
Indian bow, rested with a vast and eternal composure. The
rays of the sinking sun threw its forms into relief and deep indentations and the shapes of pyramids were shadowed forth
in a rosy glow. The mountain sat there beaming—spread out
in the bliss of effortless being. The lesser peaks linked themselves to join it; shoulder to shoulder they supported the central, massive curves. There they all waited, snow-capped, glowing like unearthly flowers, a garland of mystery beyond the
known world. Not a house in sight! Not a human being! The
wide, soft desert sweeping away to the half-circle of mountains whose central curve was twenty miles away, its right
hand reaching the canyon rim.

"Oh, where is Taos?" I exclaimed, eagerly.

"Well, it's over there at the foot of that big mountain," replied Mr. Craft without enthusiasm.

Now that the sun had set, the desert all around us was darkening rapidly, while the sky was filled with rose clouds and the
mountains turned into still, violet-shadowed masses. The air
was quieter now and had an icy touch upon one's face.

We started across the intervening sagebrush plain upon a
dry, rutted road that wound indirectly towards the "big mountain." Sometimes our wheels crushed the sage, and it was a
lovely perfume in our nostrils—a smell that made the heart
beat faster. It grew dark in a few moments and we were

unable to see anything except the waysides and the lighted stretch ahead of us, where sometimes a rabbit hopped across our path, illumined brightly for an instant—and quickly blotted out.

"Coyote," Mr. Craft said once, flicking his thumb towards the right; and I heard a high, hysterical laugh coming out of the darkness.

Quite soon it was bitterly cold, but fortunately it did not take us too long to reach the village, and we were entering it through an avenue of great trees and going up upon what was some kind of street, almost before I knew it. Dark, low dwellings were on each side of us, some lighted from within and some not. It was the darkest town I ever saw and the emptiest. Not a soul in the place.

"I don't know my way around here very well," observed Mr. Craft. "I ain't never been up here but once. But I think we go round this here Catholic church." I couldn't see any church until I squinted into the blackness and finally made out something that had an ecclesiastical façade.

We wound in and out and reached a dark plaza. It was almost without any lights: quiet, empty, deserted; yet it could not have been more than half-past six or seven o'clock. A long, low building at our right had some lamps shining through the windows.

"The Columbian Hotel," Mr. Craft announced.

We stopped before it and bundled out and our voices sounded bold and resonant in the cold, still air, so we lowered them instinctively. We went on inside, while Mr. Craft untied the bags on the rear of the car.

It smelled so lovely outside in the air, but inside again there was that hot, stove-heat, mingling cigar smoke with human odors. Two or three men looked up from their chairs, surprised and interested to see travelers arrive.

I felt conspicuous and as though I had burst in upon a dream ever since reaching this place, anyway, and now in the dim hotel hall it was like falling from one planet onto another, judging from the stale, startled faces of these men.

"Can we get some rooms here?" I asked, apologetically, of one of them.

He rose, wearily, with a great effort, and went to a swinging door, then through it to the rear of the house. We heard the sound of voices as he passed, and dishes: kitchen noises.

A stout Mexican woman bustled in from these regions. She took us into a huge room that led off from the lobby, a room whose windows were low and opened upon the plaza. Great brass double beds sprang into view as she lighted the oil lamp; huge, dark cupboards and wash-stands. The beds had thin springs and thinner mattresses. Below their crocheted spreads, they curved into wide hollows.

"Nice room, no?" inquired the smiling landlady. "Where you come from?"

"Santa Fe!" I answered in an ingratiating voice. "How much is this room?"

"Oh, dollar and half. And meals, too," she replied. "Santa Fe, hey? Well!"

"Can we have some supper?" asked Maurice.

"Oh, sure. Come on." We left the bags Mr. Craft had hauled in, and followed her out through the dim hall where those men still sat observing all our movements with impassive faces and lack-luster eyes. They seemed resigned to discouragement and were totally without the glow our hostess radiated. We were in a dining room and she brought an oil lamp and set it on a table. This made an island in the big, stuffy place. She bustled away as we all three sat down. Maurice, I saw, was looking dubious.

"This seems to be just about the end of the world," he murmured in a low voice.

"Well, I wondered what you folks wanted to come to *Taos* for!" Mr. Craft put in as he raised his glass of water to his lips. He raised his eyebrows over it, smiling archly across at me. "They say they got some artists living here, but nobody ever *comes* here, except them traveling men." And he indicated with his thumb the melancholy watchers on the other side of the swinging door.

"*Traveling* men! What do they *travel* for?" I giggled. I felt an excitement in me that seemed quite uncalled for. I wanted to laugh; I felt stimulated and gay and delighted.

"Firms," replied Mr. Craft, laconically. "Shoe firms, grocery firms, clothier firms, and all."

The lady rolled back with some plates of very thin soup. We ate it. Maurice was cheered by the soup as men always are. He began to ask questions of the beaming hostess.

"You're right up in the mountains here. Do you have much snow in the winter?"

"Oh, *yes!* After Christmas. Lots o' snow! Sometimes roads all fill up and nobody go in or out o' town. And *cold!* Nice, though." She smiled.

"It *sounds* nice," answered Maurice, trying to choke a laugh. I immediately felt like defending Taos. Taos *was* nice. I couldn't see it, but I could smell it, and I loved it already. It was not love at first sight, but it was love. Some other sense had already accepted it and I had fully decided to come back here and stay. I felt at home.

"Are there any houses to rent here?" I asked her.

"Oh, I don't *think* so!" She looked surprised. "People here live in their houses."

"But maybe somebody would like to rent a house and go away for a change," I suggested.

She looked at me in surprise. "People don't go away from Taos."

I wrinkled my forehead and began to worry.

"Well, I tell you," she added, "after supper you go see Doctor. Maybe he know somebody."

"Where does he live? Near?" I perked up.

"Oh, up the street a ways. I show you."

"Now, really, Mabel," began Maurice.

But I swept his words back into his mouth. "I have *decided,* Maurice. You must just trust me. This place has a feeling to it that is just *right*. I know my hunch was a good one—wait and see. There is something *wonderful* here."

"Gee!" said Mr. Craft.

Maurice said, "Well, it may be wonderful for you, but *I* have to see if I can Work here. How can I tell till I *See* it? You're not going to try and rent a house before you *See* the place, are you?"

"Yes, I am—if I can. I *have* seen it.—With my mind's eye," I added, pedantically.

We ate slices of meat, and boiled carrots and mashed potato in small dishes, followed by stewed prunes and a really good cake. The meal over, Mr. Craft selected a toothpick from the glass on our table, and he joined the group near the stove while the landlady went out into the plaza with us and pointed out the way to Doctor's. Maurice had his flashlight with him, fortunately, for otherwise we could not have found our way. We moved like spooks silently in the silence of the place, around half of the plaza and up a wide street.

DOC MARTIN

MR. MANBY

We could not see much on either side of us: nondescript adobe walls, a dark store on the corner before we turned, then just house-walls along the dirt sidewalk, with an occasional light inside behind the drawn curtains.

How tell of the influence of places upon one, the spellbinding that does not have to come from sight or sound, though maybe smell plays a part in it? Anyway, Taos took me that dark winter night and has held me ever since. I am glad I capitulated in the dark, blindly but full of faith. It was a real conversion, and something accepted on trust—recognized as home.

Two horses passed us, their unshod hoofs almost silent on the dirt road, their riders wrapped in white, like shrouds.

"*Indians!*" I whispered to Maurice. "Don't they look wonderful? Like a dream!" They passed on into the plaza in silence.

Now we reached the door with the sign swinging over it:

DR. MARTIN

It was a house of total darkness. The flashlight showed a bell on the office door that one twisted round and round. We twisted and twisted before anyone came. Finally a young woman opened it a little, gave a gasp, as the light of her lamp fell upon Maurice's vivid face, and shut it again upon us. I gave the bell another angry whirl. She returned and opened it, exclaiming rather hysterically, I thought:

"You startled me. We don't see many strangers. At night, too! Come in; I'll call Doctor."

We sat down in the ice-cold waiting room. There was quite a smell of whiskey around. I gazed at the beautiful photographs that covered the walls. Indians. Indians on horses, Indians beside streams, Indians dancing. I stood and looked at their faces and they seemed to me full of quietude and nobility and wisdom.

The doctor came in. He was a tall, middle-aged man, with gray hair standing up on end, and pink cheeks. His small, green eyes were shrewd and lively. He was collarless and he had a paunch and his checked suit was spotted, but there was something robust about him that I liked. I knew instinctively that one could come up against him with all one's might and he would rally. He could stand a lot of living. He had stood a lot of it, one saw, and he radiated amusement. The funny, incongruous character of life was apparent to him at all times, and this had marked his face more deeply than disappointments or disillusion. A real, stalwart man, though tricky as an elephant, and with the eyes of that animal.

He looked us over quite completely. Then, "Well?" he inquired in a ready-for-anything voice.

"We want to rent a house for the winter," I began, firmly.

"We thought we might look around," added Maurice, trying to modify my words.

This seemed to be something new for Doctor. He looked at us with quick, speculative eyes; but with a swift adjustment, he replied:

"Well, I don't know of any house you could rent here in Taos. There aren't many of us here and we just live in our houses."

"But surely there must be *some* sort of little place we could take," I pleaded.

"What do you want to *do* here?" he asked me curiously.

"My husband is an artist and he wants to paint Indians," I replied, glancing at poor Maurice with a forbidding look. This was understandable, apparently. A look of partial comprehension swept over the doctor's expressive face.

"Oh, so you're one of them painters," he said, with a touch of relief, turning to Maurice.

"Well, I paint," Maurice admitted, somewhat wryly, and looked at me like a bear caught in a trap.

The office seemed to be growing colder. We were standing up all this time. The woman who had let us in stood behind in the shadow. Nothing seemed to move in any direction. Suddenly the doctor found a solution, or maybe he only offered it to get rid of us. He said:

"Well, I'll tell you. There's an old fellow lives next to me here. He has a big house; he might rent you part of it. He's cranky as the devil, but you might persuade him—savvy? You go and see him in the morning—you'd never get him to open the door at night. Tell him I sent you, get me? Maybe he'll take you and maybe he won't. He don't have to. He's got plenty of money. But he's the only one I can think of. Name's Manby." He moved towards the door with a smooth habit of dismissal.

We moved after him, and I said faintly, "I'll try him, then." It seemed doubtful. Outside, we stood in the darkness and Doctor held his lamp in our faces from the doorway. He lowered his voice, confidentially, as he said:

"He's a god-damned Englishman, savvy? And a regular crook. He don't speak to anybody in the place except me, and nobody speaks to him. But if you want rooms, he's got 'em— if you can make him give 'em to you. You tell him I sent you, get me?"

We made our way back to the Columbian Hotel in the little beam of light from Maurice's flashlight. When we went into our room, the look of dubiousness on his face seemed to be permanently engraved there.

"This is a fr-r-rightful place, dar-r-ling," he murmured wist-

4 *

fully. "How do you expect me to Work in such a place?"

"Well, I *like* it," I answered. "It feels so *real*. And I bet you'll be able to work here. Just wait and see what it's like in the morning."

"I never *heard* of such a thing! Deciding on a place you've not even seen, when *every*thing is against it. You're so contrary! I was all nicely settled in Santa Fe."

"Well, here it's more *real*. People here *live* here. They're not just sitting on the surface like those friends of yours down there. Why, those people don't belong there, and we would never really belong there, either. I want to be in a place where I can sink in and be a part of the life."

"Oh, nonsense!" said Maurice.

So I closed myself away from him and went to bed. The sheets were damp and icy and the blankets, of coarse woven red and yellow wool, were heavy as lead. *Serapes.*

The night was utterly, utterly still. Not a sound came in the opened window from the village outside. I went to sleep with my thoughts out there upon the mountain that we had hardly seen, but that guarded, I knew, the whole valley, all the little creatures in the desert around us as well as this village, safe in its deep shadow. It was cozy and secure, dominated and neighbored by a mountain watching over it. In some way I knew that everything and everyone here was somehow under the influence of that great mountain and that there was no use to oppose that influence. "Everyone except those traveling men," I thought, dreamily, "and they are lost."

Chapter Five

WE WERE awakened the next morning by the sound of wagons passing outside in the plaza, and by people going by the windows, talking in Spanish. It didn't seem possible that we were in the United States. Even the room looked foreign to me, with its low ceiling and white-washed walls. The air was so cold that the water had frozen in the pitcher, and I wondered how we would ever be able to get up and dress.

Soon, however, a black-haired child of sixteen knocked and came in, a bundle of firewood in her arms. *"Buenos días, Señora,"* she cried, smilingly. In no time she had a roaring fire going in the thin, round stove. A lovely perfume filled the air and warmth crept over us.

Maurice dressed hurriedly and went out to find some coffee for me. Soon the child brought breakfast, in thick, white dishes on a small tray and afterwards I dressed, with my heart beating fast inside me. Everything seemed so thrilling.

When we stepped out into the plaza and looked around, I did feel slightly disappointed. It was not particularly beautiful. Long, low buildings with shops faced with columned portals, lined it on three sides, and the bare trees in the center were pinched and shrinking. Only the full, yellow sunlight over all gave it a certain look of richness.

Long, wooden bars marked off the square of dusty yellowed grass where the trees grew, and to these were hitched wagons and saddle-horses. If the people in Santa Fe had seen only the plaza, they were certainly right in saying there was nothing to Taos. But there was more to it than that, I felt sure. I could feel it coming to me through the air—the gay, compelling charm.

We hurried up to Mr. Manby's house. We hadn't much time, for we had to get an early start for our long day's journey back to Santa Fe.

Next to Dr. Martin's, a high adobe wall continued his house wall, and an arch of adobe over a wooden door was evidently the garden entrance. There was a metal sign nailed into the side of the door that spoke of some land corporation or company of Taos Valley.

We rang the bell and waited, then rang again. Quick footsteps approached the door; it was opened a crack, and a heavy old, unshaven face appeared. His eyes were rimmed with red and were bloodshot—a most unprepossessing person. He was glowering at me, and I said, timidly:

"Are you Mr. Manby? Dr. Martin sent us to you."

"Oh, he did, did he?" The voice was gruff and rude but with an unexpectedly cultivated accent; it was rather a pleasant voice to hear, to tell the truth.

I smiled at him and tried not to see him. As a matter of fact, there was not much of him to see, for he kept holding the door almost closed. So I addressed myself to his voice, for I knew that wherever in him that came from, there was something to appeal to.

"Mr. Manby, we are looking for a house to rent. Will you rent yours?"

He opened the door and said, "Come inside." And led us into a beautiful little patio. He was dressed in the dirtiest clothes I had ever seen on anyone. Filthy riding trousers and an old gray flannel shirt with a frayed waistcoat under it. His thick neck joined his heavy shoulders like a bull's, and he held his head lowered, looking up slantwise at us like an angry bull. He leaned upon a stout cane, and his whole personality breathed out a dark and bloody anger to the world. He looked us over, too, and said again:

"Come inside."

We passed through the small patio, towards the house, and he led us into a dark hall. Several dogs, as angry-looking as their master, were chained beside the door of another patio that lay on the inner side of the room we were in, and they set up a frightful barking and tugging at their chains when they saw us.

"Quiet! Down!" shouted Mr. Manby, menacing them with his cane. "One needs them, but they are a great nuisance," he explained in his charming voice.

"*Why* do you need them?" I asked, curiously.

"There are reasons," he replied, looking at me with a rather sinister twinkle in his large, pale, bloodshot eyes.

Maurice was peering at some small watercolors that hung upon the dark adobe wall.

"These are very good, very nice," he said, appreciatively.

"Yes, they are excellent. My mother painted them," Mr. Manby answered.

They were, indeed, very small, but painted broadly and with a certainty that is lacking in most pictures. They were of the essence of the English scene—the cathedral, the large country house and garden, copse, dale, lake, and mountain—suggesting Wordsworth! I knew they represented the past of Mr. Manby and that his beautiful voice came from the same place they did.

The hall was a dark brown place full of things that had died: heavy furniture, some bronze animals, several Eastern weapons hanging upon the wall, a few dingy oil paintings.

There was an ugly, musty smell in the air. When we sat down, a slight cloud of dust rose from the old upholstery and danced in a long ray of sunshine that was coming in through the glass window of the inner patio where the dogs occasionally growled and stirred restlessly.

"Well, Mr. Manby, *will* you rent us something? You have a great big house—and I am sure you can't use it all!"

I could see it through the window—long, windowed walls disappearing down one side of the patio. I suspected a length of house that must lead far back into a garden. It seemed to me a huge, rambling place. But could one live near this individual? Could one bear it? He was repulsive in his deterioration and his furious blood made the world about him seem poisoned. The man had gone completely negative all through. He was looking at us speculatively, studying us.

"Come along—I'll show you the house," and he led the way, leaning on his heavy cane. There were really two houses connected by a long corridor with a patio for each one. The portion that he lived in himself was towards the street, and the wall of Dr. Martin's office provided the wall of a small storeroom in his patio. Next to it came his bedroom, whose wall was that of the doctor's bedroom; and the old walls, two feet thick, insulated these from each other.

Mr. Manby showed us everything. His own bedroom was terrible, from the sense of decay that lay over it, but it still had the vestiges of a cultured life lingering in its ruins, like his delightful voice that issued from caverns of depravity.

There was a library table near the window with piles of faded papers, a gigantic old bronze ink-well, and stained and tarnished implements lying about: paper knives, a magnifying glass, and pen-holders resting in a dingy bronze tray. Several luxurious chairs stood drawn up to the table, but they were stained and torn and the stuffing was bursting through the broken coiled springs that showed here and there.

The light that came through the dirty western windows fell depressingly upon all this, showing up the thick dust that coated everything, showing up—oh, horror!—the sagging cot bed in one corner of the room, unmade, without sheets, its filthy, gray-toned blankets tossed back, showing a coverless pillow darkened by the head that nightly rolled about in it, uneasily.

There were more watercolors upon the brown walls of this room, fresh and clear behind their glass. One could note the gardens where doubtless Mr. Manby had strolled beside his mother in his youth: the rose garden and the long avenue of elms, the typical English park. He noticed our interest in these, and he took a tattered portfolio full of sketches from a drawer in the table.

"I studied architecture a long time ago," he said with a twisted smile. "Here are some of my plans for developing this valley. Look at this! Here we will build a great hotel in the Spanish style—right here where this house stands." His painting of it was excellent, really talented: a perfectly huge, low building with archways and outside stairways. I actually saw it materialize, years later, though on a smaller scale, as the Biltmore Hotel in Santa Barbara—but at the hand of another architect!

"East of here, towards the mountains, we will develop the residence quarter. A fine boulevard will circle around below the hills; it will circle the whole valley." My heart sank.

"*When?*" I asked.

"Oh, in the time to come," he answered. "My company will develop all this," he said loftily.

Maurice gave me a slight grimace, and all at once I realized that this old man was mad.

"Come, now, I'll show you my kitchen," and he led us through to a room that stood between his bedroom and the storeroom next to the doctor's office.

It was far more orderly than the other rooms we had seen. Evidently he swept and dusted here. Along one side, there were rather well-designed cupboards and shelves stained brown with glass doors above them. A stove was burning at one side of the room and a hot water kettle steamed upon it. Bread and marmalade waited on the kitchen table. But no, it wasn't really clean; as one looked, the greasy stain showed up. The superficial order of the room was underlaid by layers upon layers of grime.

"What do you eat for breakfast?" I asked him, intimately. I was treating him as though he were a human being and he liked it.

"Oh, tea, of course. And I make myself porridge out of the yellow cornmeal they grind here at the mill. Delicious—and very nutritious. And see here: I make *enough*—and what is left over, I pour into a bowl—like this—and it hardens. For lunch I have an excellent pudding out of it—with sugar and cream and a little currant jelly on top of it! Oh, one contrives all sorts of things in this country!" And he laughed, looking up at me sideways, for though he was taller than I, he always held his head bent towards the ground.

He took us back through the house to the dismal hall. Yes, it was all laid out like a gentleman's country home—but it was not gentle, and it was not a home. The symbols were all there, but no life infused them. Disintegration had gained a march upon the old English tradition.

He unlocked each of the long row of rooms that connected

with this end of the house. Their doors opened upon the sunny corridor whose glass sides showed the central patio of the house with its trees and shrubs all withered now, and dry. Their large embrasured windows were on the garden side of the house, and they had heavy iron bars upon them like many houses in Italy. These bedrooms were huge and dark. They faced the north and were shaded from a garden path that ran alongside of them, bordered by large lilac trees. A full-branched apple tree in a plot of grass stood just beyond and filled the sky. The thickness of the wall made the rooms seem cavernous. They were furnished with heavy walnut and mahogany double beds, ponderous bureaus, and wash-stands bearing heavy China "sets." The ceilings had white cotton cloth stretched over them.

The bedrooms were separated into two groups by a passage-way that ran between them. Here there was a door that opened from the garden, giving a private entrance. This outside door was very massive and had an iron bar across the inside of it.

We poked our way into all these dim rooms. The corridor alongside was bright enough—Mr. Manby kept referring to it as "the sun room." It had shelves all along under the windows and these were laden with shells, fossils, specimens of ore, Indian arrowheads, war clubs, and stones of all shapes and kinds. Mr. Manby kept calling this his "collection" and persisted in showing us odds and ends of it. It was quite dead, totally unmagnetic and dull, as are all objects that are no longer in use. Why can't people realize that nothing exists except in use, and that most "collections" are only symbols that once had life and now are dead—and not only dead but deadly? They would, and maybe they do, sap one's energy, for everything tries to live.

"The sun room" led into a large room at the end. It had an

adobe fireplace built in one corner, a high, barred window in the eastern wall, and the west side of it had a window opening upon the patio. This room was furnished with a round dining-room center table, several dilapidated chairs called "Morris," and a rickety sofa. In a deep niche, an old couch was covered with a beautiful brown and green serape; and several blue and white serapes were flung over the sofa and chairs. There was a safe built into one of the walls.

Another kitchen led off from it, with a few pots and pans hanging on the walls and a dirty, rusty stove in it. An outside door led to the "kitchen garden," Mr. Manby said: a yard walled in, empty, paved with dirt, and lined with outhouses. There was a toilet, some stables, a well in the center. The whole place looked ruinous, but rather orderly, and I saw I could make the living room habitable if I got the chance.

There was an old-fashioned hanging oil lamp above the dining table: and I could imagine us sitting under its yellow light in the evenings. But could we lock Mr. Manby away in his own part of the house? It would be terrible to see much of him.

"Well, will you rent this end of the place to us? The bed-rooms and this?" I queried, pleadingly.

Still he did not answer. He led us out to the garden.

It was a great wide place, well laid out in broad paths lined with lilac bushes and bordered with irises. One saw the dry stalks of hollyhocks in long rows, and squares of withered grass were bordered with them. The paths led away in long vistas and at the end of them the Mountain loomed blue. Yellow sunshine flooded the garden and warmed the long, low, pink adobe house with its row of black-barred windows. The broad road, way down at the western side of the place, was outside the high wooden picket fence and it was hidden by a row of high trees. We looked at this avenue of beautiful trees, their pale gray branches almost meeting overhead. Mr. Manby saw our eyes upon them and he said:

"Beautiful, aren't they? I planted that avenue years ago. Antonio and I brought hundreds of trees down from the mountains and laid them out here on my place and along that Pueblo road. They go winding in fine curving avenues all the way over there," and he motioned over to the east where a long, low range of hills showed between the thickets. "Some day my avenues will open up on the Taos Boulevard beyond my property. . . . But I am sorry to say that Phillips has planted those dirty female cottonwoods over there on *his* side of the road." He motioned to the outside world.

Maurice was beginning to look nervous. "We have to leave, you know," he said to me in a low voice.

Mr. Manby heard him and threw him a nasty look; then turned to me, ignoring him.

"You see that mountain up there?" He pointed to the big one. "The Indians call that the *sacred* mountain. I could tell you some things about it if I wanted to. It is full of *gold* and *silver*, but those devils won't let anyone prospect up there. . . ."

"But listen—won't you rent this to us?" I interrupted him. I began to turn towards the outside road, slowly leaving. He followed, hitting out at dried garden things viciously with his cane.

"Hum! I'd have to have a very good rent, you know. It means a lot of trouble for me, getting it ready and all. And losing my privacy," he added, looking hatefully at Maurice.

"What do you *call* a good rent?" Maurice asked in a particularly cautious tone.

"Well, I would have to have seventy-five dollars a month, and for not less than six months."

"Six *months!* Who knows where we'll be in six months!" exclaimed Maurice. Little, indeed, did *he* know! I must have known more than he did, for it seemed perfectly certain to me that I wanted it for that length of time, and I cried:

"All right! We'll take it. We'll go back to Santa Fe and we'll come back here on the first of January, and we'll live *right here* until the end of August!"

"Dar-r-r-ling!" exclaimed Maurice with a desperate look.

Mr. Manby tried to wither him with a glare of distaste. "Are you *German,* may I ask?" he inquired, coldly.

"Russian," I offered, hastily.

"Indeed. It seems the Russians are falling into great confusion. The war monopolizes a large part of our thought these days, but the end is in sight."

"I never even *think* of it!" I exclaimed impetuously. "It *bores* me!" Mr. Manby looked at me suspiciously.

"I think of little else," he replied, "but there are no intelligent minds here in this place to talk it over with."

"Don't you talk with your neighbor?" I asked, smiling.

"Oh, Doc? Doc's all right in his way, but I wouldn't say he has an intelligence, exactly! Give Doc a bottle of whiskey and he'll give you some tall stories. But of course one can't discuss anything significant with him." The beautiful voice spoke gently and was modulated to express all the delicate shades of his English insularity.

But suddenly it broke into a thick, rough brutality. "Besides, he's a damned liar, a low-lived, vulgar rascal. I could tell you some stories about *him!*" He broke off and cast a sideways glance of fury up over the roof and, presumably, down into Doctor's house.

Heavens! These people don't like each other much here in Taos, I thought.

We left with further promises; and Mr. Manby required
the first month's rent in advance. Mr. Craft had come after
us in the Ford, and we waved good-by to Mr. Manby as he
stood behind the garden door watching us leave. He looked
remarkably sinister, peering out one side of it, half concealed,
lowering.

"We better be on our way," remarked our driver.

"But we've *got* to go to the Indian village and see it just for
a moment! How far is it?"

Mr. Craft pointed up the broad, tree-lined road. "Up there
a ways. I don't know as we should take the time. . . ."

"Oh, *yes*," I begged, and he gave in.

Taos village ended at Mr. Manby's place. There was only
one other house beyond his, an ugly square wooden one
painted gray. Beyond it there was a crossroad, with a graveyard at the corner; and in it the graves were marked with
white and pale blue crosses—a very pretty cemetery! After this,
empty fields bordered the road and we were in open country. Not desert, however: the land was cultivated and the
brown, plowed earth looked opulent. The pale stalks of corn
yellowed some places, but in others the land lay bare and
dark and warm. Clumps of soft, rose-colored willows showed
here and there like the glow of a gentle fire marking the
creek that flowed down from the mountain. We crossed a
rickety bridge and on our left, miles of level pasture land
swept away as far as the eye could reach, with a great number
of small horses and cows wandering about, grazing in it. On
our right, a long, full line of lavender-gray cottonwood trees
paralleled the road, the breadth of a field away from us. I soon
learned to know that cottonwoods always followed water.

Now there seemed to be a mild happiness pervading this
land. The sun made everything luminous, and bathed the

5

earth and the trees in a high light that brought out all the subtle winter tones. I had never seen so much color anywhere before this, in December—not even in Italy. There were pale yellows and pinks and mauves, and dark shades of wine and bistre. Everything glowed and pulsated; the usual immobility of the dormant months was replaced here by a gentle vibrating life, and the blue sky overhead, showing between the bare branches of the lacy trees, was of the most ineffable transparence instead of being hard and opaque.

We saw the sacred mountain ahead of us at the end of the road. It was greenish black with violet mists shadowing it. A gray, rugged tooth of rocky crag a mile high thrust upwards beside it, and the range continued northwards until it tapered away on the horizon.

"I never realized the ether before," I told Maurice, "whatever ether is. But here one can *see* it. Look at those veils of blue and violet and plum color upon the mountain! I never saw anything so lovely! And don't you feel something different in the air here, Maurice?"

"That's altitude," cut in Mr. Craft.

"Oh, it's more than that," I answered him, impatiently; and went on to Maurice in a lowered voice: "It's as though one were nearer than before!"

"Nearer what?" Maurice asked.

"I don't know—that's just it! How can one know?"

We finally came along close to the mountain. It swept away above us, and there at the foot of it. was the Pueblo, guarded by its heavy, green magnificence. On either side of a sparkling brown stream that rushed down from a canyon on the right were two piles of brown cubes, like children's building blocks, that rose in pyramidal-shaped masses, like the things I used

PUEBLO ROAD   *by Ernest Knee*

to build when I was a child, or like a design by Gordon Craig.

The two big community houses were standing there in a smooth, clear space of earth, absolutely stark and undecorated, as economical as beehives, with little square holes for windows, but no window-frames, plain doorways, and with many ladders, hand-hewn out of trees, leaning against the walls at all levels from one roof to another, so that the people who lived away up at the top must climb half a dozen of them to reach their houses.

Now, strange to say, although the village seemed austere and certainly anything but domestic, yet one got a feeling of home from it. The very essence of it was of the home. Why? I do not know. That was the feeling it gave out richly. A stab of longing and of nostalgia went through me like lightning.

Pale blue smoke was coming out of dozens of chimneys all up and down the piles of the two houses, and the air smelled marvelous, for it came from burning piñon wood. There were no other cars there, and a crowd of dark little boys came tagging after ours as we drove up to one end of the plaza and quickly turned and came back. Mr. Craft seemed to want to get away as fast as he could; it meant nothing to him but so much time wasted. So the first visit to that Pueblo was only a sketchy impression of the earth rising in square brown blocks on each side of a stream in an atmosphere of snug content.

"Earthworks, aren't they?" I turned to Maurice and saw that he was quite excited.

"Why, it is *wonderful*—those pyramids composed of cubes! How mystical! And that mountain back of it—entirely made up of triangles! It will be *wonderful* to paint."

As we reached the little adobe church at the entrance to the village, I looked back and saw two Indians wrapped in

5 *

white sheets standing upon one of the higher roofs. They had their heads together and they were looking after our little car. All of a sudden I had a realization of the illimitable distance between us and them—and of something powerful but quite undefined that shut us off from each other. It was as though the Pueblo had an invisible wall around it, separating the Indians from the world we knew—a wall that kept their life safe within it, like a fire that cannot spread. "How self-contained it seems!" I thought, "and how contented it feels!" I mused to myself. "I *wish* I belonged in there!"

Chapter Six

THE NEXT day was the day before Christmas and we were on our way over to Santo Domingo Pueblo in the little Ford car that we engaged with the Burlins to take us there and leave us, and then to return for us.

It seemed a long, tiring trip, for the road south was rough and sandy, and a cold wind blew the fine grains into our eyes so that we had to keep our heads down against it. But between whiles I stole glances at the beautiful, mysterious landscape we were passing through. Out of the level desert over to the left rose a group of little hills, flat and blue and suave like those in the Da Vinci backgrounds, and farther beyond them stretched the distant desert with a high range of purple mountains against the sky. Like peaceful islands they seemed to float, these small hills with a quavering outline, upon a gray-green sea; and the same earthly sea surged up gradually behind them to the mountainous horizon. There was no disturbance in the scene, nothing to complicate the forms, no trees or houses, or any detail to confuse one. It was like a simple phrase in music or a single line of poetry, essential and reduced to the barest meaning.

We reached the rim of the high plateau we had crossed, that desert eight thousand feet high, held up in space with its vibrant and revealing light; and then we had to zigzag down the face of the wall to another desert which looked to be thousands of feet below. The road ran steeply down, doubling upon itself with hairpin turns, and at times we could look over the edge: a sheer drop downwards that was terrifying, and made the senses reel.

Far away, down below, I saw a row of telegraph poles miles long, like pins stuck in a map and as we ran along the mountainside before making the turn to reach a lower level, they changed position and from uprights they melted together and formed a single black line like a wire stretched across the land—and I realized I was seeing a mathematical formula demonstrated in front of my eyes where before it had been only words in my mind.

I had a sudden intuition right then that here in this country life could come to one more concretely than in other places, and that meanings that were shut up in words and phrases out in the world could incorporate themselves in living forms and move before one. Ideas here might clothe themselves in form and flesh, and word-symbols change into pictured, living realities.

We reached the plain and journeyed on along the rutted road until we came to a great water-tank beside a railway track. A wind-swept, gray station house was labeled "Domingo," and across from it a big store was marked, "Bernalillo Trading Company." Outside it, several Indians with bright bands of silk folded around their black heads, watched us curiously as we stopped to rest and relax for a while, inside, away from the bitter wind.

These Indians had a friendly aloofness in their faces. They did not seem to think we were people like themselves, but that we were objects of speculation; and I could see between them and us sufficient difference indeed! They were lightly clothed in wide, flapping cotton trousers that were slit up the sides, and in loosely hanging, flowered or striped homemade shirts, open at the throat. On their feet were soft, Sienna-colored moccasins, fastened up the sides with silver buttons. Their heavy, shining, black bangs came down to their eyes, and these eyes were glowing and alive. Right at that first nearness to the Indians, at the door of the Domingo store when I was close enough to look into their dark eyes I saw how living and aware they were, and I gradually learned these are the most marked of Indian characteristics.

A couple of miles further on through the sand, we reached the Pueblo lying near the river. On the outskirts of the village we passed one of the squat, adobe Catholic churches the priests had dropped wherever they found a group of Indians. It had an upper balcony across the front made of pale, weathered wood, with two prancing horses painted on the wall, one red, the other black and white.

I imagine that when the Spanish priests and soldiers first arrived and set up the images of their religion, the horses they rode seemed no less divine than the gods they introduced, and were accepted as part of the foreign hierarchy of the saints, for the Indians frequently decorated the alien churches with them, and in some Indian villages I learned they have religious ceremonies to ensure the fruitfulness of these animals, and these rituals always take place under the protection of the Strangers' church in corrals attached to the rear for this purpose!

The low, one-storied houses of Santo Domingo Pueblo were built of pale adobe and with white-washed porches, faced out upon broad, parallel streets. The village had all through it a blond and bleached cleanliness. The pale wood of the beams that projected over the house-fronts and supported the porches, was of the color of the dry, delicate, gray deer-horns, hung trophy-wise here and there, jutting out like branches of the gnarled, dry cedar upon which they were fastened. There is no material with a greater integrity than cedar wood. Stuck in the ground, it will never rot; no weather can destroy it; and the older it grows, the more beautiful it becomes. Little wonder that for the Indians, it is the sacred tree.

I heard the singing and drumming as soon as we reached the Pueblo, and it drew me strongly and I left the others and ran hurriedly towards it with my heart beating. Eighty or ninety elderly men stood close together around a great drum, singing, with eyes that seemed to look, but to be looking inward. They produced a volume of sound that was the glad, solemn voice of the tribe, and at the same time it was like the wind that rose and fell above us. This secure and sumptuous music was not, as with our orchestras and chorals, the expression of one man, drawn from one heart and rendered by the obedient many to tell his experience: it was the expression of many, told altogether.

While I listened, I thought: Communal music is not the voice of the individual; it has in its totality more than the sum of its parts; it reveals the over-soul of the tribe, the entity that is invisibly made up of many single units. It is easy to believe that a tribe composes the body of some vast Being, and that its health and strength must depend upon unison in the tribe. There is a group-spirit in the flock, in the herd, and in the swarm. And in the tribe there is one.

For the first time in my life, then, I heard the voice of the One coming from the Many—I who until then had been taught to look for the wonders of infinite divisibility and variety, for the many in the one, the elaboration and detail of a broken infinity. My world, all through my life, had been made of parts ever increasingly divided into more intricate and complex fractions. By our contemplation of pieces of things we had grown to believe that the part is greater than the whole; and so division had motivated all the activities of people I had known, of books I had read, of music I had heard, and of pictures I had seen.

Knowledge is power, was the belief behind all the activity of the students of the world—but it was a knowledge of the infinitely divisible atoms of that world. Out of the endless breaking up and recombining of elements, the numberless taking-to-pieces of things, the examination and the observation—out of all that knowledge people had learned how to move faster, how to transmit electrical force, and how to be more physically comfortable. The practice of infinite divisibility had produced an enormous number of devices. Indeed, the whole world was cluttered up with devices. Knowledge is Power—and with the power they gained, they learned to make electricity do their living for them. The more singleness, separateness, and individuality became the habit of our development (so that everywhere everybody was breaking away from old patterns of social and family life), the more ways there were of escaping mechanically. Actually, the conquest of machinery was to promote the separation of the individual from the mass; and the by-product of scientific conquest was become the elaborate, unhappy, modern man, cut off from his source, powerful in mechanisms, but the living sacrifice of his scientific knowledge.

The singular raging lust for individuality and separateness had been impelling me all my years as it did everyone else on earth—when all of a sudden I was brought up against the Tribe, where a different instinct ruled, where a different knowledge gave a different power from any I had known, and where virtue lay in wholeness instead of in dismemberment.

So when I heard that great Indian chorus singing for the first time, I felt a strong new life was present there enfolding me. Bubbling up like a spring, it came up and surrounded one in sound. But what *is* sound? And in what archaic past did those sounds first emerge? Did they lift themselves all at once, fully created, from a hundred throats? Or were they slowly evolved from layer upon layer of shared experience?

The chant sounded so fresh and spontaneous as I first heard it that it might have been coming into being at that instant. But no! It was unpracticed and unmechanical in its vigor and impulsiveness, yet the precision and perfection of its unanimity meant centuries of continuity. It was fresh and new as the water of a bottomless spring is ever new, yet forever the same.

The sonorous drum fused the voices of the men and the volume of it all together was strong and good and very masculine. The waves of sound penetrated the diaphragm, shaking atrophied cells into life, awakening dormant tissues. All the earth elements sounded in that music: the water and the wind and the sun and moon. Only nothing of mankind whimpered there! The human heart was silent. The spirit of the tribe, unseen, lifted up its voice: a great, fiery Being without name, without heart, without sorrow or pain, but with purpose and wisdom.

Oh, fellow mortals out there in the world! Until you learn how to join together once more, to fuse your sorrowful and lonely hearts in some new communion, you can never make true music. The sounds you produce will continue to be but the agonized expression, called "modern," of separate and unshared life, the wistful, sorrowing complaint of individualism before it has reached the new communal level for which it has been creating itself. Until then, science, science, science—but less and less life. But afterwards—magic again: magical power instead of scientific power. When will the time for it arrive? When will we get together again and make a happy sound?

On the warm music I tried to travel into the Indian life. The volume of it was warm and full, but not with the heat of Negro music, nor with its plaintiveness. Feeling, yes, but not sensation.

Long lines of dancers made patterns with the women's bare feet and those of moccasined men in the loose dust of the broad space between the rows of houses. Like the ephemeral design left by the sea upon the shore or the delicate imprint of ferns upon fossils, the patterns of Indian feet dancing recalled again to one how all the elements in nature bear resemblance and relation to each other, having a common expression whether it is left written by fluid or solid; and doubtless, could we see the writing of wind and gases, light and sound, these, too, would show their similarity. The creative force is as limited as the universe. Essential form is infinite in variability, like the markings upon finger-prints and leaves, or the metabolic rate recorded by the kymograph, but it is only infinite in variability. There are not innumerable forms of fingers or leaves or faces, or of other objects and forces.

The dancers' faces looked deeply fulfilled and were unmarked by fear. Indians are safe from fear by virtue of a living religion that has its source in love, unlike the African, which is inspired by apprehension. From love arise all nobilities, every reverence and every certainty.

The Domingo Indians radiated a self-contained joy. They glowed. Their downcast eyes burned, withdrawn in contemplation of their positive knowledge. Their flesh and their hair had a radiation and gave off a sparkle of vitality. Taken in terms of flavor, they had more savor and tang than we, as the trout in a moving stream have more than those fish raised in private pools, or as wild game has more than domestic beasts. It seemed to me I had never seen real human beings before. How could I penetrate this kind of being?

All day long they danced in the cold air under the hot sun. They themselves were neither hot nor cold. They did not sweat or shiver in their nudity. They danced effortlessly, borne by the shared rhythm. And my companions and I looked poor and outside life as we squatted on the ground, able only to watch them. The doom of our race, I thought, is to watch things. We travel around or we stay at home, but wherever we are, we are only looking at life, not living it. Looking at it and telling about it, not being it. We have even learned to make a virtue of this substitution of modes. . . . Our attitude, wherever we are, is the one we assume towards the purple cow: "I'd rather see than be one!"

"Well," I thought, "I'd rather be a part of this Indian thing than anything I've ever seen."

But there was little likelihood of that, apparently. The Indians, inside their magical circle, did not even seem to know we were there. They did not exclude us, they did not have to: we were, in reality, not THERE where they were. We did not know what they knew, nor experience their mystical communion which was as natural and inevitable as the communion between the cells of the body, and similar to that. No, lonely atoms like us could never participate in their rich, shared, companioned being.

We form dancing classes, we try to do things in groups, we strive for a group consciousness, trying to raise our vibrations to greater heat by some means or other, desperate, like cold flies at the end of the solar year, crawling separately up the frigid, unfriendly walls of our cooling spiritual universe. But it is all no good. We have reached the last outpost of the warm and loving world of our kind of relationships. Our solar year is ending. We will give out and fall to the floor of the world and be swept away. That one or two among our kind will carry over into a new life, may or may not happen. Perhaps we must come to this communal way of life again at a higher level; possibly evolution proceeds spirally, repeating itself. Maybe. How does one know? Some such thoughts as these ran through my head as I watched the Indians dance through the hours.

But though my thoughts were rather dismal and envious, I was surprised to find how I felt after it was over, after it had ended in a sumptuous accelerated outpouring of forces, the dancers beating out the dance in two joined groups, to the drums and voices of two choruses who were singing contrapuntally.

I felt made over. Renewed, refreshed, filled with life. Sometimes, after a deep sleep in fresh air, one awakes restored and full of unjustifiable hope—ready for inexpressible undertakings. The day in the Pueblo had given me a sense of new life, like sleep can give.

I looked at Maurice and I saw he felt it, too.

"It's wonderful, isn't it?" he said. "How it smoothens one out!"

The characteristic I liked best in Maurice was his ability to feel things, and to benefit by them, and even to know he was doing so. No, he was not so dead or so ruined as others I knew.

"Yes," I answered him. "It's marvelous. And it's hidden here where no one knows it! Why, if people *knew* about what is here, they'd rush upon it and simply eat it up. And there's no one here except just us! Why, that's extraordinary. I hope no one discovers it!"

"Why?" asked Paul Burlin, who overheard me.

"Why?" I repeated, staring at him in amazement. "Why? Do you want to see it eaten up?"

"Oh, I don't know what you mean by that. I think an Art Form like this should be known to the world, so people could enjoy it. There's no question of its being eaten up, as you say—"

"Yes, there is, too. This isn't an Art Form. It's much more than that. It's a living religion—it's alive like the Greek religion was alive before it became an Art Form and died out! Heavens! If people come in here—don't you see?—they'd grab all this and commercialize it somehow. As soon as religion is commercialized, it has turned into an Art Form! Commercial value is the standardized, accepted foundation of acknowledged Art. It is Recognition! I'd *hate* to have these Indians get recognition! Why, it would be the end of them!"

"Well, I'm going over to Geronimo's to see if I can get some songs," broke in Natalie Curtis, who was bent upon her book of Indian music; and we followed along.

"Come in. *Entre!*" said Geronimo, with a hospitable manner. One could not see whether he was glad to see us come or not. He had gladness in him, anyway, and some of it flowed over us. The room was large, with white-washed walls, and there were bright, clear-cut colors about in blankets hung on horizontal poles, and black and white, clear-cut patterns upon great jars. A fire burned snugly; he gave us straight-backed chairs and bade us be at home.

"Will you give me a song, Geronimo?" asked Natalie Curtis.

He nodded indulgently, smiling. His manner was slightly condescending, as to children. He started to sing a little song in a gentle voice, beating the measure with his hand. He sang it over and over. As he sang, two or three young Indians entered silently, and without any effort to make an entrance. They just flowed in and became a part of the scene without ostentation and without disturbing the composure of the room. Geronimo generously sang his little song over and over. Natalie was listening intently—humming it along with him.

"Now you try," Geronimo said.

She started to sing. She had caught the simple phrase, she had the time and the tune: but not the feeling! She injected something into it that did not belong there. It became sweet, and had a willful virtue in it. Indian music is not sweet, and neither is it moral. She made it sound virtuous, even sentimental—Protestant!

Geronimo smiled, kindly. I saw a smile flash between the other Indians.

"No," said Geronimo, very kindly and like a patient teacher. "Not like that. You make a white man's song. Like this. . . ." And he sang it again in his own way. It was strong and gentle, full of life, but quite impersonal. No complaint in it, no need to fulfill.

She repeated it again after him, trying her best to imitate him. But it was impossible for her to sing it as he did. One had to come to the conclusion that their vocal cords were different, that different experiences had created different vehicles of flesh and bone, so much we are an expression, concrete and material, of the life we live.

Natalie Curtis couldn't reproduce the sounds the Indian psyche used to utter its meaning of life. She *had* to be sweet, resigned, and good, or whatever it was that was coming out of her. What a gulf opened between us in that room! Between the Indians and us. I felt lonesome. The young men rose and flowed out silently, laughing and murmuring to each other. Not rudely, just amusedly.

6

The queerest part of it, perhaps, was that Natalie had not seemed to notice the difference between her singing and Geronimo's. She was writing down the song in her notebook, humming it sweetly to herself. She continued doing this until she had compiled a big book, which cost a good many dollars to buy. I think she never knew the Indians laughed kindly at her way of singing Indian music. She never knew she was unequal to the transcription.

Chapter Seven

JOHN and I went up to Taos alone, for Maurice took so long to pack all his paints and paraphernalia I couldn't wait. Leaving orders at stores in Santa Fe, I expected boxes of provisions to come up to us every week; for I felt one wouldn't be able to buy *anything* up in that village, far away from the railroad. I even ordered dry things, like coffee and sugar and cereals! It seemed to me I was going into the wilderness and leaving the world behind me, and I loved that, for it was a new thing to feel.

We reached the high desert of Taos Valley at twilight and saw the sacred mountain, twenty miles away, standing out in startling bright distinctness, lighted by a sun that had already sunk below the horizon. The snow patches on the three peaks of the bow-shaped crest were transparently pink, and all the deep flanks of the southern slopes were purple plum color. The low light of the dusk made the shapes like pyramids stand out so clearly the range seemed made up of cones, piled one upon the other. Very huge and splendid it was. In the high sky over it, a few rosy clouds floated; the pale blue sky seemed still and peaceful, bearing breathlessly the soft, warm, pale clouds over the massive, voluminous earth beneath it. Looking at this definite, sudden, precise earth-form that towered there so still, I saw something again that I had never noticed in nature. It seemed to me the mountain was alive, awake, and breathing. That it had its own consciousness. That it knew things. If I needed John or some man beside me to enable me to be somebody with a valid, objective existence, this mountain was Itself with no outside aid. "I am I" the mountain breathed to me— or so it seemed. "I am what I am—nothing can add to me or take away from me my own being. But it is because I am a part of all the rest of Nature." The mountain seemed to smile and breathe forth an infinitely peaceful, benevolent blessing as the light faded away from it.

We reached the Manby house in the darkness of a silent country street. No one moved outside the mysterious adobe houses. Lights burned behind curtains, but no movement crossed the windows.

Everything, everything left behind; just John and I alone, beyond the known things. John being there with me gave me a sense of identity. He made me feel "I am I."

Manby let us in, helped us with our bags and bundles, helped us light lamps and fires, for the house was cold as death as we came into our end of it through the thick side entrance door of the garden. In a short time, though, it came all alive. When I had the kitchen stove burning and potatoes and eggs and bacon frizzling upon it, we were Home!

John was thrilled by it all and so was I. The old-fashioned, ugly hanging lamp shone down upon the center table in the living room, upon dishes and forks and knives, and we felt cozy and shut away in there from cold and darkness and obliquity—as complete and self-contained as birds in a cage, and content to be in the warm prison.

While we sat there together alone, Manby having at last taken himself away into his own quarters with a baleful smile over his shoulder, I suddenly said to John:

"I want to cut my hair off! I've always wanted to! Let's do it now! Can you do it for me?"

"Sure I can," he exclaimed joyfully. He had always liked to

MABEL

brush and comb it, to twist it into different shapes. I fetched scissors, and a mirror that I propped up on the table in front of me.

"Just straight around—just below the ears. . . ."

He clipped and clipped excitedly, and laid the long brown tresses in a pile.

"I love doing this!" he murmured.

Soon it was all off. Straight across my eyebrows, then down a few inches and hanging heavily over my ears in an angular bob. I had no precedent for this kind of hair-cut. No one I knew or ever saw wore short hair like this, but I remembered Maxfield Parrish illustrations and medieval pages. That was the way I wanted it to feel, and that was the way it looked when it was finished.

I tossed it back and forth and felt the satisfactory swing and freedom of it. Never had my head felt so like my own— not since I had cut it off years before, under Seward's influence. Something in him had made me want to cut my hair, and I had done it. But then I had had to hide the outrage under a false "switch." No one left me in peace about that. The outlandish, short-haired girl had offended every eye.

"I don't know *what* Maurice will say!" I was walking enthusiastically about the room, feeling the change. "He'll be furious! I've tried to do it before, but he wouldn't let me!"

"I don't know what business of his it is!" John cut in truculently.

"Well, he thinks it is, anyway!"

"I wish he didn't have to come! I wish we were going to be alone here. . . ."

I didn't answer him. Poor Maurice.

In the evening when he came I met him at the street entrance. He was getting out of the dark car, his back turned, dragging at bags.

"Look, Maurice. I've cut my hair off!" I cried, shaking my short locks at him, gaily.

He turned, and the most woebegone expression passed over his face, smudged quickly out by anger.

"I don't like it at all! Why did you do it? Your lovely hair! You look dreadful!"

"She didn't do it. I did it," John said, poking himself in front of me. "I think it looks great."

Maurice didn't answer him. He continued to unload the car and carried things into the house. His arrival was spoiled for him. Something was knocked flat in him just by that haircut, and all that evening he remained silent and separate from us.

The old adobe house with its two patios, its long corridors and many rooms, all iron-barred, was full of an atmosphere of mystery and secrecy. It seemed to have things to tell that one could not hear. It was impregnated with the thoughts and the acts of Mr. Manby. And it was not long before Pinkie emerged. Poor little Pinkie!

"I bought this eiderdown for Pinkie," Mr. Manby explained one day. Dr. Martin told us she was a little girl seventeen years old, the third of Manby's wives. She had been practically immured in there with him for a year and then had escaped with the barber. He had not pursued them. He just let her go—like that. In the complicated affairs of Manby's life, beset as it was with lawsuits over land, breach of promise, gold mines and what not, Pinkie must have been like a kitten, hiding with terrified eyes among the coils in which she was entangled.

The garden was like a frozen replica, in its bitter winter

rigidity, of the deviations and turns and twists of its creator. Manby, I found when spring came, was a wonderful gardener. Things sprang eagerly into life for him. The lilac bushes were heavy with clusters of bloom, poppies flamed everywhere they got a chance, and his hollyhocks grew ten feet high. But the garden and the land behind it were laid out in all kinds of paths that started straight but either curved away or ended nowhere. There were borders and squares of lawn, and away from the garden, just outside the length of the house, long avenues curved and meandered away towards the eastern foothills: avenues that were bordered with all kinds of trees which Manby had transplanted from the canyons in the mountains.

There was a pool he had constructed, a quarter of a mile away from the house near the end of the curving, tree-shaded way. It had willows drooping over it and rustic benches beside it. I never saw anyone sit on them. This avenue was designed to enter the Boulevard that would encircle the valley and that existed vividly in Mr. Manby's imagination. Many of the townspeople had never been inside the house or the garden.

Dr. Bergman stood looking at it for the first time, after we came. He said:

"Very nice; but Englishmen hate the straight line, don't they? With them, everything must curve."

Inside the house, it was all light and shadow, scented with burning piñon wood. The rooms were dark with heavily dark furniture, and the full yellow sunlight would burst into a corner like a blast and make a Rembrandtesque effect.

Maurice fitted into this somber, deep, and bright-slashed interior. He needed a strong realistic background. The suggestion of violence and desperation that the house somehow seemed laid out for was not unbecoming to him. It suited him better than the white living room at Croton, where the canary sang.

In his flannel shirt, with corduroys tucked into high boots, he stamped purposefully around with a pipe in his mouth. He looked like what we had heard that intriguing new race, the Bolsheviks, looked like. Quite soon he developed an expression of evasiveness, eyes downwards and a hasty passing, that made Mr. Manby watch him closely with a dubious eyebrow raised.

Manby's suspicions were always ready for anything except himself. He did not realize Maurice was occupied only in trying to avoid him and his long garrulous tales of self-defense. He was a boring old man with his manias and his madnesses. I was kinder. At first. I let him talk for a while, sitting beside me on the slippery horse-hair sofa . . . tell me how he killed the two men who attacked him when he was in the stagecoach, how he caught the ones who were purloining nuggets from "The Mystic Mine," about Fergusson, the dead partner, the disappearance of people. . . . It was all a phantasy of murder and gold and heroic self-defense that he talked about in his charming English voice. Closing one's eyes, one could imagine an Oxford dean, who might be reading aloud from the annals of Deadwood Dick.

Like everything in my life since early days, this new phase was all a story-book to me; but these few months I am about to tell of are the last ones that had that fictitious feeling, as though things were happening around me but not to me. This book must first tell a little about the people that were there in Taos, who lived on the fringe of that other life that was esoteric and unknowable to them. But this Taos village was not then more real for me, did not belong to me any more than the Buffalo world, or the Florentine world, or the New York or Croton worlds had. It was fantastic and funny and parts of it were delicious. The light and the air in those high regions were solemnly beautiful, but the people who lived in that beneficence were like the money-changers in the Temple. Few were there except to make something out of the Indians; and the village had grown up on the outskirts of the Pueblo upon land stolen from them and settled by priests, traders, merchants, and finally artists. Even the pretty blue and white court-house held no title for the land it stood upon, and no one had a title that had any real validity. There was no foundation to anything, no rights, no roots, and no security, in Taos village. There was no law, no reverence, and very little beauty of living. But the small population thought it was real. They were spending their lives gathering enough money to remain on land that was not theirs, in a country that lacked everything they considered most desirable. Many of them went about on their short, routined paths, dreaming of New York, or Germany, or Philadelphia. Some of them even dreamed with homesick remembrance of Texas or Kansas. But they stuck there in Taos, always hopeful, always thinking it was going to be different. Before I tell about the real Taos, and the sunny, real life I entered into, I must describe some of these shadowy characters, these Americans from Europe who lived next to, but never knew, reality.

Ralph Meyers said to me once:

"It's queer, but one just can't get ahead in Taos. Nothing succeeds here. It's as though there is something working against us. We struggle and plan and it doesn't come to anything."

"Maybe the Indians won't let you," I suggested.

"It looks that way," he answered, glumly.

Chapter Eight

OF COURSE the white people clustered together in the village; there were very few who lived outside it. For instance, in the village of Ranchos de Taos, five miles away, that one passed coming in, there was only one white woman.

There were several hamlets in the valley entirely made up of Mexicans, and these were lovely villages where streams ran, bordered with great cottonwood trees and red willows. Arroyo Secco to the north, Arroyo Hondo to the west, Ranchitos southwest of Taos, Ranchos de Taos at the southeast, and Cordovas over south, this last a stout, compact row of thick-walled adobe houses plastered in very light mud and with pale blue window-frames and doors. At the rear of Cordovas the desert rolled straight over to the dangerous opening of the Rio Grande Canyon where marauding Apaches used to emerge above the rim and rush down upon the village. There was a round adobe fortress behind among the corrals where the women and children would be hurriedly hidden when this happened.

In the summer, if one climbed a little way up the slopes of the foothills behind Manby's house, one could look down over the whole valley and see Taos like a green oasis with cultivated fields around it, cultivated and cleared by the Indians in the bygone days; and the other villages showed up, too: minute clusters of houses and trees and fields, and Randall's orchard like a neat, striped square. Where all the streams ran down from the mountains, the cottonwoods and willows showed distantly like heavy, dark green blobs in the summertime, and in the winter like pale, spectral, gray, half-solid mist.

Besides the groups who lived together, isolated houses were dotted here and there like oblong notes cut in a music-box reel, so the landscape looked like a musical phrase that no one knew how to play. I never saw one, or two or three together, of these simple, sudden adobe houses set clearly on the earth, when riding or driving about, that they did not seem to me like musical notes in a piece that no one heard.

The Mexicans always had geraniums blooming in the windows. In the winter time, the round leaves flattened themselves against the glass, reaching out to the sunshine, and bright red and magenta flowers lighted up the adobe color of the house as though a fire burned within. They always seemed to me to be a symbol of the Spanish drops of blood. Much-traveled flowers, these beloved geraniums—taken into Spain by the Moors, and brought from there across the sea ages ago to this continent. The same is true of the pale yellow Castilian rose that grows busily in so many gardens here. How many times slips must have been shared with neighbors since the first plants were carried here. They have been divided and sub-divided like family trees, but outside in the world it is called the rarest rose in America.

The native Mexican houses and gardens are austere but complete. The older adobe houses, made without benefit of plumb-line, have an irregularity that sweetens their rectangles and gives them a hand-made look. The windows are set in a trifle crookedly, and doors lean a little so that nothing is exact; and the askew and unmechanical result is attractive and naïve.

I learned early that Mexicans never want trees, bushes,

or vines near the house. I don't yet know why. The houses
stand on a hard, bare, earthen floor that is swept as often
as the earthen floor inside. At a small distance away, there
may be a round bed of flaming magenta flowers in the summer, or the familiar Castilian rosebush and a few iris plants.
But there is nothing creeping up the walls or growing against
the house. Perhaps on account of insects or snakes. The wood-
pile is the most noticeable thing in the bare yard, and it is
usually decorative, for dry piñon logs and cedar have lovely
colors: one pale gray, the other of burnt-sienna—and the shapes
are clear.

Inside the house there is the same swept and almost bar-
ren look. A large bed adorns the living room, and a few upright chairs stand upon the mud floor. In 1917 there was always a hand-made Santo or two up on the walls, and in
most of the houses there were old carved boxes that had
been wedding chests and then became granaries; and there
were cupboards with hand-turned spindles. A perpetual smell
of beans and coffee is the characteristic odor in Mexican houses,
and has been for centuries.

The Mexicans in Taos Valley seemed a sad lot to me when
I first came. Apparently they hadn't much gaiety. They looked
pinched, discouraged, and baffled. Their forefathers had come
here ages ago and nothing much had happened to them since
except conquests, so it seemed as though the most they had
accomplished had been to keep alive. They are almost all of
mixed Indian and Spanish blood, except for a few families.

It was so short a time ago that this whole country in the
Southwest was a part of Mexico, and these Mexicans the
slaves and soldiers of Spanish overlords that the resignation
of defeat may linger yet in their blood along with the hatred
and fear of the white American conqueror, who came eighty

years ago. These feelings, and, added to them, a half-con-
temptuous, half-envious regard for the Indians who have kept
themselves to themselves through everything from the Spanish
conquest and on through the American conquest, these dreary
feelings seemed to me to rule them and sap their vitality and
their hope.

But it was not long before I became attached to these
people and enjoyed being with them, for they had a wistful
pleasure in small things like the plant in the window and
the handwork upon bright woven serapes or crocheted rugs.
Whenever one entered their houses there was a welcome there.
They were simple and brave and capable of enjoyment, possessing a quick humor and a warmth that was lacking in
the more dispirited "Anglos," as they called the white people.
They were capable of passionate loyalties once they became
one's friends, and there was a thin, rugged tenacity about
them that humanized and dignified their lives.

The Spaniards found another Indian pueblo at the village
called Ranchos de Taos. The priests built a large mission
church there, facing their plaza, and the soldiers married
the unresisting Indian women, and after a while all the Indian strain melted into the Spanish and became Mexican.

There seemed to be a happiness in the Mexican life, due
to the Penitente exorcisms, wherein they flayed themselves,
unconsciously perhaps, to diminish the accumulated bitterness
and despair that they could not pour out upon us. They came
out of these ceremonies apparently refreshed. Turned inwards
upon themselves, they drew their own blood, identifying themselves with Jesus Christ, who died for them, and who is still
dying for them, in their flesh.

Their social and political life is still entangled with religion. Their Catholicism is violent and their violence is cathol-

icized; and since the preponderance of the population in this part of the state is Mexican, the vote is a Penitente vote. Their *bailes* on Saturday nights frequently end in bloodshed, and the ensuing trials are decided by Mexican juries who rarely convict one of their own race. Even penitentiary sentences are usually remitted after a few years by the pressure Mexicans can bring to bear in this state upon those in office. Though they have a kind of power, they don't know yet what to do with it, how to pass laws that will lift their standards, or how to secure schools that will ultimately improve their conditions when their children are grown. The education handed out to them in the local public schools is unenlightened and it seems more calculated to keep them in ignorance than to raise them out of the darkness they exist in. The convent schools are, however, of a higher order of culture and the children benefit more from them than they do at those others called "High," because the gentle association of the nuns does a great deal more for them than the influence of non-sectarian teachers who are in general apt to be drawn from an uncultivated environment. There are occasionally real teachers who by vocation or aptitude find their way into these pathetic southwestern schools but they are rare.

Besides the *bailes,* where the dance often ends with a knife or a gun-shot (attributed by the white people to "the altitude" rather than to the state of suppressed intensity in which they are driven by the white people themselves), they have the colorful pleasures connected with going to church, and with *velorios* and funerals. When someone among them dies, they have a gathering that lasts all night. It resembles an Irish wake and it is called a *velorio.* They meet and sing and pray and eat and have a rich time.

Their churchyards are very pretty. The graves are marked

with turquoise blue, or white, or black wooden crosses, and are quite gay with flowers in the summer. On All Souls' Day, they decorate the graves with wonderful tissue-paper flowers and garlands of all colors, and these flutter and cling to the bright crosses, fading and falling into shreds as the cold winds come across them. The wintry churchyards, covered with deep snow out of which the pale crosses thrust themselves, with tattered paper roses clinging about them, are lovely under a happy blue sky.

The churches were originally built like the Indians built their houses, with ceilings supported on huge pine beams, from which the bark was peeled when it was green. Then hand-hewn planks were laid across them, or rows of small saplings. Upon these, thin willow-branches were spread to cover the cracks, and then quantities of mud, mixed with straw, to a depth of a couple of feet, was tamped and stamped hard and flat. Wooden *canales* or water-spouts stuck out on either side of the roof (which had a border of adobes a couple of feet high) to drain off the rain and melted snow. But the roofs were quite flat and often the water collected in puddles and finally leaked through the layer of mud. When, as sometimes happens in this country, a cloudburst occurred, these roofs let the water in faster than it could be controlled, and then it was miserable indeed.

As priest succeeded priest, down through the years, and traders began to have building materials in the country stores, finally Father Joseph Giraud arrived in Taos. He was a Frenchman from Lyons—and a practical man. He began by tearing the old roof off the Taos village church. He threw out the fine carved corbels and the old beams, had the mud lifted off, and replaced the ancient roof with a tin one that sloped up in the middle so the snow would slide off, and completely

7

spoiled this fine church. Gerson Gusdorf salvaged the corbels and the beams, and when he made his store over into the Don Fernando Hotel in 1926, he incorporated them in it.

The Ranchos church has always belonged to the community where it stands, and Father Joe couldn't touch it. There it squats, its massive rear heavily buttressed, painted a hundred times by the artists who have lived here and by visiting ones, its roof still leaking after cloudbursts, but as handsome as the day it was built.

Only inside it, the Mexicans tore out a hand-carved balcony, and one day Bobby Jones found the pieces lying on the floor and brought some of them home in a wagon—and we built them into the big gates of our house.

When Bobby came he was spellbound by the leaning and irregular lines of adobe architecture, and the crooked crosses, all askew. He was, for a time, impressed by the curious powerful influences that linger around the Mexican Penitente *moradas,* those private chapels standing in remote spots, windowless and windswept, where unimaginable effluences escape into freedom. After his first visit here, he returned to New York and produced "Macbeth," a semi-abstract construction that made audiences feel faint and ill, that made Dr. Jelliffe himself stagger out of the theater, exclaiming: "But this is murder!" "Til Eulenspiegel," at the Metropolitan Opera House, with its fantastic towers and houses leaning and bowing towards each other, came out of Taos, too, after that visit.

The interiors of the churches had altar-pieces decorated with incredible naïveté, and Santos painted on hand-hewn boards with paints made out of earth and vegetable substances. When the pioneering priests and soldiers came, they had to have images to worship, so they sat down and made them. They made everything they needed, and the painting and carving they left here is the only true primitive art America has ever had. Life-sized, bleeding Christs, with black Spanish beards, carved out of pine wood and painted realistically, hung in these churches on wooden crosses in no way different from the crosses the Penitentes dragged from the *moradas* up the Hills of Calvary all about the valley, and upon which they hung by ropes a member of their Order during Easter week, until the priests were told from Rome to stop them.

The bells in the low towers of these churches and chapels were secured with difficulty. The one that was in the Ranchos church when I came had been hauled up from Old Mexico, where it had been welded of copper and the contributions of jewelry sent down from here by the women. A few years ago, the Ranchos people decided they wanted a new bell, and offered to sell this one for a hundred dollars. I had not the money then, and Gerson Gusdorf bought it and hung it in the lobby of the Don Fernando, where it kept company with the corbels and beams from the Taos church until the hotel burned down.

There have been all kinds of priests in the valley, along through the years. One comes upon traces of the earlier ones from time to time. Padre Martinez, alive here during the life of Governor Bent, the first American Governor of New Mexico after the American invasion, became a legend. He ruled here powerfully. He did not believe in celibacy and a great many women loved him and apparently they all called their offspring Martinez; so his descendants of that name are to be found at all the cardinal points of the valley. Magnetic and resolute, when he was excommunicated from the Catholic church, he set up a church of his own, taking his whole congregation with him. I have a charcoal drawing of him, made by an admirer from Ranchos de Taos, showing a fierce, bullet-shaped head, intense eyes, and a lower lip that pushes the upper lip up like an iron brace.

The Mexicans in the valley resented being run over by the Americans. They preferred to be exploited by the Spaniards, and they plotted to murder Governor Bent, and to drive out the handful of white people. Whether Padre Martinez had anything to do with this plan no one definitely knows. The Mexicans went out to the Pueblo to the Indians, who were living peaceably behind their wall, minding their own business and not much concerned with the affairs down in the Mexican-American village. The Catholic church had raised its little temple at the entrance to the Pueblo, like a sentry box, but beyond that it had not interfered much with the people, as it had in the south in Old Mexico. These Indians had never intermarried with Spaniards or even with Mexicans, and they had no mutual concerns. But the natives from the Taos village wanted their help. They told them these Americans would be the end of them all—of both the Mexican life and the Indian life. This fitted in with what the old men had always been prophesying about a white race that would come and swallow them up so they would almost disappear from the earth—except they be strong and keep the eternal fire burning in the mountains, so when the Mexicans asked them to help to drive the strangers out, they agreed. They agreed only to help, but the Mexicans got everything started, directed perhaps by the shrewd Padre, and when the fighting was going on, and the American soldiers were sent up from Santa Fe to put down the rebellion, the Mexicans seemed to fade away and leave it looking solely like an Indian affray.

Governor Bent was killed, and so were many of the Indians, whose share in all this had turned into a defense of the Pueblo, during which the church was cannonaded and fell. The Indian women in the houses loaded and reloaded the muskets for the men; they all worked together to save their homes, not understanding at all why the militia were bearing down upon them so heavily, not realizing yet the defection of the Mexicans. They only understood it later, when the fighting was over and our government ordered seven of the head men of the Pueblo to be hanged, as a punishment for the killing of the American governor and for the whole uprising.

The Governor of the Pueblo, the War Chief, and some of their officers called upon Padre Martinez and asked him to save them now. They had been told a good deal about Fatherhood. There was the Great White Father in Washington who was their father and who had given them a silver-headed cane —were these Fathers connected with the Church that stood there in the Pueblo? Surely, if a father was anything, he was first a protector. But Washington was too far away, so they went to Father Martinez. They had heard, anyway, that he was managing all this business.

The Indians asked the Padre to save them, and he asked them what they would give him to save them. They said they would give him a big piece of land adjoining their pastures. They bargained back and forth and finally came to an agreement. The priest drew up some papers and the Indians signed with thumbprints and crosses. The end of it was that despite his efforts he got the land and the Indians were hanged. He had no jurisdiction over them, nor any influence with the United States Government—and anyway, possibly it was he who had always intended the Indians to be the scapegoats in this attempt to defy the Americans. The highway north to Colorado runs through this land that he got from the Indians and the houses of descendants of his stand on either side of

7 ★

the road. This story is the account of one of the land deals
of Taos Valley, as it is believed by the Indians here.

Father Joe, who had been in Taos for a good many years
now, had a kind of geniality. He was cheerful and convivial.
A square, black beard adorned his red face, and the thick
lenses of his spectacles prevented one from reading his thoughts.
When I first came to Taos, he drove about in a high buggy
with two black horses, his driver a Mexican with a grim smile
who helped him in his house and in the church, hard by.
Father Joe had him ring the church bell for the Angelus, at
six in the morning, and again at noon and at six o'clock. This
was always called "the Padre's time," to distinguish it from
"Santa Fe time," for instance, or "railroad time," which one
got by telephoning over to Taos Junction. Needless to say,
these times were all quite different from each other.

Father Joe lived on the street behind the church. There
was a high wall in front of the house, and it went all around
his big garden at the back. All summer long he worked early
and late in this garden, which was laid out exactly as though
it were somewhere in provincial France. Long neat rows of
vegetables and square beds of flowers—all the flowers from
roses to hollyhocks. At the rear there was a tangle of plum trees
and some apples. Father Joe of course had strawberries, rasp-
berries, gooseberries, and currants in his garden, and at one
side of the house there was a corral where there were always
a few sheep fattening to provide him with mutton.

The Indians gave him a "tithe" of their crops. A special field
is sown for the priest in wheat and farmed by the young,
unmarried men, whom the church considers more holy than
the married ones. They provide all the wood he burns, and
more besides, which some priests have been known to sell,

CATHOLIC CHURCH AT TAOS PUEBLO   by *Ernest Knee*

although they should have kept the church warm on Sundays with it.

Later on, when he got his glassy Buick sedan, Father Joe used to drive out to the Pueblo on All Souls' Day and say a mass in the "new" church, and bless the dead in the graveyard of the old, ruined church. Two Mexicans waited for him at the door of the church, and at the conclusion of the service, they shoveled into the wagons the great heaps of corn and wheat that always lie waiting on the floor of the church that day to go to the poor.

I once was in Father Joe's house at noontime and he asked me to sit down to the table with him—and how like a French curé he was! The dining room was cold and gray-looking, the deal floor scrubbed spotless, the deal table scoured until it was worn down. The curtainless window, looking out upon the garden, faced north and of course the repellent light of the room was due to that. But such good food brought in by a disgruntled-looking Mexican woman: a leg of lamb, and succulent green peas from the vines near by, crisp French salad in a bowl, with plenty of garlic, and beside his plate, the round, brown loaf that tastes the best when it is broken and not cut.

Father Joe poured wine from a glass pitcher into tumblers. A good French *vin ordinaire* that he made himself, perhaps, and plenty of it. His face reddened more and more and grew quite glossy.

Father Joe was saving money, but what for? What did he do with all the money that was brought to him in silver dollars and laid timidly upon his desk in the office in the front of his house? Money to pay for masses, for marriages, baptisms and funerals. For all kinds of odd jobs. The Mexicans were forever creeping into that front office and laying silver dollars down upon the desk in an apologetic way that was evoked by his practical, efficient, and business-like manner towards them.

He didn't assume this manner. He was but acting as he felt and as he believed he should feel towards his parishioners. With those who did not belong to his church, he was free and easy—but with the Catholics he was a stern disciplinarian and supremely indifferent to their opinion or their comments.

In the winter, he grudged the wood for the stove that was to warm the church so often people caught cold Sunday mornings. He himself strode in to conduct the service, warm in his full-skirted cassock and ruddy from his wine, and during the service he would look up and frown slightly if there was too much coughing. No one dared to ask him to heat the church better. They only protested with coughs and sneezes.

Pneumonia was a frequent cause of death in Taos Valley and Father Joe generally officiated at burials and he would collect a fee for the ceremony.

Father Joe wouldn't have an old painted Santo in his church! No, indeed! Everything was brand new to go with the new tin roof. There were shining new brass candlesticks on the altar and a number of statuettes in pale blue robes, with meek, Nordic faces. Virgins and Sons of Virgins closely resembling each other—and all produced by factories.

On one side of the Padre's house and garden, the Sisters have their Convent. Like his, it is painted a cold, serviceable gray. It stands back from the street and beside the walk up to it there are planted small, symmetrical evergreen trees, and flower borders. There used to be silver poplars lining this sidewalk, but Father Joe said evergreens were better, because they were nice in the winter; so he had them all cut down and replaced with the little evergreens that take so long to grow. In the flower borders, purple iris came the first thing in the spring. In the summer, there were pansies and phlox, that started in various shades of pink and red, but which relapsed into magenta in that way it has.

The Sisters had a school for little children. It was quite a pleasant, small school, but the children were hypnotized by Father Joe. There was a perpetual terror that he might come in and find someone without a clean handkerchief or a tidy shirt.

Chapter Nine

THE DAY after we were settled in the dark, warm interior of Manby's house, John drove Maurice and me out to the Pueblo. I wanted to see the Indians, to know them, for, as they passed up and down the road outside the house all day long on their hard-bitten, gaunt ponies, I searched their faces and tried to penetrate their infinitely unfamiliar souls. But I could not. They seemed to have a barrier raised between themselves and the world—my world, anyway. Their eyes were not empty, but they were distant in expression. Sometimes cold, and sometimes smiling, but though they were alive and glowing, they seemed to keep a distance between us.

I took a bag of oranges out with me, for I had heard somewhere that one could ingratiate oneself with small presents like that.

Just inside the Pueblo, across from the little Catholic church, there was a group of houses that looked less blank than some of the others. The doors were open, and when we stopped to decide what to do and where to go, a couple of small children ran up to us in a friendly way. Then a beautiful woman stepped to one of the open doors. She was full-breasted and her black cotton dress, sprigged with white, was brought in at the waist by a broad, red, woven belt that was wound twice around her and tucked in, so that it supported her deep bosom like a corset; and below it, the full skirt hung stiffly away from her, trim and rotund, while an inch or two of white embroidery showed underneath the ample folds.

She had a warm smile on her small, perfect face, and her eyes were dark and warm and amused. I got out of the car and just naturally went towards her and the others followed. Determined to make a good impression, I reached out to her from inside myself, and smiled a hesitant appeal as I approached her: but no hunter was ever more calculating, or ready to sprinkle salt on a tail approached unawares.

Near the door, I stopped, for I heard a low singing and the soft beat of a drum, and I became deprecating. But she made a smooth, round gesture with her small hand and murmured, *"Entre!"* in a voice that was low and rich and deep-toned.

Over the threshold and we were in a large, bare room with white-washed walls that had along their base rows of rolled mattresses covered with white sheets and colored blankets. The room went far in and was shadowy at the end; but near the entrance, a bright fire burned and perfumed the air with wood incense, and sunshine came in at the door.

There was a tiny little window in the left-hand wall, without glass and only thin bars of wood between it and the outer air. This little window, set high up in the thick adobe, let a beam of light come streaming in across the room, and suddenly reminded me of the window in the bedroom at Pierrefonds Castle, where Violet and I slept together. Maybe it was the thickness of the walls, and the way the light cut across the enclosed space like something ponderable.

A man sat beside the fireplace on a low wooden hassock. A thin, gray blanket came over his shoulders and fell in folds around his moccasined feet, and he tapped lightly on a little water-drum that rested on the floor between his knees. He was singing in a low, far-away murmur, and his eyes were on the drum, his head bent so I could not see his face at first, and he didn't look up, even when we came crowding in, the three of us.

The woman motioned to the low, white bedrolls with a gesture that was grave and quiet and respectful to the song, and we tiptoed in and sat, in an atmosphere that was new to me. The room was impregnated with a fullness of life. It had a rich, slow peacefulness without being in any way solemn. Maybe the drumming and the song gave a measure in which one could relax and spread one's breathing fuller and deeper, maybe the deep being of these people enriched their surrounding air. Anyway, whatever it was, I had never felt more satisfied and at ease, although my attention was set upon trying to fit in and be a part of it without seeming to try.

I knew I could arrive at this unconscious, full equilibrium, but that I could only do so by adapting myself. I longed to simply *be* so, as they were, but I knew I must make it for myself as I went along. Not for me, alas, the simple, unthinking harmonies of life; but for me—yes! I thought fiercely—this sumptuous peace and content, this sunny gravity and fire perfume in white-washed walls at any cost, at any sacrifice.

And as I was thinking so, the man stopped singing and raised his head and looked at me for the first time, with a quick glance that penetrated to the depths with an instantaneous recognition, and I saw his was the face that had blotted out Maurice's in my dream—the same face, the same eyes, involuntarily intense, with the living fire in their depths. He bowed slightly, faintly patronizing.

"I sang you a little song," he said, gently.

"Thank you ever so much!" I answered, feeling really deprecating, now, and not having to pretend. "Would you like an orange?" I asked him, timidly, and offered him one. He bowed again and took it graciously.

Maurice, trying to be sociable, said, "What are the words in that song?"

"Got no words. Just song," he replied, coldly, becoming aloof and keeping his eyes on the orange as though he would not injure them with the sight of us.

The woman got up and altered the stiff moment by placing a stick of wood upright on the diminishing fire; so I got up, too, and said we must be going; and the others followed my example. I walked up to the man and held out my hand and said:

"Thank you! I wish you'd come and see us down in Taos."

He said, "I seen you before, already," and he gave me another glance, swift and passing, but deep in the eyes, so that something vivid was etched into both of us. "Where you live?" he asked Maurice.

"Well, we are staying at the Manby house. I want to paint the Indians. Maybe you could come and pose sometime?"

"Not me. Maybe the others." He smiled, indulgently, as though generously overlooking a *faux pas*. The woman laughed and shook her head, raised her thin eyebrows, tossed herself a little, humoring us, laughing with politeness, but still, laughing at us.

I hated to go out the door and leave that good and lively feeling behind me in the room, for not in any room I had ever made and lived in had I achieved such a plentiful and active sense of living. Not with Genoese velvets and Renaissance chairs, nor with the repercussion of dangerous ideas fearlessly told, nor by any manner of means had I ever come so near before to the possibilities of abundant life, as in that empty place where firelight played upon bare walls and the air was sweet with wood-smoke, while some man unfathomably unknown to me, yet immediately recognizable, beat upon a small drum and sang a little song.

The moment we were all in the car together again, the ease was gone, for on the invisible stage where we lived and had our being, our spirits clutched at each other and strangled freedom. All three of us, entangled together, were tensed in strange and subtle ways, and strove both to grasp at and to repel the others' claims on life.

It was too bad—for all about us, out there in the Pueblo, there was a free and easy mode of life that we could see and smell and almost touch, that we might emulate, only we did not know how, for we did not know what elements it was made of.

The air was cold, keenly cold in the shadow, and the earth was frozen hard; but in the sun we felt warmed through. The great mountain rose massive and mysterious in its shadowy folds which seemed full of a dark blue light, and Indians were passing back and forth from the canyon that circled around one side of it and let the river down through the Pueblo.

This river had a coating of ice upon it, and there were some black holes broken near the brinks where the women went and dipped out their water and where the men bathed at dawn. There were horses and dogs and children about, and it was all very happy, with a kind of subdued merriment, for there were no raucous, uncouth noises such as I was familiar with in almost all villages. The high, clear air amplified the voices so that one heard them, round and clear, even at a distance, and the sounds were like soft, dark flowers falling gently into water.

An elderly man came to the door of his house and called

a little boy to him. He asked him something, and the child replied in the same tone the man had used, a gracious tone that seemed to have a full permission in it. No hustle, or roughness among these people: but indulgence, tolerance, permission. The keynote of their relationships is like that, I saw. I had felt it in the house we had left. No hindrance of each other, no embargo, but a mutual sanction of life in each other. This made an ease that my people have forgotten.

We drove back to Taos town and left this pleasant, acquiescent atmosphere behind us. At the Post Office, on the corner of the plaza, we stopped to secure a letter box, and met Manby there, striding out with lowered head and sidewise angry looks to right and left of him at the other village characters who hung about the entrance. I caught a muffled and obviously malicious comment directed after him by one of the dingy loafers who leaned against the wall, and his companions broke into jeering chuckles. The whole neighborhood was colored by hateful thoughts and feelings and I hurried away from it. I carried letters from Bobby Jones and Andrew Dasburg and Agnes home to read.

Our rooms had a home-like feeling already. That is, though they were dark and warm, fires gleamed in the living room fireplace and in the stoves in the bedrooms, and there were cedar branches over the chimney place and on the round center table.

Maurice had taken a studio in a house a few doors down the street and was all ready to work, he said. But this meant he was ready to start preparing to work, for there was the usual elaborate business of art to get in order: canvases to fix, paints to grind, and all that.

"It's queer, Mabel," he said at supper that night. "I never

8

really wanted to do sculpture so much as I do here. These Indians are so plastic—they have such wonderful Form."

"Yes, they have real faces," I answered. "Well, I hope you will, Maurice!" Was my aim to be accomplished at last? What I had gone through to make that man into a sculptor! I looked at him more comfortably that evening. As we sat at the table with the cast-iron hanging lamp bathing us in the yellow light of kerosene oil, and the rest of the solid, prosaic room dark except for flickering gleams of firelight, I felt a kind of peace and relaxation I hadn't had before. It seemed awfully real, for once: the plain, not very good food that Anita trotted in and out of the kitchen with, the firelight and lamp-light and Maurice sitting there in a blue flannel shirt looking thoughtful and less nervous than usual and even John poring over a fascinating old copy of a Montgomery Ward catalogue, all of it seemed somehow genuine and down to rock-bottom and away from the pretense and the artificialities we had always lived with. Of course I had to see myself into it and some-how play the role of being really in it, but it came easy to me.

Anita was a diminutive Mexican girl of eighteen whom Manby had secured for us. She was very small and hardly came up above the edge of the table! She cooked beefsteak and coffee and fried potatoes for every meal until we couldn't bear it any more and Andrew and Bobby came along bringing a cook from New York. But that was a month or more later. Just now we were as on a desert island, away from the world and all we had known before, and it was good for us to be so.

That evening after supper there was a singing silence in our house, only broken when a page was turned. I remem-ber how I lay on the old sofa and listened to the high, hum-ming silence of a lonely winter countryside in one of the altitudes of this earth. The air is very thin and seems to be more penetrable than the denser ones of the lowlands, and it is as though all kinds of ethereal essences and elementary perceptions creep through from beyond our usual plane and we become aware of the life in things—in trees, and rivers—and there are curious messages, only half received, borne to us on the movement of the winds.

A few days later we stood in the gray air of the Pueblo darkened by thickly falling snowflakes. Several hundred Indians clad only in deer skins, padded up and down in two long lines, bent forward on the deer sticks they carried in their hands. They uttered harsh animal groans and yelps as they followed the two implacable women who led them. The two women danced backwards with mask-like faces and eyes downcast. They were majestic in their ancient Indian dress, and utterly compelling in their irresistible female way. They carried small pine branches upheld in each hand, and they shook them slightly to the rhythm of the chorus of singers.

The snow fell quietly and unnoticed upon the deer people, who were naked save for the hides that were belted around them. They bore the heads of newly killed deer upon their own, their identities blotted out beneath the branching antlers. Among them, little boys were hidden beneath the skins of fox and wolf and mountain lion. All the beasts that came from the forest seemed spellbound by the magical women.

The air was muffled by the snow, yet alive with the desperate and doomed utterance of beasts. Drawn along by those two proud women, the men followed where they led. The older men sang a strong invulnerable song in a chorus that seemed as full of the beat of fate as the waves that pound in upon a beach.

As they moved along, following the women, outlaw, clownish hunters pelted them with frail straw arrows—they caught a deer or a fox from the ranks and, flinging them over their shoulders, made off with them to the river. Rescue came when it was possible for the grave head men of the tribe to catch them before they reached it. The head men were clad from head to foot in newly tanned white buckskin. They walked along beside the shuddering, spellbound beasts, guarding the game that was theirs.

The power of the tribe was invested in the two women who gently danced before the helpless creatures, leading them to their doom. An old—perhaps the oldest—allegory was confronting us there. The feminine principle is the strongest one in nature—and the wild animal must follow where it leads, must be sacrificed, assimilated, and converted into a new energy. What matters the interpretation of the white man who told us what the dance represented? One of the painters murmured his story of the ceremonial in my ears. He had had it from an Indian, he said.

"Years ago there was no meat for the people, for the game was scarce. So the council sent two of their most beautiful women up into the mountain, and they made magic and lured the animals down into the Pueblo where the head men seized them and everybody feasted. Ever since, they have danced the Deer Dance to commemorate the occasion."

The sun suddenly broke through a faltering cloud and the mountain seemed to laugh. The cries and the shuddering remonstrance went on beside us. The old men continued the strong beat of the chorus, and the two women turned slowly and led the rows of subjected animals back to the kivas. The soft furs and brown bare legs disappeared into the snow, and the sound faded away. We were among our own kind again, a little handful of white people from Taos.

"May I present Mrs. Harwood?" said Mr. Phillips.

"How do you do?"

"My feet are cold. I think we'll be getting along."

I wondered where the man was I had met the other day, but I did not even know his name and did not like to ask.

We drove home in a soundless landscape that had whitened since we left the house. The whole world was white and still, and we saw nothing that moved except a little hawk that was perched upon a cedar fence post and rose with its curved beak outstretched and flew a little further to the next one, and thus alternately flying and perching, preceded us into town where I lost sight of it.

"Marvelous!" exclaimed Maurice as he stamped into the house. "These Indians have a real Art of their own."

But it was their life that seemed so real to me every time I got near enough to it to feel it. Real, real, and deep as fate, and full of wisdom and experience.

8 *

Chapter Ten

SOON a couple of women friends came to stay with us.

They drove up from Embudo on Oscar Davis's stage and arrived late in the evening, because the car had broken down somewhere along the rough canyon road. Julia was gibbering with delight. She was the nervous kind of woman who welcomes trouble because it is an outlet.

They were enchanted with the mysterious house and the strange, dark rooms with their brown adobe walls. Even the scrambled eggs I hastily cooked for them pleased Julia because it was all so "different."

The next day I took them out to the Pueblo and as I saw the Indian woman I knew in the doorway of her house, I drew them over there. We went in and it was all as it was before. The man was singing beside the fire.

When we left, Agnes said:

"Your friend has beautiful eyelids!" I knew what she meant. His downcast eyes were nobly shaped under the three-cornered, veiling lids. The face was like a noble bronze—rather full and ample, with a large nose and a generous mouth. He had not seemed to look at us, though maybe he did. When we were going out the door, he gave us each a handshake and said he would come and see us some day. Like the first time, I carried away a sense of deeper being and more easy breathing. I began to be happy, then, in January.

The snow covered the whole valley from that time, so we were only able to go to the two villages at either end of the three-mile road: down to the plaza where the few chilled-looking Americans went for their daily groceries and the Mexicans drove in from their huddled houses in the distant corners of that sleeping plain, or up to the Indian community—and the snow was soon too deep to drive there easily.

The Indians did not come down in their high-seated wagons, but rode in occasionally on ponies whose white winter coats made them look shaggy and blurred. It was a year before I learned that after Twelfth Night the wagons are not used for forty days, nor any hard-nailed boots to tread the Pueblo earth, for then the earth is sleeping quietly, is left to her quietude, because in the delicate, breathless period before germination, nothing must vibrate harshly or strike the sensitive Mother with iron or any other metal.

I longed to explore the roads leading across the valley to the north and up the canyon to the east, but found no way to go, so I could only gaze across the white reaches of snow that rose and fell in long, mild levels, broken here and there by groups of lacy cottonwood trees or warm-colored willows, and wonder what went on over there and over there.

The sun moved across the valley all day long, circling the house that was the new center of my life; and fell early, with blinding rays of purple and red as it sank below the faraway horizon. After five o'clock, when it would be gone, the sky showed a long, narrow bank of rose and yellow, just above the dimmed blue-white distance. The winter evening came quickly all about us in the village street, even while the west held its color for a long time. Then there was a magical, hushed feeling in the air and people's voices, out-of-doors, dropped to a lower key in unconscious reverence for nightfall.

Once, at this twilight hour, I came in the adobe archway

that held the garden gate, after I had been to the Post Office for the evening .mail, for I had the lifelong habit of letters and I still believed that sometime *the* letter would come that would make all the difference. I had three letters in my hand, but none of them was it.

I passed along the path beside the long house on my way to our entrance door, and as I moved in the cold, creaking snow, my heart began to beat tumultuously for no reason. I looked behind me, and then I saw a figure standing motionless at one side of the path down by the gate, under a tall, round lilac bush. Like a still column, he stood there swathed from head to foot in a dim gray blanket that covered all but the dark eyes that stared through the dusk. He faded into the surrounding gray evening and he seemed as immovable as the earth, and only came alive in the glance he bent upon me as I returned to where he was.

"You not see me if I don't want you to," he said, gently. "I can come and go and if I don't want you to, you can't know it."

It was half in joke, but half serious, too.

"Come inside," I said, "and get warm."

"I not cold, but I guess I come in," he answered, and we went into the underworld atmosphere of that house where it was dark although the lamp was lighted and a fire burned in the chimney corner.

He sat down in a large chair beside the fire and never said another word. I took off my coat and hat and fidgeted around the way one does, making a lot of motions. I turned the lamp up higher, opened the door into the kitchen because I knew Anita was there, shut it again, and finally came back to the fire. He had pushed the gray blanket off his head and it coiled around his throat like a wrapped toga.

GOING DOWN THE RIO GRANDE (SUMMER)   *by Ernest Knee*

GOING DOWN THE RIO GRANDE (WINTER)   *by Ernest Knee*

His hair was pushed back from his brow, which made it look very open and candid, and his face was perfectly composed and serene as he stared into the fire.

"Do you know what fire is?" he asked.

"Do *you?*" I returned, not knowing what to answer, for I didn't know.

"Yes, I know. He is alive. He feel. He is my friend. I know what he say."

"Does he know what you say?"

"Of course. Natcherel!" Anita opened the door and came in.

"Hello, Tony!" she exclaimed. So that was his name: Tony.

"Do you know Anita?" I asked.

"'Course. I know him since she born."

"Tony was a friend of my father's," Anita exclaimed, and then burst into a cataract of Spanish.

He listened to her and nodded from time to time in a kindly but distant way, as though indulging a child. They both of them forgot me and I left the room to look for Julia and Agnes.

"I have a visitor," I told them when I found them in their dimly lighted bedroom.

"Not Mr. Manby again, I hope," cried Julia. Mr. Manby loved to come in and see us. He was growing to be a problem.

"No. That Indian."

"What Indian?"

"Oh, the one whose house we were in. You know—with the nice eyelids."

They made a move towards the door as though I had announced an entertainment, and I followed them back to the living room where Anita was setting the table for supper now.

"Put another place, Anita," I told her, boldly, I thought. "Will you stay for supper with us?" I asked him, timidly. And he replied briefly:

"All right."

"How do you do?" Julia was urbane, and Agnes was smiling graciously. Although the question had been purely rhetorical, he answered again:

"All right."

We all sat down and conversation was started.

"I think Taos is beautiful!" Julia broached. "Is the winter very long here?"

"Long enough to make summer. Got to have winter. And snow. Then everything come right."

"Oh, yes! Of course! But we want to see the country and we can't get about!"

Then Agnes said, "You have a fine mountain. Do you hunt up there?"

"Boys hunt when we want meat. Fishing pretty good, too, in summer. Do you like that mountain?" he asked, turning to me.

"Oh, yes!"

"I take you up there when summer comes."

Maurice came in, stamping his new black boots.

"Maurice, this is Tony." Maurice came up smoothing back his long locks. I saw his thoughts as they ran through his brain. "This is my chance," he was thinking.

"How do you do?" he said and smiled.

"All right," Tony replied once more, and looked at the fire. I looked at it to see what he saw, and it darted slyly and flickered into jolly, small excitements. Maurice sat down and began:

"I am almost ready to Work! And now I need a good model. Can you recommend one of your friends to come and pose for me?"

"Some will and some not like to. I ask Pete. She used to work at some artists."

"She?" queried Maurice, obtusely, I thought.

"Yes. She very nice-lookin' boy and artists like him."

"Oh!" answered Maurice.

"Well, let's eat supper." I hastened to the table and they all gathered around. I put Tony next to me, protectively, though I need not have done so. He has always been able to take care of himself, liking to—even after I put him next to me because I wanted him there.

Both he and Maurice paid a concentrated and undivided attention to their food. They were alone with it, and we women were thrown back upon each other, so we chatted conscientiously, not caring to have silence fall upon us. I kept nervously passing things to our guest, who checked this perfunctory service by saying, "Not yet," and this made me pause.

I saw Julia and Agnes studiously avoid looking at him so as not to disturb him, but I saw, too, that it would not have bothered him if they had. He was the only perfectly poised person at the table. He seemed to have the ease and the unconscious balance of a rock on the edge of an abyss. The room, the house, the earth, were whirling faster and faster around him as he sat in his imperturbable equilibrium, but he did not know it, or, if he did, he never let on.

At the end of the meal, he turned to me with a large, bright smile and made a gesture of thumb and forefinger with his left hand raised to his throat. "Full up," it said. Then he gathered his gray blanket into a thick twist around his loins and strode rapidly over and laid three fresh logs on the neglected fire.

"Good!" he exclaimed, as the flame spurted up. "You got a drum?"

"Oh, dear! I wonder if Mr. Manby has one?" I cried. "Oh, Maurice, go and ask him!"

"I don't like Manby's drum. Better no drum," Tony said, stopping Maurice as he was going. "I sing, anyway."

He started in quite a loud voice, beating time with his hand. It was a fast beat with strange sounds in it. He drew his breath from deep down and sent the sound out roundly, and soon the room was full of it. As the waves rolled out to the corners of the room, he sent new ones rapidly after them, not leaving any interval for the volume to diminish, so the air was full and more full of strange new patterns of sound, one chasing the other, leaping across, and followed immediately by more. We were immersed in the flood of it. He put all his energy into the room, going out upon it through his lips until we knew we were surrounded by him, by his living emanation, his essential being. No escaping the subtle, surrounding ether animated by this man's vital principle. This was something new in singing—magic in the air!

A knock came suddenly on the door, breaking through, and Mr. Manby came in. His head was lowered and he glanced sideways, more like an angry bull than ever. His bleared eyes flamed red at the rims as they swept across us and rested on the singing Indian who stared at the fire and continued the song. He sang and Mr. Manby gazed, and no one spoke. It was a momentary duel, won at the beginning. In a moment, the old man took a step backward and drew the door closed upon himself. But the magic had been disturbed; other elements had entered the room to mix with the older sorcery and confuse it.

The next morning Manby stopped me at his gate. "You want to look out for those fellows from the Pueblo," he said. "I have a lot of valuable moccasins and things around they're liable to help themselves to."

"Oh, not that one!" I exclaimed, shocked.

"Well, Antonio is a pretty good chap, we planted many trees together, but he's an Indian, remember. I know his father-in-law well. One of the most intelligent old rascals out there: a born lawyer and statesman. But I wouldn't trust him with my back turned."

"Oh, Mr. Manby! I don't see how you can stand having a point of view like that."

"Well, when you've lived here as long as I have, you will have it, too," he answered, and glowered at me.

Sometimes in the winter three or four Indians came to see us in the evening and they would dance before the fire while one of them tapped our new drum quietly (not to arouse Mr. Manby) and sing a dance song.

Always in that music there was the same heartening lift, never a complaint, never a wistful note. As in the dance Indians lift their weight and place the emphasis on the upward movement never thumping it down onto the ground but raising themselves as though dissolving upon the air, so in their singing. They do not lay their burdens upon the earth. To hear them sing, one might think they have never known individual sorrow or pain, for it is not recorded in any expression of theirs, for it is tribal music and tribally they do not suffer; tribally they are free. Listening to them, I thought perhaps the only way to go free is to live as a group, and to be part and parcel of a living tribal organism, to share everything, joy, pain, food, land, life, and death and so lose the individual anguish and hunger as well as the little sips and sups of pleasure that come to one here and there along the line.

For certainly a shared misfortune must vanish when so divided, and joy pooled must gain immeasurably beyond the slight nervous spasms we know in our aloneness.

When we grew enthusiastic and showed how we loved this gay and gentle art, the Indians said several times:

"Wait till summer comes. Then we all dance out of doors together."

So that was something else to look forward to: besides the valley and the roads in it leading away to the mountains we could wait for the Indian life and get to know it and perhaps to join in it a little.

Chapter Eleven

THE WEEKS passed. Maurice was working on a bust of Pete, a Buddhistic-looking young Indian who slept on the model stand, much to the artist's irritation, but the head and shoulders, modeled in black wax, grew daily more solid and suave. Two long braids came down on either side of the strong neck, the eyelids drooped, there was a slight smile on the voluminous countenance.

Occasionally, large wooden boxes were delivered to us, containing groceries from Santa Fe. These were unpacked in the stable yard at the far end of our part of the house, and stored in an empty pantry. But we were growing tired of Anita's unvaried cooking and I was unable to teach her anything, for I had not learned to cook anything more complicated than beefsteaks and eggs.

Then we heard that Dasburg and Bobby Jones were coming to visit us in answer to my enthusiastic letters about the simple, beautiful, remote valley, and I wired them: "Bring a cook with you."

Julia and Agnes had gone, now. Julia promising to return later in the spring. Her brother was spending most of that winter in Chicago reorganizing a newspaper, so she joined him there: the trip seeming quite short, only two nights and a day.

Andrew and Bobby drove up from Embudo on Oscar Davis's touring-car stage, and they had a pale, gentlemanly stranger with them whom they introduced as William von Seebach. He was the cook. He was better dressed than either of them, and his bags were of the best, while theirs were only imitation leather. He seemed to be in the last stages of some nervous horror, while the two boys were excited and gay, and I hastened him into a bedroom beside the kitchen, so that he could compose himself.

"He was scared of that revolver the stage driver keeps in the side pocket of the car," explained Andrew. "It's lucky we had him along, though," he went on. "He's the only one who had any money. We only had a bottle of Scotch and nothing to buy meals with, so we shared it with him and he bought our food for us!"

"What *is* he, anyway?" I exclaimed.

"Well, he's the new cook. But he *says* he can cook. We got him at an Employment Bureau."

"The day we left Chicago, he got confidential and told us his uncle is General von Seebach," Bobby broke in. "I think I've heard of *him*."

"But how embarrassing! I won't know how to treat him! Do I call him William?"

"Certainly. He's the new cook."

William soon recovered his poise, and he really could cook. He used to go to the plaza to do his shopping every morning, and would come home with a little Mexican boy carrying a basket. He charged everything and I didn't think much about that, though I did sometimes think the soups were very rich and the roasts very sumptuous. The beefsteaks he occasionally served were far nobler than Anita's thin slabs—and such sauces!

Maurice and Andrew had a map of Europe pinned to the wall of the living room, and every evening they discussed the progress of the armies and stuck little pins into it to mark the advances. They were quite pro-German, and wholly free to admit it in their talk in this outpost of the world.

William hovered in the dark background of the room, and his eyes shone like cats' on a black night. Bobby was rather a German sympathizer, too, for he had had those years in Germany and loved it; but he didn't pay much attention to battlefields and he spent his evenings drawing things he'd seen on his short prowls around the village.

As for myself, I maintained the broadminded attitude I had tried to keep since the war started, and to remain impartial and uninvolved in the war-time manias. The Germans were just other people to me, I thought, and the war a stupid misery. But I have to confess I felt slightly exasperated that those whom I was shut up with should happen to be prejudiced on the German side, for I had fewer affiliations with them than with the Allies, but I choked my irritation back into myself and became a little broader-minded, that's all.

Gradually I began to know people in the village. There was Mr. Phillips, across the road, who was one of the first artists to come to Taos. He was a small, worried-looking man with a long, straight nose and kind brown eyes. He and Manby had not spoken for years, though they were constantly meeting each other. They had developed a feud because when Mr. Manby planted the long avenue of cottonwood trees along the road, Mr. Phillips had also planted some along the stretch that passed his house. But *he* had planted the female cottonwoods and in the autumn all the air in the neighborhood was full of the white fuzz. Mr. Phillips was married to Dr. Martin's sister, and he had a boy and a girl about John's age.

Around the corner from his house on the side street lived

the Bateses. He had been one of the mounted police somewhere in Canada, a young tough with a baby face, married to a woman older than he, short, plump, with pale, protruding eyes and the look of reformed dissipation.

The village seemed to live on feuds. Almost everyone had some kind of cherished hate for someone else. There were the two stage drivers, Oscar Davis and John Dunn. One drove to Embudo station, and the other to Taos Junction, but they did not speak. Oscar was handsome in an Irish way, with black hair and merry blue eyes, large bony features and an attractive look to him; but John was immeasurably tall and lean, with a drooping, tobacco-stained mustache and melancholy eyes. He had a Yankee drawl that came out through his nose and he emphasized it because it made people laugh. Before these days when he drove the car slowly and cautiously down into the canyon and up the other side, over through the opposite valley of Carson to Taos Junction, he had driven a stage with horses that crossed the Rio Grande further north and went to the station of Tres Piedras. He was a character —but so was everybody here. One thing one knew about him in spite of anything he did or said. He had a sense of justice buried in him and though he was supposed to be lawless one trusted him. He was a real man.

The little group of Germans who had come from the old country, years before, and owned the first store that provided for the Mexican and Indian trade, had grown rich here: Mr. and Mrs. Alec Gusdorf and Mr. and Mrs. Gerson Gusdorf.

It did not take long for William to find an affinity with the Gusdorfs, for forty or fifty years in Taos had not altered their blood stream. I began to realize that soon after breakfast he would pile up the dishes, pull a cap on his gentlemanly, sleek head, and plunge through the door in his slightly huddled way and disappear towards the plaza. He didn't return until nearly noon.

This made me mad. My mother rose in me and made me feel it was not fitting. So one morning I decided to track him down, and I hurried through the melting, muddy snow that the sun softened every day and the frost froze again every night.

I found him in Gerson Gusdorf's store in converse with that merchant. They stood near the big stove with their heads together. Gerson's gold teeth shone in an amused smile, and the sight of their intimacy enraged me still more. I marched up to them and exclaimed:

"William! I wish you wouldn't leave the house in the morning until you have done your work!"

He gave me a look of mingled surprise, horror, and utter rejection, and slowly fell straight over backwards in a swoon, striking his head on the cement floor with a loud crack. There was something in him that could not stand being addressed like that, and perhaps he wished he'd stayed at home to fight an honorable war.

Gerson and two clerks were raising him up when I walked out; and he soon came home and cooked an exquisite lunch in dignified silence. I tried to make up for wounding him by talking to him sometimes, and gradually he grew communicative. We were mystified, one day, when he brought a couple of Rembrandt etchings from his room to show us after supper.

"I know you're all artists," he said. "I thought you would appreciate them."

We did. They were beautiful. Another time, he brought out a lovely little Italian bronze.

9 *

"Subtle, isn't it?" he asked, turning it in his refined fingers.

"Wherever did you get them?" I asked, with ill-suppressed curiosity.

"Oh, they are little things I picked up!" he replied, ambiguously.

Chapter Twelve

WHAT a long quiet winter!

We were all so anxious to see what the valley was like and there we were hemmed in by the snow, reduced to the circumference of the village for our satisfaction while, we imagined, in every direction there were most beautiful things to see and know.

We could look up eastward across the shining white stretches of desert, to the long undulating range of near-by hills dotted with black cedars poking through the snow. (Once, an old Indian, describing the valley when he was a child, said, "The Buffalo were as thick as cedars on the hills.") And there were vistas to be glimpsed of the far western horizon over miles and miles of shining snowfields that changed color every hour of the day, now appearing coldly blue in the morning, then a glowing rose towards sunset.

The huge, crumpled sacred mountain had snow so deeply covering it even to the trees upon it that it lost its black and purple depths and became a monstrous, gray, silvery, and gleaming form with mauve streaks marking its forms.

High drifts bordered the wide street we lived on, and the snow was piled high around the plaza, and it never grew black-dingy and soiled as in cities, for here there was no coal smoke or soot.

We realized everyone in Taos was interested in the doings of his neighbors, and quite interested in us, though they did not seem to do much about it. I know Doc Martin was always keeping his eye on us and of course Mr. Manby watched us day and night.

Hardly anyone seemed to like anyone else in the village, for there were about two specimens of every kind, and they were always rivals. There were two doctors, too. There was Dr. Bergman, who was called "the Indian doctor," and was supposed to cure the Indians and keep them well for one hundred and twenty-five dollars a month. Besides this pueblo that he was required to visit (at the schoolhouse three times a week where Indians could come and ask him for medicine or treatment), his contract required him to go over the mountains to Picuris Pueblo twice a month and take care of them. Usually the road was not open in the winter and he had to ride over on horseback.

There were also two butchers. We went to Mr. Cummings, a pale, ascetic man with a sad, green eye—the least like a butcher of any I have ever seen, for usually they are rosy and like the beef they handle, possibly through the law of attraction.

After William had been with us a month, the first bill came in from Mr. Cummings. It was about seventy dollars. When I went in to pay it, he apologized to me.

"I've been telling folks," he began in a mournful voice, "I don't know what that cook of yours does with all that meat. He buys more than any four families here put together. I hope it's all right."

"Well, he's always making soups," I explained. I felt rather apologetic myself.

"Well, he never buys any soup meat!" exclaimed Mr. Cummings.

There was a large family of Witts who were intermarried with many other families in the valley. Mr. Cummings had a

Witt for a wife, and John Dunn had had one, but she divorced him.

"I've had three wives in this here high altitude," he said, "and now I've got me a Mexican."

Dr. Martin was the source of almost all the gossip I picked up. Gossip was the nourishment of this energetic, pent-up man. Every morning he walked up to the plaza to visit the bank, of which he was a large shareholder along with Alec Gusdorf and John McCarthy. His first stop was at the Telephone Office a few doors away. All the telegrams were telephoned from Taos Junction, so the operator listened in to them. "Well, what news today?" he would inquire, and she would tell him. It never occurred to her not to. All along the way, Doc stopped people he knew to find out what he could, and always in return he passed on the best bits he had gathered.

I think, from the first day, we were objects of passionate interest to him. And, of course, not less to Mr. Manby. Maurice and Andrew, marking armies on the map at night, began to notice noises through the ceiling of the living room. They seemed to be near the chimney that stuck out a couple of feet on the flat, dirt roof.

"Someone is up there listening through the chimney," Andrew finally said.

"Oh! Who?" I couldn't imagine who it could be—out there in the bitter cold night."

"Maybe old Manby! I've noticed he watches us very suspiciously," Maurice said, nervously.

"Oh, everybody's suspicious in this place," I cried.

"They live on it," Andrew said, crossly. "I never saw such a lot of poisonous, ingrown people as there are here."

We gradually learned the sounds of the quiet neighborhood, and they were few. In the early morning before we left our beds, the wood chopping for breakfast fires could be heard behind us or across the street, and the country sounds of chickens, horses' hooves or cows mooing became an unconsciously familiar accompaniment to our own voices. Once in a while late at night, waking in the cold, still house, I heard a faint, rapid drumming, very eerie and far away and I thought of Indians awake beside their fires singing strange songs.

I was dying to go sleigh riding the way we used to in Buffalo when I was a child, and I inquired around the village for a sleigh, and actually found one down at Pedro Trujillo's stable. Pete Trujillo had the most wonderful big barnyard at the side of his long, one-story adobe house. It had a high fence of cedar posts around it and inside all kinds of animals lived at large: sheep and goats, some angora, with long, sumptuous wavy fleece, and others with elegant spare outlines, very stylish, like tailored persons.

Cows and chickens and horses, pigeons and pigs, all these creatures lived there, feeding off a generous haystack, trampling the thick straw, huddling together in the small cedar post sheds on cold nights, and always making rich, warm-hued, Flemish compositions.

In the winter time the coats of animals were longer and deeper-toned and more gleaming, the horses shone like burning metal and the cows were coppery or like polished ebony, so with the thick yellow sun shining on this richness, one could penetrate into color more deeply than one ever had before, except in painting.

It was here in Pete's stable I found an old frail spider called a cutter. It had a small, narrow seat, upholstered in faded and threadbare red plush; its runners were long and keen, the seat poised high. It was like a remnant of dream, fragile and attenuated, standing in its spiderwebs in a dark corner.

TAOS VALLEY   *by Ernest Knee*

Andrew was all for a sleigh ride, too, so Pete harnessed a horse to it and brought it up to our house the next afternoon, when we started out about half past two, overflowing the edges of the little seat, with a big fur robe around us. The six silver bells on each of the shafts gave out a peal of piercing laughter and made the occasional pedestrian lift his chin out of his muffler and smile as we went by. The horse from the rear view had a puzzled look on the back of his head and kept turning to right and left to throw a glance behind him. But he seemed to get used to the novelty of bells quite soon and he plugged along in the snowy wagon ruts.

Andrew and I both wanted to get up onto a long, flat mesa that ran across the western end of the valley, and he found his way over to it by various turns in the road. We climbed gradually up onto the wide, level top where we were lifted above the whole country and could see for miles on every side. It was wonderful! And so quiet and still! Up there the snow was deeper and the road fainter, but we kept on and on for miles, never wanting to turn back.

It was stimulating and strange to us who had been in cities for too long, or in domesticated countrysides, to be up there on the top of a wide, empty world where the village of Taos was only a vague dark huddle far away, and where in the middle distance, all one saw of human existence was an occasional immobile, rectangular house that looked like an adobe brick dropped by a giant in the big landscape.

Way over to the north we saw two long, low, brown pyramids and that was the Pueblo, looking like foothills of dark clay beneath the mountain.

Now the sun goes down early here in the winter and all of a sudden, I think, we noticed it was level with our eyes, itself looking at us like a large, red, surprised eye, as it dropped miles fast to the red earth line. The sky was growing green and the air was nipping.

"Well," Andrew exclaimed, "I guess it's about time we went home." As he spoke, the horse stumbled and sank up to his neck in snow and stopped. We were off the road on the steep slope.

"Why, look at those fence posts," Andrew said, pointing with his whip, and all I could see was the tips of them sticking out of the milk-smooth drifts.

The sun was hurrying so to get down that we knew we'd never find our way back in the quick darkness that falls. We wouldn't be able to make out our tracks and turns. Knowing these valley horses as I do now, I imagine that smart fellow would have taken us straight home without a waver. But we didn't realize that then.

Andrew tried to find a way to drive down the side of the mesa and get onto one of the main roads, but over and over again the horse floundered and sank deep into the unbroken snow up to his neck, and this frightened him so he quivered and white vapor rose off him from the evaporation of his sweat.

I was scared. I knew we couldn't stand it, out all night in the sub-zero hours on that mesa. Andrew never expressed a word of how he felt, he just got a kind of grim smile on his face, and his cheeks were bright red from the cold and he stuck out his arms and urged the horse on over and over again.

After many failures he actually found a way down. It was over an unbroken space between tips of fence posts we could now only just distinguish in the twilight. We drove home with the horse galloping for joy and it was dark when we reached the house and everyone had been frightened about us—as well they might.

But I had loved it, even with its anxiety. It was one of those afternoons one will never forget as long as one lives. How few hours stand out glowing like that!

Everything was apparently going smoothly—but only apparently. Mr. Manby was getting the wind up. The first thing I noticed was his almost theatrical hostility towards William. He had a way of narrowing his eyes and gazing sideways to register suspicion that dated back to the days of Edwin Booth. He turned this sidelong look upon William whenever they met in the garden, which was too often.

But no one paid much attention to anyone else, now, in our house, because when the rigor of winter broke, it broke with a loud jubilance of singing birds, singing brooks, and singing hearts.

Chapter Thirteen

NEVER had I known a spring to awaken with such a sweet violence as it did in Taos Valley—after weeks of sunny rigidity while the earth was either hard and white, or hard and brown, then suddenly something happened. From one hour to another a sort of heaving and the change came. There was breathing in the valley, all over the valley, in fields, in flesh, in people, in cattle, in birds, and probably in the gay fish flickering in the rivers. Now all the larks were singing on the fence posts, and in the pastures the shaggy, ungainly bulls struggled to mount the passive cows.

Walking along the road one came upon country couples standing in awkward postures beside a bridge or under a tree, their arms about each other, and their dark, sullen eyes velvety and soft. There was a fortune teller who lived down Canyon road and in these days many were the females who passed in and out of her gate. "Ladies want to know their fortune in the spring," she said.

It was not like the hot and sudden spring I had grown accustomed to in Florence. Although once the tremor started through the land, the earth never froze hard again in March or April, yet there came one snowfall after another, deep snow too, but to no avail. The heat breathed over the land and the land struggled to overcome the white heavy snow and drew it down into itself—deep. It drew the moisture down many inches to the roots of trees, and strong flowers like the hollyhocks and delphinium, and to the coarse alfalfa.

So, though we had to take it on trust many times, yet we knew spring was there. It was really there. But sometimes it was funny to see some little premature animal, a lamb or a calf, knee deep in snow, looking quite amazed, or to see the bunches of snow and frozen steam on their fuzzy heads after they nuzzled beneath it to find the short hidden grass.

Never mind! It was not really so long before the plows were cutting open the wet steaming furrows and there was a smell of flowers in every breath and breeze. Hastily the spring dug and delved among the tissues of earth and the men and beasts upon it. It made the hearts in all of these species to swoon and bound again, and the blood was renewed and freshened on its course. All over the valley the coupling went on to an accompaniment of singing birds, and a delirium of bleating, mooing, whinnying, and barking. The perfume of spring caused a madness in the nerves that was stronger than all caution and restraint. A girl was raped in a near-by village . . . a boy was knifed in Peñasco; all through Lent the Penitentes gathered in the *Moradas* and sang on the roads to Calvary Friday nights.

Each of us in that house was happy in our own way. Maurice was a sculptor at last. He saw the Indians in the round, plastic fullness of another medium than paint. Wax, clay, plasticine occupied him all day long, while Pete dozed on the stand before him.

"Really, da-a-rling—you were right, I believe. . . ."

Andrew had started hunting, an instinct that awakened in him every once in a while, made him breathless, eyes darkened, fully engaged. He hunted the old Santos painted on hand-hewn boards that we had discovered soon after we came to Taos. No one had ever noticed them except to laugh, but here was an authentic primitive art, quite unexploited. We

were, I do believe, the first people who ever bought them
from the Mexicans, and they were so used to them and valued
them so little, they sold them to us for small sums, varying
from a quarter to a dollar; on a rare occasion, a finer speci-
men brought a dollar and a half, but this was infrequent.

They were hanging in every Mexican house and chapel
when we came here; and even in Manby's house, two or three
of them hung on the wall. In his own rooms were several that
he made himself, aping their rude simplicity with a creative
urge that never had been wholly repressed in him. The naïveté
of the Santos was of the most genuine kind, their wistfulness
utterly touching. They were pressed out of nowhere by inar-
ticulate and untutored men in their extreme need for something to answer their religious needs, something to hang their
love upon, something tangible that would picture the inner
image.

We started collecting them whenever we saw them. It was
not long before the little population knew we bought them,
and they began to bring them to our house. One night, two
Mexican boys of fourteen or fifteen years came knocking at
our thick door. We let them come in and show us a package
wrapped in paper. Two beautiful Santos!

"Do you really buy these old Santos?" one of them asked,
his eyes sparkling with wonder and hope.

We did. I bought them for a dollar apiece, and they are
set in the doors of the black cupboard in our kitchen to this
very day.

Andrew was soon absorbed in saint-hunting. He managed
to hire an old horse and buggy, and he went all round the
valley looking for them. He became ruthless and determined,
and he bullied the simple Mexicans into selling their saints,
sometimes when they didn't want to.

At night, at our round table under the lamp, he washed them in kerosene oil to demolish the bedbug eggs with which they were generally incrusted, and to remove the top layer of dirt—the dirt and grease of a century or more, in some cases. The colors emerged, rich and real and true, colors made out of vegetables and weeds by people who had no paints: the yellow of sage, the lovely brown extracted from Brazilian nuts that came up with traders from the south, red from cochineal, and beautiful greens, too.

He grew more and more excited by the chase, so that the hunt thrilled him more than what he found; and he always needed more money to buy new Santos. I usually bought from him each night some of the ones he did not care for, so those and the ones I found for myself made a real collection before long. I had them in our house for years, until I gave them to the Harwood Foundation, for I finally came to feel they should be kept together and never leave this country where they were born.

It was Andrew who started a market for them, and people began to want them and buy them; and I was always giving one or two away to friends who took them east where they looked forlorn and insignificant in sophisticated houses. People always *thought* they wanted them, though, and soon the stores had a demand for them.

Stephen Bourgeois finally had a fine exhibition of them in his gallery. All this makes them cost seventy-five, a hundred, or two hundred dollars today.

When Albert Barnes ran through our house like a madman, he ended up in the kitchen and saw my two Santos in the cupboard doors. He had already bought all the best silver and turquoise he had seen, and serapes out of vaults, and many saints in curio shops; but he felt he had to have just those two of mine. He begged me to sell them, but I refused. They had been there so long. After he left, he wrote from his house about them. He said he simply had to have them. He said I must not be egotistic about them, but I must take an objective attitude.

"They belong here with my primitives," he wrote. "They will fit in perfectly. Think of how many more people will enjoy them in my gallery than where they are." (In my kitchen!) But I couldn't help it. I didn't let them go. He never wrote to me again, and dropped me from his acquaintance.

John had a young tutor named McKenzie, whom he liked pretty well, and they did things together. Soon they could drive the Ford around in the muddy roads. I did not see them very much, for I was all caught up in my own interest. I walked out to the Pueblo every day. I was teaching the Indian girls to knit—not for soldiers, but for themselves and their babies. I sat in Tony's house and slowly and patiently taught Candelaria, his wife, and his nieces how to make long scarfs and shawls. I walked out along the pasture road and skylarks sat on fence posts and trilled the loveliest songs. I walked fast, and it took me half an hour there and half an hour back again. I left after breakfast and came home only in time for lunch.

On one of the first false spring days that come sometimes in March, when all the earth is black and moist and steaming under a hot sun, and there is a faint, imaginary odor of hyacinths in the air, which comes in reality from old, manured ground, William encountered Manby on the lawn. I was unfortunately in the rear of the house, where we lived, and the lawn was near the front fence, so I missed the preliminaries. But afterwards, William said he said:

"Good morning, Mr. Manby." And Mr. Manby said:

"Don't speak to me, you god-damned Hun!"

Anyway, we all heard a cry and a scuffling noise, and reached the garden in time to see the old man on the ground, sort of rolling, unable to rise without help, and William standing over him, bending and looking down with an expression of joyous surprise on his pale, aristocratic face; and he seemed to be saying to himself, "Why, I didn't know I had it in me!"

We saw Mr. Phillips's head stuck out of his patio door across the way, simply pop-eyed with curiosity and gratification. Doubtless, he'd mentally rehearsed such a scene dozens of times, with himself in William's place.

Andrew ran to help the old man up. His eyes were unusually red-rimmed, and his venerable white hair stood up on end. He muttered to himself as he stumbled ignominiously away to his own front patio; and perhaps from that day he started to revenge himself on us all. No, not all of us. He actually liked me, probably not for my own sake, but because I was a woman and belonged to what undoubtedly he, since boyhood in England, had considered "the gentler sex," and was a harmless ornament to be treated gently with a slightly quizzical, unserious attention.

One day he stopped me when I was going out.

"Listen to me, my dear," he said, in a low voice, in his charming accent. "Something may happen today and I don't want you to be alarmed. But I don't believe you will be. You have fearless eyes." He was peering into my face with his own pale, bleary ones.

"What is it?" I exclaimed in delight, for I adored excitement.

"Oh, nothing. Maybe nothing will come of it, but we are living in strange times." He hobbled away and his departure cleared the air of an odor of stale sweat and a foul pipe.

That afternoon, Maurice was summoned to the house of the

10 *

ex-mounted-policeman Bates to meet an Inspector from Albu-
querque, who, we were told, had come to investigate us. An
Inspector! Maurice looked so helpless that I went along with
him. Mr. and Mrs. Bates looked embarrassed when we went
in, and she said apologetically:

"This gentleman just wants to ask you a few questions,
dearie." Bates was walking up and down with his hat on and
his hands in his pockets. He always looked like a big bad
boy—the type that often becomes a policeman. The other man
in the room was different. He was small and compact and had
a glittering peer in his pale eyes. He was smoking a cigar, too,
which made me anxious to leave.

"Well?" I said as Maurice said nothing and was looking
foolish. We sat down. The Inspector drew his thin lips together and examined us in silence for a moment, with his
eyes half closed and a frown on his brow. Then he said:

"Well, lady, a report has been sent to our office about your
household, and I was delegated to come up here and look
into the matter." He hesitated. I was looking colder and colder,
and Maurice had lost his usual slightly guilty expression in
such a childish confusion that he seemed to be on the point
of babbling.

"Well?" I asked again.

The Inspector nerved himself, and told it all in a breath:
"You are suspected of pro-German activities. It is said you are
receiving arms and ammunition almost weekly in large boxes
and storing them in your house; that one member of your
family is going among the Mexican population and enrolling
them; that you, lady, are inciting the Indians to rise. . . ."

I was amused and I was mad and I was also scared, for I
knew what a village like this one could do to us if it were
allowed to get going. Already the Bateses were looking less

embarrassed and more ready to act, upon hearing in words the atrocious accusation. A glare was coming in Bates's eyes.

"Well, what is the idea?" I asked, smiling in a friendly way. "What are we supposed to be doing all this for?"

"Why, this is the gate to Colorado and the rest of the states, up this Rio Grande canyon," he answered.

"The gate for whom?" I cried, not understanding.

"For Mexico!" exclaimed both the Bateses and the Inspector, simultaneously, in a great burst.

I broke out laughing loudly. "Well, really! So we are arranging an invasion, are we? Well, listen. The boxes we receive are filled with groceries; the member of our household who is visiting the Mexicans daily is collecting old paintings; and I, I am sorry to say, instead of inciting the Indians to rise, am teaching them to knit! Furthermore, I should like you to know that my stepfather is Rear-Admiral Reeder, several of my relatives are majors and colonels in the Army, and I demand an immediate apology from your office for this ridiculous accusation!"

Never had I felt so patriotic and so allied with our Allies! At the Inspector's words, I had recognized that it was an insult to be considered pro-German. He was looking foolish now, and turning his hat round and round in his hands; and at his disadvantage, my anger rose still more.

"I shall report you immediately to Washington," I said, though I hadn't an idea to whom to report him, for I didn't know anything about military hierarchies. "I shall report you for stupidity, for libelous accusations, and for invading our privacy upon insufficient evidence. Who turned in this ridiculous report, that's what I want to know? Who did it?"

"Lady, we don't know. It came in a roundabout way."

"Oh, there's been a lot of talk going around here," Bates

broke in, blusteringly. "They say you got that German cook that ain't no cook, and that he's putting up provisions for the future. You got one of them war maps in the house, and it's the German armies you watch. Besides, people heard you all talking. . . ."

"When? Where?" I interrupted.

"Oh, nights," he answered, taking off his hat and scratching his head.

"Oh, on the roof?" I inquired. "Do our neighbors visit our roof of an evening?" My sarcasm stimulated him.

"Well, look here." He turned on me. "Don't you *know* we been watching you? Don't you know, when those lady visitors you had went away, Judge Moore went along with 'em in Oscar's car and opened that there box at the station they took along before they got on the train?"

I *had* wondered what that was all about. When Julia and Agnes left, I motored down to Embudo with them in the stage. Oscar had looked rather queer as he stopped to pick up Judge Moore, the Justice of the Peace, who had on a collar and a suit of clothes instead of overalls.

I liked Oscar. He was a hardy, handsome, bold Irishman, with a pistol in the side pocket of his car. He liked me, too, and for years, while he drove the stage, he always brought me up the first pink almond blossoms of spring from Velarde, long before we saw it in bloom in this valley. It was on his account, perhaps, that I had liked to motor to Embudo to see Julia and Agnes onto the train.

When we arrived there, I remembered, Judge Moore had leapt out of the car and seized all the bags and the box of Santos Agnes was taking home with her—and simply disappeared. When I started after him, Oscar said:

"That's all right. You all wait here. We're early today. Some time before the train comes in!" After a while, the "Judge" returned, with a baffled look on his face.

I remembered all that, but I hadn't thought a thing about it at the time. These people out here all acted differently from people I'd ever known before, and it was like being on another planet, before one came to understand them and their ways. It must have been the same for them, where we were concerned. I cannot imagine what that J. P. garage man thought when he opened Agnes's wooden box and discovered those "old Santos"!

And our mysterious habits! Andrew driving round the valley all the time; and I tramping daily to the Pueblo where no white woman ever went except when there was a dance going on, and not many of them then. Of course, all this flashed through my mind in rapid circles, my anger and impatience chasing my realization of the others' point of view.

"Oh, I see," I said, frigidly, to Bates. "You've been watching us, have you? And this 'investigation' is the climax! Do you know who that friend of mine was, whose bags you had examined? It was the sister of B——." Already his name was one to conjure with in America. "Well," I went on, "we'll have another investigation soon. We'll have this Inspector inspected, and these smart investigators investigated. I guess there's plenty to find out if one goes about it carefully! We'll go home now, and if you care to come and search our house, you're at liberty to do so!"

"Lady, I guess we just made a big mistake!" The Inspector seemed quite crumpled, now.

"Pulled a boner," murmured Mrs. Bates.

We walked across the muddy road and into the house, and Maurice was looking rather queer. I marched up to that map and pulled out the little flags and threw them on the floor.

"That's enough of *that,* I guess," I said haughtily. Then I sat down and wrote a letter to the War Department in Washington; just tossed it into the air to fall to earth, I knew not where.

But it had George Creel's name on it! So it was not long before two strangers arrived in town. They did not come to see us, but they were closeted a couple of times with Mr. Manby, who seemed to be helping them. The Bateses were very chastened, after that, and did not remain in Taos very long. I never knew where they went. As for the Inspector . . . "I heard he lost his job," said Mr. Manby. "Another incompetent!"

I never let him know I knew that he had started the whole thing, and that *he* had done a lot of "inciting" among our neighbors. He never realized how much I knew of all his underground treacheries.

Chapter Fourteen

LENT was coming to an end, and just before Holy Week people began to tell us the Mexicans would soon "whip" in the *Moradas*. There was one of these isolated chapels over behind Manby's on the Indian sage-brush land, where the Penitentes had a long lease from the Pueblo so they could have their strange secret rites in undisturbed privacy away from the townspeople.

John told me some of the boys went out there at night and hid behind the sage and cedars to watch them come out of the *Morada* and drag their great crosses up a long, sloping, cleared space they called Calvary, to the final cross planted at the end. He said they sang and whipped themselves with the cactus plant bound into balls. It was a dangerous thing to go and hide over there, because if the Mexicans found them they threw stones at them. They were all tense and concentrated through Lent and during Holy Week, ready to shed blood and suffer relief. This they needed to do in secret and undisturbed for only they knew why they expressed themselves in this fashion and they resented the prying, cold curiosity of those who did not understand their strange ecstasy. It was a strong ecstasy, with such joy in it for some that they found complete fulfillment in its experience and never turned to women after they were initiated into the Brotherhood.

How curious, I thought, to find these different religions alive in this unfamiliar state of New Mexico, and of course I was all

eagerness to go out at night and see something of it. I went
in to see Doc Martin about it, but he discouraged me.

"You'd better lay off Penitentes," he told me. "I'm a Repub-
lican and I'm their official doctor, but I wouldn't butt in on
their doin's."

Indeed, I knew he never even left his house after dark, but
put out the lamp in the front room and went to bed in the
rear with the newspaper.

I liked to go in and talk to Doc before he went away to
Fort Worth. He was one of the most energetic men in the
village and he was always ready to do anyone a good turn.
His office was a caution! Along the broad windowsill, there
were all kinds of instruments: forceps, pincers, scalpels, hypo-
dermics, mixed up with bottles of pills, pamphlets, loose rolls
of absorbent cotton, surgeon's plaster, dust, and copies of the
Journal of the American Medical Association. Several very
large bottles labeled Castor Oil and Milk of Bismuth, and a
variety of disinfectants stood on the top of a chaotic roll-top
desk, and on a shelf along the wall ranged smaller bottles
of pills: aspirin, rhubarb, antipyrin, and so on.

There was a huge waste basket usually containing wads of
cotton with dried blood on them, where they'd been tossed
any night after a wounded Mexican had been brought into
the office, and the floor had a good many bloodstains on it,
too. The walls were covered with the beautiful photographs of
Indians, and the long window that went all across the front
of the room had fish-net curtains with many rents in them.
Two Morris chairs faced each other under this window, for
doctor and patient, and they, too, were ominously stained.

"How do you mean, you're their official doctor?" I asked
him, full of curiosity.

"Well, they sit in those hot *Moradas* and then go out along

THE MORADA BEHIND OUR HOUSE

the Calvaries with nothing on but their short white pants and they ketch pneumonia. They whip themselves raw and then they get blood-poison; sometimes they crucify, or pretend to, and they hang a man up for hours in these cold spring winds and he gets pneumonia or shock, savvy? And then they send for me. I don't interfere with 'em or ask 'em questions. If they pay me, I doctor 'em. But I don't get mixed up with 'em, do you ketch me? There's a lot of stuff in this valley to keep away from. Indians is one, and Penitentes is another, and then some. Get me?"

"What else?" I asked, encouraging him, for he had just given me a tentative wink out of his small green eye.

"Oh, that god-damned Englishman next door," he said in a lowered voice. "He's up to all kinds of trouble. He's got enough gold buried somewhere on that place of his to sink a ship. Keep that under your hat, savvy? He's a killer."

"Gold! Where'd he get it?"

"Oh, that Mystic Mine over to Baldy he and his partner were in. Partner's disappeared! Old Fergusson up the canyon here, he was in with 'em, too, but he's gone mad."

"Well, he certainly doesn't seem to get much fun out of his gold!" I said, cheerfully. I had seen no signs of luxury, certainly, in our landlord's house, though once he had instructed me where I could find a great tidbit that he occasionally indulged in: it was preserved tongue in glass, and could be bought at Burch's store. That was the nearest thing to it, however.

"He's going to make a get-away some day," Doc whispered, raising his bushy eyebrows and making a face. His restless, energetic mind had to think up things, it seemed to me, that it could browse on and be stirred by, and he had a sensational twist to his thinking.

But if he did, so did Manby. In the same lowered tone, Manby recounted horrors about Doc, while his poisoned eyes searched out the corners of the empty room and his voice guarded itself from penetrating the thick wall that stood between him and Doctor's back bedroom.

"That old fellow's as thick-skinned as an elephant!" he told me. "I could tell you stories of his practice!" And he proceeded to do so.

"But he's a good doctor, isn't he?" He seemed very astute to me.

"Oh, certainly he's a good doctor. He's a splendid diagnostician because he's intuitive; then he'd had an enormous experience here these thirty years. He's seen all there is to see of sickness. He likes a fight, too. He'll sit up, night after night, fighting a pneumonia case, and then he'll get drunk for twenty-four hours afterwards. He's a pretty good friend if he's afraid of you, and a bad enemy if he's not."

"Mercy! What a character you give him!" I cried, dumbfounded at such talk.

"Oh, Doc's all right. No worse than most of the others in this neighborhood, for they're all of them poisoned by something . . . the altitude gets nearly everybody. Of course, Doc's worse trouble is that he can't keep his mouth shut. He talks too much," Mr. Manby said, giving me a meaningful glance, full of warning. He made me feel uncomfortable, so I left him.

It was like that with nearly everyone I talked to in the village. Take any simple conversation, and though it would start all right, in five minutes one felt a blighting influence coming at one, sapping one's vitality and lowering one's enthusiasm. Everyone in the place seemed to have gone negative except the Indians. I avoided the villagers more and more, for I wanted to see through the Indians' eyes. They were polarized towards the positive and beneficent spirit of this place, the spirit that dwelt in the sacred mountain, which even the outsiders, these prisoners in the valley, recognized was full of richness, attributing gold to it, that most powerful symbol; murmuring, too, legends of the Eternal Fire that burned in its center, guarded by the keepers of the unseen shrine.

Still I remained curious about the religious expression of the Mexicans, and so I went and asked Mr. Phillips how to see something of it.

Mr. Phillips had acquired a sort of authority for us, ever since an evening, some time back, when those two Mexican boys who first brought us Santos, had burst into our quiet house with an Indian serape for sale—for we were collecting blankets as well as Santos. Beautiful old blue and white ones, dyed with indigo; Brazilian ones dyed in lovely browns and greens with nut juices and sage; or the later kind, colored with Diamond Dyes in exquisite patterns, the tones somewhat faded with washing.

Sometimes Tony went with Andrew and me around to the Mexican houses and it was he who taught us to feel the cotton quilts, for under the old calico we frequently discerned the weave of warp and woof; and if they let us slit them open, a fine blanket occasionally appeared. They had sewed them up in a covering, sometimes to save them, sometimes because they were wearing out. There was often a worn, thread-bare place in the center of the serape, we never could find out why.

Tony would knock at a door and say: *"Tiene cosas antiquas, y cuanto hay?"*—and we would push in behind him, especially Andrew would push eagerly, and occasionally we would find perfect treasures. In the evening, Andrew sat under the lamp with a blanket over his knees, patiently darning the worn places. He got quite good at it and his collection grew.

So that night the two boys unrolled their bundle. Their eyes were popping with excitement and fun. It was made in stripes of dark blue and black, with a white circle in the center, and in the center of that a square, black cross—and out to the edges went dark red stripes to the four sides. A very grand blanket, it seemed to us, and having great dignity and beauty. It was in perfect condition, too, and of a fine, smooth weave. I bought it for fifteen dollars, and the boys went off grinning.

In the morning, we called Mr. Phillips over to see it, for he knew about blankets and had some good ones himself. He opened his eyes and said:

"Oh, it's a beauty! It's a real old Chief's blanket! These are very valuable, you know." He examined it rather carefully before he went away, it seemed to me. I was feeling very proud of having it, for I had a little of that collector's spirit in me, too, by this time. I pinned it up on the wall.

Alas! That same night a knock came on the door and when I opened it, a tall, slender, sandy-haired man stood there, grinning a little. He was unshaven and had keen blue eyes, twinkling under drooping lids. When he came under the light, I saw he had only one arm.

"I'm the Sheriff," he said. "My name's Lee Witt."

This was our first acquaintance with him. "Well," I answered, surprised, "come in."

He came into our lighted room and there was Andrew patching an old serape. Maurice was smoking and making a drawing, and the others were reading and it looked home-like and comfortable.

"Well, I came to arrest you folks," said Lee Witt, genially, fishing a loose cigarette out of his pocket and lighting it. Everybody looked dazed.

"What's the matter with us?" I said, amused.

"Been receiving stolen goods, seems like!"

"What stolen goods?"

"I guess that's the one up there," answered the Sheriff, pointing to my new Chief's blanket. Oh, dear! "Phillips reported to me you folks had bought a serape that's mighty like one of Couse's, so we got into his house today and looked, and sure enough, it's gone—and signs around of other things messed up. One of the windows was busted.—Who sold it to you?" he went on. And I said:

"Oh, two Mexican boys."

"I guess I know the ones. We haven't got any other thieves around here. Well, I'll be going," he drawled, taking the blanket off the wall and folding it up. "Now I'll go and make my arrest."

Then I was sorry for those gay kids who had had such fun looking for a good serape for us.

"Can't I pay the fine for them?" I asked.

"They ought to go to the Pen," he said. "They're the real thing. 'Specially Pete."

"How much will the fine be?" I pleaded.

"Oh, I guess twenty or thirty dollars," he answered.

Then Mr. Phillips arrived. He looked apologetic, but relentless. He liked being an authority and he was always proud to show off the oddities of the neighborhood and to tell the fables that distorted minds had invented for their own relief.

Now I went over to his house and asked: "Can't you take us to see the Penitentes? We want to see them."

"Why, yes," he answered. "We can go out there in the sagebrush and hide on Good Friday night and you can probably get a glimpse of them as they go up the Calvary."

It was a pitch black night when Maurice, Andrew, and I followed him over there, but he knew the way and we kept in his footsteps. He led us on a roundabout trail to avoid the Mexican houses, over hard fields and into an arroyo a few feet deep that we wound along deeper, where we crept as quietly as we could.

It was early in the evening so we could find places before they came out of the *Morada*. The stars were trembling in the sky near us, and a cold wind blew along the narrow channel, buffeting us. The mountain was invisible and we could scarcely see the one who walked ahead of us. Mr. Phillips turned and whispered:

"Now we are directly behind the Cross. I'll climb up the side here, first, and take a look."

We waited, hearing him scramble. The arroyo had deepened so it must have been ten or fifteen feet to the top where he stood now.

"Come on up. There's no one about yet," we heard him say in a low voice above us; so we followed as best we could, up the steep, dry side, digging our feet in and our hands, too.

At the top, the wind hit us harder. We were on the level sage-brush Indian desert and a far half mile or so beyond us we saw a little yellow light burning that was different from the white stars.

"That's the *Morada* down there," murmured Phillips. "Now all we have to do is to wait till they come out."

"How long?" whispered Maurice, for he was already chilled.

"Well, it's hard to tell. Probably they are waiting until they think any people or boys watching for them are tired out and gone away!" So a waiting game began, and it seemed to last for hours. There we were, squatting out in the empty desert with no company but the stars and not a sound but our own breathing and the fitful wind in the sage. It smelled lovely and fresh and I crushed the small sage leaves in my fingers and inhaled them. Once a coyote barked in the hills, and instantly a chorus of maniacal laughter followed as though a dozen insanities were giving voice in the silent night. Then all was still again.

"The coyotes make a circle and dance round and round," whispered Mr. Phillips. Again a long silence, and then we heard a rustle over to the left of us somewhere: creeping feet and sibilant whispers.

"There are the boys." Somewhere, John and McKenzie and Ralph were finding bushes to hide in. Who knows how many souls besides they were crouching in the dark, hearts beating, nervous laughter choked back into their chests, allured by the necessity for secrecy, attracted by the mysterious byways of the spirit that must choose an empty desert in the blackness of the nighttime in which to issue forth and find the solace of expression?

Hours we waited. Sometimes I remembered the Indians in their quiet Pueblo, only two or three miles away in space, but how far away in a reality different from this! I knew how quiet it would be in those white-washed rooms, where the mattresses were spread out on the floor and, straight and calm, the dark bodies slumbered in an untroubled serenity. Sleep, for an Indian, I thought, is so complete and active, a collecting of himself in composure, and having a dignity which white men lost in unconsciousness. How much better off they were to stay aloof in their peaceful village, instead of skulking in the desert like ourselves to spy upon the ways of other men.

The night cold stiffened us, and once in a while we moved a little to lessen the tension in our cramped limbs. Andrew, especially, was terribly irked, for he had such a strong, restless energy in him that he never could be quiet for long at a time.

"Shall we give up?" Mr. Phillips murmured once.

"No," I answered, obstinately; and we went on for another age of time.

Then, suddenly, "Look!" Maurice hissed, giving me a poke.

Far down the line we saw several moving lights: little lanterns swinging this way and that, and then suddenly assembling in two rows; and presently the weird song was borne to us in snatches on the night wind.

What strange sounds! High and low, the voices mingled in the peculiar chant that dates back to Gregory, but carries with it all the slow accretions of agony since that time. Mingled with this eerie anguish that issued from the depths of the pit that is the soul of man, the fantastic notes of an archaic wooden flute played fitfully up and down in trills and sudden gay flights, like eldritch laughter.

The little procession was approaching us slowly, head on, making for the great, gaunt cross that we knew stood planted there above us; and soon we began to hear another sound, rhythmical and heavy: the dead bang of the cactus lump as it was flung backwards over the shoulder, *bang* on the solid, resilient flesh, *bang* on the wet, strong, unresisting flesh. We could feel the heavy thong, the heavy ball at the end of it, and the *bang* it made on the bloody back, driving in the needles, coming against that surface of flesh and bone solidly, no resistance to it, the stubborn body of man that gives no sound when it is struck, because it is not hollow like a drum, nor hard like wood, yet has density and mass and fluidity and endless endurance, not wearing out for years.

They plodded towards us in the pure, dark night, twenty or thirty men, some singing, some whipping, and others, we soon perceived by the sounds that accompanied the singing and the bangs, were dragging the heavy, new, ten-foot crosses we had seen lying beside the *Morada* some days before this Friday night. Every once in a while they all stopped for a few moments and the lights lowered and were still; and Mr. Phillips whispered:

"They are praying at the Stations of the Cross. Little piles of stones mark them."

As they came slowly nearer to us, very slowly, really, it seemed, I began to feel we should not stay and share their secret worship. I stumbled up, making a crackle in a bush, and a stone whizzed past me. We all dropped to the ground and slid down the side of the arroyo and began to run slowly in the confusing darkness, falling over sticks and stones, until we had gone some distance and the singing sounded now like a faint, plaintive moan, far away. Awesome, and utterly separate from any way that was familiar.

"Would they really hurt us if they found us there?" I said, panting a little from our haste.

Mr. Phillips answered, "Oh, they're all good fellows. They wouldn't hurt you."

"Who are the Penitentes and who aren't?" I demanded, curiously.

"Well, nobody knows for sure about all of them. It's a secret order, you see."

Later on, I told Tony about our night. We were sitting under the apple tree and it had some small pink buds on it and Tony was whittling a hard plum branch to make a drumstick. He laughed as a grown person sometimes laughs at the ways of a child.

"Indians got different ways," he said. "We have springtime, too, but not like that."

"I saw some of them going through the fields, though,

carrying a saint and singing, going towards the Pueblo. There were some women, too. The Indians let them come, don't they?"

"Oh, yes, to visit," he said. "They bring their Saint to visit our Saint in the church, and they sing, but no whipping. Once my uncle, when she young man, visit a Penitente *Morada* one night over in Costilla because they invite him. He didn't know what's going on till they take him way inside beyond the chapel room and then they began to whip theirselves. He was so scared he ran back into the chapel and jumped right through the glass window and run and run and run till she tired."

He whittled carefully for a moment, musing, and then went on: "But over in Picuris Pueblo, sometimes Indians walk in parade with Penitentes. I don't know what for they do that, unless they all mixed up with Mexicans, now."

Chapter Fifteen

ONE NIGHT Mr. Phillips brought some people to call on us. They were English, and the woman was nice-looking, though she had restless brown eyes and her smile was held up at the corners determinedly. The man was tall and attractive, with a very youthful air. He had almost a turned-up nose, and long, dimpling grooves in his lean, ruddy cheeks, and his green eyes were full of light and laughter. They had a pretty little girl with them and their name was Young-Hunter.

They had been in Taos only a day and had fallen in love with it: one of those instantaneous affinities that happen occasionally. We saw each other sometimes, after that; Jack Young-Hunter had a longing to know the Indians, which had been awakened in him when he was a little boy in London and Buffalo Bill had taken his circus over there.

They lived in some rooms in Miss Lena Scheurich's big house, just off the plaza, and they used to walk up to spend the evening sometimes. In that way, Jack met Tony and they became friends, liking each other from the first.

It wasn't long before Jack began to talk about buying a little piece of land here, for he thought this valley was the most beautiful place he had ever been in. Mary was more hesitant about it, but Jack was sure. One day Tony said to him:

"I show you a place quite near to here—east. Nicest place, I think."

So Jack said, "All right, let's go now and look, can we?"
"Come on, then."

So we three went together and Tony led us back behind
the house and along the curving, tree-lined avenue Mr. Manby
had laid through his place, until we came to a barbed wire
fence that separated his land from the Mexicans who lived in
this neighborhood. I had ridden past it with Mr. Manby once.
We walked across a low-dipping field of alfalfa and up over a
wide, dry ditch to the big cottonwood tree the old man and
I had stopped under when we rode over here, and Tony said:

"This the nicest place I know 'cept the Pueblo. Little bit
high up, good air, and you see all over." He waved his hand
across the south and west and north, just as Manby had done,
where we could see the whole valley stretching out beyond
the town, and the sacred mountain looming dark and secret,
so solid there at one side where it faced towards the narrow,
southern canyon entrance up from the outer world, over across
the level sage-brush land, eighteen miles away.

The sacred mountain was the high point. It sloped away
northwards in the range that ended in a low, crescent curve,
and east to south became the hills that were the other end of
the crescent. Those eastern hills were at our back when we
stood beneath the gigantic tree, a lovely skyline, sensitive and
alive. How often, in the winter, I had looked across to them
when I came out into the garden, and wondered what it
would be like up on the crest! Once, even when the snow was
on the ground, I told a friend of Tony's, named Juan Concha,
how I wished I could go up there, and he said:

"Come on. Let's go!" Juan was a small, slight Indian with
a very subtle, fine face that often twinkled with his thoughts.
I had hurried into "arctics," heavy coat and muffler, and we
had started out over the same way we had just come on this

spring day; over across the fields until we reached the big
tree, and past the Mexican house along a wood-trail that led
up towards the hills. Juan marched placidly along, step after
step, the snow getting deeper now. He moved easily, unhas-
tening and sure, but I hurried and lost my breath. He walked
smoothly in his thin moccasins, while my heavy arctics im-
peded me, and I came down heavier and heavier with every
step. Juan never seemed to put his weight down on the ground,
but to carry it up. He had a new balance I was unaccustomed
to, as though he was hung from the center of his body, and
it was as easy for his weight to go up as for mine to go down.
He had a different law of gravity, and his inertias were in
other centers than mine. For where the earth pulled me down
to it, he seemed to be free of that tug, and nearer to bird life.

"How far *is* it?" I gasped, finally, after I had plodded for
a long time and we seemed no nearer to those blue, snow-
sprinkled hills.

"I don't know. Not far. You tired?"

"I'm not used to it," I answered, panting.

"Indians never get tired," he said. "Guess you think too
much."

Well, we had turned back to the house, and when we
reached our warm living room, where the fire drowsed in the
dark chimney place, and I had taken off my heavy coat, I
was all damp with perspiration and tired out, and my hair
was wet; but Juan was the same as when we had started, except the soles of his moccasins were soaked, so he stretched
his feet out to the fire and dried them. . . .

"Oh, yes! This is a lovely place," Jack murmured. "I like
that little house with those apple trees in front." He pointed
to the two-roomed adobe a little distance away to the south,

along the level space above the curving ditch-line. "There is another big tree over there, too."

"That the place I thought for you," said Tony, leading us towards it over the bare ground.

"And what place did you think for me?" I asked in fun.

"This one," he answered, gravely, turning around and pointing first to the big tree and then over to an adobe house set back a little way, with the sage-brush desert behind it and the clean-swept Mexican space in front that all these houses had. It was set down there like a toy block from the hand of a giant child. A dark-faced man stood in a doorway smoking a cigarette and staring at us.

"Jack going to buy over there, and you going to buy here."

I laughed aloud. The idea attracted me, and at the same time frightened me a little, too.

"What do I want a house for?" I queried, wondering at him.

"Don't you want a studio?" Tony asked, seriously. We were walking along over to the other end of the little hilltop to look at the place he had designed for Jack, as though that was the first thing to attend to, and the other all settled, as a plan to be carried out unhurriedly, which could wait.

"I thought all Americans have to have studios."

"Well, that's an idea," I laughed. "Perhaps I do!"

The little place under the second big tree was perfect for Jack and his family. He didn't want much land and it had not much; just where the house stood, with the space in front where the red-trunked apple trees were planted in the Mexican fashion, so close that their branches interlaced. At the back, the Indian desert land came right up to the wall.

There was a cowboy named Braselton living in it, and we found him at home. He showed us inside, and it had beautiful old smoke-darkened ceilings made of saplings. He tried not to act surprised when Jack asked him if he would sell, and he promptly asked three hundred dollars for it.

When we left, it was as good as sold.

Tony led us back to the other end of the small settlement, telling us what the few houses were along the row. Outside Braselton's, there was a two-roomed one that belonged to a man named Tenorio, then came a little one that he said used to be the Penitente *Morada,* before the Mexicans leased a portion of the Indian land behind this place, and built a larger one on it so they would be farther away from town and have more room. Then came the place where the trail went between these adobe houses up past the desert *Morada* leading to firewood in the hills. It wound up from town and crossed the ditch over a rickety bridge and over the open, wind-swept space, through the Indian land.

On the other side of it, there stood another two-roomed house—then, at the end, the one Tony had designed for me. That made five little, bare, unadorned houses in a long row of three or four hundred feet, with the deep mother-ditch the Indians had laid there hundreds of years ago curving around them in a watery embrace that made the big trees grow larger every summer.

Below them lay a large alfalfa field, with an apple orchard at the north end of it.

"The field and the apples go with this last house. That why I like it," said Tony.

Heavens! Did he think *I* wanted an alfalfa field and some apple trees? Well, perhaps I did.

Jack was looking at me and laughing, now. He thought this was very funny. Tony left us, quickening his step and going up to the Mexican who had never stopped watching us; and they went into the house and shut the door.

"It *is* a lovely neighborhood," Jack said. "Why don't you get a piece if we do?"

"Why, I never thought of such a thing!" I exclaimed.

"But Tony has," he laughed.

After a while, Tony joined us. He looked serious and solid and immovable.

"That Mexican want fifteen hundred dollars for all this," he said, waving his hand. "Pretty good house. Good piece of land."

"Well . . ." I hesitated.

"Never mind. Don't have to decide today. That Mexican, he named Trujillo; they call him old Chimayo; he my friend. He live there with his sons and his grandchildren. We come and talk some other time. First Jack buy this place, then you."

We turned to leave, and he waved his hand back towards the house. "My father and I work on that when I a little boy," he said. "My father made those windows in that last room and I help him. Then we eat our dinner under this big tree, and drink water here. This *good* water in the summertime. We rest under the tree. Very happy place."

When we were at supper that night, I said, suddenly, "I believe I'll buy a little piece of land here and have a studio of my own."

Maurice looked up quickly.

"We aren't going to stay here forever," he said. "I have to go back east by August, anyway."

"Well, maybe I'll stay on," I said, noncommittally.

"*I'd* like to," John broke in.

I kept thinking of that big tree and how nice it would

SPRING AROUND THE CORNER   *by Ernest Knee*

be to rest under it in the summer and drink the nice water from the stream.

I took Julia over there one late afternoon, and showed it to her. We sat on the bank and looked into the field and over the western horizon. Mr. Manby's trees were growing up, so the tops of them pricked into the skyline.

"It *is* a nice place, isn't it?" I asked her.

"Lovely! I think you *should* buy it," she cried, encouragingly. "You ought to have a little place of your own, and do some work of some kind."

I didn't care for that. I just thought it would be nice to sit on the edge of the stream and watch the horses feeding in the field below. That was what drew me more than anything else.

Tony didn't say anything more to me about buying it; but while he helped Jack secure the other little house, the idea of it worked in me.

Chapter Sixteen

NOW WHEN the spreading apple tree in the center of the lawn was white with blossoms the time to remember the Indians' promise had come.

I asked Tony to make a dance in the garden and I invited all the Taos people I knew to come to it. I asked them for tea, not for an Indian dance, and the Indians were asked for a dance, not for a tea! I did not conceal the character of the occasion from these people. I didn't know enough to do that, for I didn't realize at all that they were not accustomed to meet "socially" as it is called, and that never before this time had the Indians danced at anyone's place in town.

Later, I found out what a strong line of demarcation was drawn between the Americans and the Indians who lived so short a distance from each other but in different worlds, and that this separation was as acceptable to one group as the other. The Indians, I knew, had friends among the artists for whom they posed for twenty-five cents an hour, and they had friends among the merchants where they spent their small earnings or traded their grains for groceries, but any deep confident intimacy or understanding was quite absent between them. There was a varying scale of vague distrust that arose from the great difference in their values and that made them mutually unable to get at each other. Perhaps Mr. Manby's conception expressed the most anti-social viewpoint of Indians in this valley, "You have to watch 'em every minute, thieving rascals," and likewise Candelaria's dictum when the flu broke

154

out among the Americans and Mexicans the following January. "That is *theirs,*" she said to Tony, who repeated it to me.

Those two opinions marked the lowest common denominator of human separation. But how could there be anything but misunderstanding between these groups, when one set of them had lived here always and raised all they needed off their land and had only the most sketchy monetary system which was still in the process of being imposed upon them by the other group, who had arrived a short three hundred years ago and who were here to make money?

When we had our first Indian dance on the grass, Tony brought about ten Indians and these were some of my first Indian friends. Juan Concha and Cristino and Pete Mirabal were there. Among the Americans I knew were some of the artists and their wives, Mr. and Mrs. Phillips from across the street, I think, and who the others were I have forgotten. About twenty of them in all, and these included some of the villagers who were not artists but who were people that had lived a long time in this valley, like old lady Gusdorf who came here as a bride with her husband, "Mr. Alec." She has always been called "old lady Gusdorf" or just "the old lady." For as long as I have seen her she has had the fine-grained pink and white skin of a child, and wide, pretty eyes. By the long exercise of curiosity and interest in human nature, she knows all there is to know about people here, and a habit of observation has taught her a fair judgment of them. She is therefore kind and shrewd, contemptuous and at the same time easily surprised into admiration. Her charm lies in the sense of wonder alive in her after sixty years here. Sixty years in Taos and still a European; sixty years in Taos and become a little *grande dame,* always speaking as one having authority.

Several of the Indians went to the end of the garden and

changed their clothes for dancing. That is to say, they removed most of what they had on and returned to the apple tree in loin cloths, moccasins, and a few silver sleigh bells.

Tony and his older friends, meanwhile, sat against the big tree trunk and chatted together while tapping the drum faintly, and "the white people," as the Indians call them, stood together in twos and threes and looked a little self-conscious.

Of course I had asked Mr. Manby to come to tea but he was nowhere to be seen. Possibly he was observing us from behind the bars of a window; undoubtedly he knew his foe Mr. Phillips was actually on his property for once.

I recall distinctly that the ones who were most at ease in the turgid first moments of the party were Jack Young-Hunter, and "the old lady." Jack was always happy to be with Indians, for it made him feel like a little boy again. He was released and twinkling as he crouched on one knee beneath the apple tree and talked to the waiting Indians. There was, curiously, something resembling them in his lean, bony face and features, and a little later I knew a man in the Pueblo who looked enough like him to be his father. Is there something innately resembling the ancient Scots in these tribes?

The old lady's eyes were alight with amusement. She thought it was the funniest thing she'd ever seen, to bring these people together at a *tea party!* Her dignity was unassailable, nothing could harm it, therefore she was able to enjoy the incongruous event.

Finally a faint war-whoopish call came from beyond the farther lilac bushes, so Tony and his friends stood up, held the drum between them by its several buckskin loops, and started to sing a glad, gay song, and as the white people turned to seat themselves on the scattered chairs and benches around the patch of lawn, the dancing boys emerged from the green shelter and danced up the dirt path in a row.

To the beat of the drum they danced a one-step, only in their unusual fashion, so unlike us, they raised themselves on the *tap*-tap and their silver bells rang the accent off the drumbeat, and this produced a syncopation unlike anything I knew. It was just the opposite of every dancing or marching musical habit I had ever known, and very lithesome and unlike the *thump, thump, thump,* the-boys-are-marching regulation with which I was familiar in America and Europe.

Once in Switzerland I was awakened in the night by a band of boys and girls hiking along, singing a rousing march song, and their feet thundered past on the accented bang of the tune until it seemed to shake the house I was in, and one understood how an army crossing a bridge in a concerted rhythm of footsteps could collapse it if they had not the sense to break the ranks. I wonder if they could not safely cross in step if they learned from the Indians to lift their weight up instead of dropping it upon the downward stroke? Every time they dance, the Indians overcome the inertia of gravity; is it for this reason they are always enlivened and refreshed by it?

As soon as they were leaping on the grass to the sound of the drum, the men's deep voices and the singing bells, everyone seemed to forget the unusualness of the hour and give way to enjoyment. It was beautiful to see the low sunlight flickering on and off the red-brown bodies as it sifted through the wide, old branches. A few white petals floated down upon them and they lifted up their faces and laughed into the tree as to a friend.

On and on they danced, stopping once in a while to rest and change the tune and time, and while they rested, they threw themselves onto the cool grass and pressed their cheeks against it, and the singers sat on their haunches and smoked cigarettes.

Everyone felt fine and relaxed. At one moment I saw Manby's furious face lowering from behind his patio door. For him the dancers were feet upon the lawn, crushing it.

After more than an hour of this pleasure Tony stood up and lifted his drumstick and swept it around at us in a summoning swoop, like conductors the world over. He tipped his head back a little and smiled gravely and said:

"Come on. Everybody got to dance. Round dance now."

A slight hysteria passed through the white guests. They wanted to, they were scared to, they didn't know how, they were frozen again to their seats, but Tony and his singers encircled the drum, started a new song, and began to pace slowly round and round in tune to it but always on the lift; the boys hastened to join them, one by one, facing in towards the drum, and round and round in a swinging slow, joyful chorus they sang with the others.

Still no one amongst us moved, inhibited to the death. Tony, standing taller than the others, raised his drumstick again. "Come on," he waved, and called to us. "Everybody dance." Now who but the old lady broke our painful immobility! She got up with a sprightly step, looking back at us over her shoulder, smiling a smile that said so much. It said, "I can do what I like. Why shouldn't I? I can make a clown of myself like this dancing with *Indians* if I want to! Come on! Be daring, be free, be as you like. It cannot make any difference!"

(Couldn't it?)

Her initiative loosened us all up, and one by one shyly joined the slowly circling dance. The Indians smiled across the ring to encourage us. They did not laugh or show by a glance that they found us funny, as we were, for without exception as we moved along with sidewise steps, we moved in our accustomed rhythm on the beat of the drum, thump, thump, thump, we all came down on the ground together as the drumsticks struck, so the outer ring of us around the core of Indian dancers bobbed up as they went down, and we went down with a bang as their dark heads lifted lightly before us, and indeed it must have been a droll sight but one we could not see ourselves. We were engrossed, all of us were, in the pleasure of this song and dance and we circled and circled doggedly as long as it lasted.

When Tony ceased with a flourish of his stick, voices cried, "Again! Again! Let's dance again!" Faces were flushed and moist but they wore a new soft look of delight. Rhythm, any rhythm, even when it is exercised in an inverted and mistaken manner, will lighten hearts, and to join for once a group of people whose magic is centered in rhythm and one of whose ideals is to have "light blood," could not help but enliven sluggish circulations.

So we danced again and again until we were weary and aching from the unusual exercise, and when we were stopped by Tony declaring, "That's all," there was not one among us who had not been given life.

All the white people went home feeling differently but the Indians went walking back to the Pueblo feeling, just the same as usual, their habitual ease and delight in being alive.

Upon the third of May in the early morning, an Indian race took place. By this time all the wheat was planted. Now the children raced along the track in relays, to give power to the earth before the corn planting would take place. They were bare and brown, with little loin cloths and feathers tied on their black heads and yellow, red and white earth paints decorated their bodies.

All along the race track beside these little runners, the head men of the tribe and council stood shouting encouragement, breezing them along with an eagle feather, running a few steps themselves. "Run! Run fast! Um a *pah!* Um a *pah!*" they cried.

In the afternoon the first corn dancers of the spring and summer corn drama appeared in the open space before the church. Afterwards the dance moved to every house in the village where a man named Cruz lived and there the young men and girls danced for him. During the summer they dance on St. John's Day and on St. Anthony's. In May there was a strange medley of spring invocation and the Holy Cross. That the cross was built just when the frost was safely out of the ground so the delicate corn seed could be planted without danger was felicitous. The saints' days and church celebrations seemed to come with convenient simultaneity as the agricultural crises. In the little church at the entrance to the Pueblo, Tony's father had painted the Queen of Heaven standing upon a crescent moon with the sun rolling large in the sky and ruddy at her right hand, and before the race the Indians were given a mass at the altar before her.

Now in May, the whole valley was filled with calves and lambs and little chicks. Everywhere they tumbled and scampered and peeped in field and barnyard. The foals stood in pastures and gazed with huge, liquid surprise at their surroundings. The young grass was succulent and tender for them all.

Now at sundown from all over the valley was heard the quick, fidgety instruction of the parent birds to their young. Such an impatient everlasting chirping and calling to bed themselves before the twilight came down upon them. Sweet, sweet, the fragrance of growing things, the natural juices of trees and fields as well as garden flowers, hyacinths and daffodils and irises and all the narcissi and tulips. Behind us the desert sage was powerfully strong on the breeze, before us the sacred mountain wafted down its pine and balsam, so we were forever in the delight of good smells, always sniffing, hardly believing it could be real. For in other places odors are not so poignant as here, as flavors are not so keen on the tongue. The seasons were more powerful here than those that I had loved before, in the pleasant moderate days of Croton or Florence, or Buffalo. I had never known anything like this intense, piercing-sweet, flashing assault called spring up in Taos Valley. It seems that here the cup runneth over.

And little by little the hard-pressed store of discontent that had caused me so much irritability and uneasiness melted and evaporated away and was dissipated upon this fresh desert air, swallowed up so that it was as though it had never been, and lighter and lighter beat that heart in me that had seemed old and worn out with more than years, with a kind of distemper of youth never outgrown but perpetuated in its forlorn and persistent infantilism. How much of this melting and cleansing must have been due to Tony? It is not easy to estimate the influence of a person like him. We have no scales to determine the benefit or detriment of presences. Just as some people are allergic to certain constituents, so may others react in some positive and virtuous way when they are brought in contact with the one that can change them. What a miracle and how little we understand it that a human being will be brought across a continent to the right one, that she may be changed truly almost in the twinkling of an eye by being with him. I would not have understood that such a power is the result of what we call love or being in love, though it is perhaps natural that true love would come out of such an experience. It is *true* love, however, that if it arose, would follow this mysterious change, this revivification and metamorphosis; true love not necessarily entangled with the senses, but true in gratitude, appreciation, even awe, and by a stirring new sense of security, happy and confiding. Such true love as this might be given to any magical personality who by his mere presence can awaken one from the wintry hibernation. Nor is it necessarily divorced from the strong sensuous response. No. It may be as it please or as the nature of anyone shall express itself. Only twice in a lifetime have I encountered this mystery of influence and change, and I have been told that many, most, do not ever encounter it. But perhaps they do not need to as I needed to, dying of starvation as I was, the dwindling forces in the organism atrophying from enforced inanition.

But though thrice I have known people who, with a seeming involuntary power in them, worked a change in being as positive as any chemical change in a laboratory, only two of these dealt with psychic elements and operated upon an invisible plane, and both of these people awakened true love in me. One completely and on all levels of body, soul and spirit, the other by a psychic intuitive love that was the high flight of understanding. To both of them my love and faithfulness forever.

Chapter Seventeen

TONY had some wonderful stories about things that had happened in the past of the Pueblo—stories his father had told him and that his father had perhaps heard from his father before him or from his grandfather.

One evening Julia, John, and I were home alone and Tony told us about Silverbird and how he got even with a Mexican woman over in Prado. I will tell it as well as I can remember it but I will probably forget a good many details, for Indian stories are long and full.

On an early morning, Silverbird opened his eyes just as the Morning Star moved across his little window. It was like a drop of white fire in the new sky and he knew the early hour it came. The air rushed down the canyon like a breath of ice.

Silverbird stretched himself and tied his blanket around him and he made a fire of cedar in the fireplace in the corner. After he had set his old black coffee pot between the upright burning sticks, he walked to the center of the Pueblo plaza where the river runs between the two community houses, and there he washed himself, and rinsed out his mouth, and then he drank from the good water that was rushing down from Blue Lake and going on to the other Indians of the South.

Silverbird was tall and skinny. There was always a look of amusement on his face, as though he were laughing at something, yet his friends never did see what he had to laugh at,

for he was all alone in his house. Nearly every Indian has a
mother or a wife but his mother had died when he was twelve
years old, when he had been apart for a long time away from
the family at the time of learning, and now he had nobody.
Every day she had come with his corn bread to the place which
he shared with several other boys who were passing the
year of initiation with him before they could be called men
and enter the tribe. As their mothers did, she had brought
him his corn meal that she had ground herself for him
and made into mush or in a loaf, or prepared in other ways;
then, after a few months she did not come any more and in
her place his old aunt brought him his food. When the old
men in the kiva had told him that his mother was dead, he
had taken it strangely; he had not said anything, but that
look of laughter had fallen upon his face and he had carried
it ever after. He had not married, nor had the old men, vigilant
in conserving the tribe and of convicting youth of indiscretion,
caught him in any of those wild pranks which are usual with
young ones. Silverbird had gone his way in silence, with that
smile on his face. He worked his powers, the Indians said
—he worked his powers as they worked their deerskin hides
and as the medicine men worked their medicines.

At dawn, that morning beside the creek, he had met a
couple of friends. These two, Eaglestar and Stonepath, were
going up the mountain that day, they said, one for a load of
wood, the other to hunt. All three, they dashed cold water
from the creek up to their faces and with wet hands they
smoothed down their hair. Each one, as he knelt on the bank,
tossed a stream of water to his mouth by a succession of swift
swooping movements, making it seem to rise to him in a
little column.

"What you up for so early, friend?" Eaglestar asked Silverbird, when they rose together and faced the east, where the pale green was fading away, and the red was coming in.

"I'm going to Prado. Our compadre Josesito is marrying off his girl today. Maybe they will need someone to work and I will chop wood for them for the fires burning in the ovens. There will be *mucho* baking in that house before nighttime."

"Hey! Cakes and pie and bread," exclaimed Stonepath. "Some Indians are lucky!"

"Well, friend, when you come back tonight with those birds, come to my house and we will eat together," replied Silverbird, his usual smile lighting his thin face.

"And I will come, too," said Eaglestar, adding, with a sly glint in his eye, "Maybe I will find something up the mountain beside my wood."

"*Bueno,* friends. We will wait for each other. Whoever comes first, from east, north or west, will watch for the others from the roof top. Let us go, then. Good hunting, brothers."

Returning to his house, Silverbird drank a bowl of the coffee which was bubbling on the embers of the fire. It was rather pale because it was made from old grounds, but like all Indians, he was used to the thin flavor, and he drank with enjoyment. He set the pot on one side, cherishing the grains for one more drenching, rolled his bed of skins into a bundle which he placed against the wall, wrapped his blanket around his hips, tucked one end under, locked his door, and started to Prado through the pasture.

It was a very nice morning, now, and there were long streams of white cloud tinged with pink lying across the dark mountains. There were plenty of horses and small cows grazing in the meadows as Silverbird moved quickly along staring straight ahead of him towards Prado with his queer smile on his face.

Before he came to Josesito's house, he heard a great barking of dogs and he saw smoke rising from the two low chimneys and from the adobe oven beside the kitchen door. When he got there and went around to the back and looked in, oh, what a lot was going on!

The women were preparing the wedding feast. The bride's mother was rolling out pie crust, the aunt was kneading dough for bread and the bride herself—her face powdered with flour to protect it from the sun—was just coming out to draw the ashes from the oven in which fire had been burning for an hour to heat it through.

"Hello, friends," said Silverbird to the women, who knew him well, for, each Indian has his friends among the Mexicans. As young girls, Silverbird's mother and Josesito's wife swapped chickens for bead work and beans for pottery, so he was an old acquaintance from childhood, and his occasional visits were taken for granted.

Josesito himself now came strolling from behind the house, and he held out his hand to Silverbird with a sweet, wry smile. He was a good man; it was as though he had honey in his veins, so good and kind and easy he was.

"*Bueno, amigo,*" he purred. "We have a good deal going on in our house today. This afternoon Domingo Martinez is coming over from Arroyo Secco to marry my Rosita. All our friends will be here. I have just killed a sheep. Come along and help me clean him."

The two men went off together. They worked all the morning, they prepared the meat and chopped more wood to replenish the fires, and then they tidied up the old shed near the corral—a big undertaking, this—only a wedding or a funeral can start such things in an easy-going land.

In the meantime, the women cooked and swept and made the house as fine as they could, breaking every dead leaf from the geraniums in the windows, while the meat boiled and roasted and the cakes baked in the ovens. The day grew hot. The hedges of white plums between the fields were white with blossoms that made the air very sweet and although there was snow on top of the mountains, the sun beat steadily, almost overbearingly, down, as it gazed in on what was going on that day at Josesito's house.

Finally the shelves in the kitchen were filled with pies and cakes; big brown loaves of bread covered with white cloths stood on the recently scrubbed kitchen table. An immense black pot filled with mutton simmered on the stove alongside another, filled with red chili. Inside the oven the sheep's ribs were roasting.

By three o'clock the company began to arrive. After lying like dead all the forenoon, the dogs suddenly came to life and barked frantically with their front legs braced, and their ears laid back.

Josesito, now wearing a clean white shirt, and a vest with a black satin back, greeted each wagon-load of friends, and Silverbird, who was still helping, took the horses into the corral while the host led the guests into the house.

In their black fringed shawls, the women stood about or sat on the enormous white iron bed. This bed had two ruffled pillow cases and a white cover embroidered with thin, red cotton cloth in a design of birds and flowers. The women, black figures against the white-washed walls, resembled the small painted Santos that hung behind them. Their faces all seemed to have a look of patience; some were pale, some were yellow, while others were sweet and pink and smiling. Still, they all had a patient look.

Several young girls giggled in one corner. They wore ready-made muslin dresses of pink or blue and big straw hats over their black eyes, covered with bunches of fast fading ribbon or stiff, nodding cotton flowers. With hands in their pockets, their sombreros tipped over their eyes, the men strolled about outside the house, smoking cigarettes, and smiling uncertainly toward the front room where the women were.

Josesito was busier now than ever, hauling water from the well for his thirsty friends, seeing that the horses were cared for all right, and sometimes selecting a friend from among the others and leading him around the corner of the house to give him a swig from a bottle that he kept hidden behind a barrel.

Silverbird was moving around, helping, too, smiling, and watching everything. When a horse kicked an unfamiliar neighbor he was unused to, Silverbird was the first one off to separate them. As each wagon came up and turned in, he was at Josesito's elbow. He said little.

The bridegroom was a good-looking boy, with red cheeks and shiny black hair, flattened down with lard. He tried to appear at ease but his black eyebrows twitched, his mouth was a tight line, and he could hardly wait for this day to be over. The marriage service, the feast, the dance; after that, he could withdraw Rosita from the gathering, and drive her in his new buggy over to his mother's house in Arroyo Secco. His parents had come and would go back in the wagon.

A fat, severe woman, Rosita's mother; she was none too glad to lose her daughter, for she was helpful to her, baking, cleaning, and weaving blankets. She knew Rosita was lucky to get Domingo—but just the same, it was going to be hard.

THE FIVE MEXICAN MIDWIVES   *by J. Valentine*

Between traditional vivacious greetings, artificial smiles, and cackles, she would throw a mean look over at poor Domingo where his new suit of bright, dark blue clothes showed up so plain in the strong light of the blazing sun as he nonchalantly strolled past the door in an effort to catch a glimpse of Rosita who was sitting, with two girls beside her, on a carved bench.

La Chiquita was a shrew and everybody knew it. Josesito had begun to call her that twenty years ago when she looked like Rosita. "She'll be a grand mother-in-law," whispered one of Domingo's friends, throwing smoke rings in the direction of the large severe woman when her glance fell on them from inside the dim room.

"Oh, shut up!" growled Domingo. Didn't he know it?

He walked over to his father to get a sense of comfort. His father, Enrico Martinez, was a tiny man with a fiery disposition. No one had a worse temper than he when he was put out. Domingo had none of his fighting spirit; he had only a strong heart for work and a strong fear of women, although he was drawn to them, too. He had a feeling that his father would be on his side when they had all become one family, linked together by the priest. The old man smiled quizzically and sniffed in the direction of the front room. Instinctive as an animal, he knew the fears that were coursing through his son.

Finally, finally, Josesito came up and laid his hand on Silverbird's arm. "Come, friend," he said, "it is all over. Now we will eat." So they stood by the kitchen door and were drying their hands on the two ends of the same cloth.

The sun had crossed over the sky and was now in the west; the wedding had taken place, and now the guests were together for the great moment of the day, the feast of chili con carne, fresh bread, roast mutton, cakes and pies and coffee. Sweat stood out in beads on Josesito's brow, but Silverbird was calm. All that day he seemed not to have felt any of the fatigue, the excitement, the anger or the fear which had moved the others. There had always been merely that look of amusement marked upon his face.

Suddenly, La Chiquita saw them. For the first moment in all those hours, Silverbird seemed to her to stand out from the surroundings as something separate. She was tired. She felt like giving that Domingo a box on the ears and telling him to clear out, but she had to remain polite and smiling to the end. But Silverbird—that Indian—was not a part in this game she had to play—no part of this kind of life of hers at all. She certainly did not have to smile at him if she did not feel like smiling. As she moved toward the two friends who stood wiping their hands, she was a fine figure of a tired woman in a very bad temper.

"Now what are you doing around here, Silverbird?" she asked in a low, harsh voice. "I thought you had gone home long ago. We got lots of people here today, so you'd better go home. No time to feed you, no place."

Josesito looked up quickly at the sound of her voice which was pitched to wound. It eased her to speak so, one could see it as she stood there.

Silverbird looked at her and went on smiling. There was no flicker of any feeling other than amusement on his face, as he said, "All right, *señora*, I goin' now. *Adios, amigos,*" he said, and turned at once toward the Pueblo.

"That's pretty damn mean," said Josesito. He spat.

"I can't help it," said La Chiquita, turning to feed her guests.

Silverbird walked home across the pasture lands, moving quickly over the dark, cropped, spongy sod, and the sun was behind him. He walked as lightly on the turf, and he wore as satisfied and intent an expression as he had worn at sunrise that morning. He could see Stonepath sitting high on the housetop in the distance. He was only a tiny speck but Silverbird knew him and Stonepath caught sight of the gray flitting figure as it came across the fields. Simultaneously they waved to each other.

Soon the sun set; a rose light tinged the snow on top of the great mountain and faded, and two figures now watched Silverbird approaching. Stonepath and Eaglestar, wrapped from head to foot in their white sheets, stood side by side, motionless, on the roof, waiting.

They met him at his door and entered with him.

With a careless gesture that masked his pride, one of them threw half a dozen birds on the floor. The other lowered a great lump of honey wrapped in leaves that he drew from beneath his sheet. Only Silverbird had brought nothing— nothing but a smile.

They quickly made a fire, as Indians do, in the early morning and evening, for company, for more life, as they say.

Silverbird's voice rose then, in a narrative, quiet and gentle. Looking into the fire—not listening with their eyes—his friends absorbed the sound of his voice as they absorbed the heat. When he had ended, they made gentle sounds of affirmation and of agreement. They showed no emotion, no excitement, but rather a kind of acceptance: not the resignation of the Mexican women, but an unyielding firmness.

After hanging the birds on a nail and placing the honey on the edge of the chimney in a pan, they glided from the house together, Silverbird leading the way, back in the direction from which he had just come—back to Prado. Once out of sight of the Pueblo, they untied their long hair and flung it loose,

1 3 *

and it was like dark water shimmering in the dusk. Then, arm in arm, they began to dance backwards, in a curious jog-trot, back towards Prado. They chanted in a low sing-song, and they raised their knees, as they swung along in their inverted dance. Their eyes were fixed. They were one moving shadow, passing backward under the stars to Prado, where the wedding feast was in full progress. There was never a break in the movement or in the song as back, backward they danced, their hair swinging at their waists like waterfalls. There was no stumbling in the grass, never a collision with a tree or a shrub and the horses lifted their heads in the stillness and watched them.

With a single intention, they came at last to Prado, and the barking of dogs and the sound of fiddles were heard on the quiet air. Unaccountably, as they passed, the barking stopped. The three-fold dancing figure backed into the light from the open door, and for an instant there was a discordant clash. The shrieking of fiddle strings, the excited voices and laughter were met by a strange harmony. The mild, united song of the Indians overpowered the disjointed utterance that poured from the big room into the silence.

Leading his companions, Silverbird entered the house. What a sight! The wedding guests had suddenly all sunk to the floor; with eyes closed, some sat against the wall, some against the bed; the fiddler lay with his head pillowed on his violin. Silverbird had worked his powers.

"Now *we* eat!" said Silverbird, gently leading his friends through the guests strewn about on the floor. Out to the kitchen went the three, where they found the remaining loaves of bread, the pies, the chili, and the mutton. In silence, seated on the ground, they ate with dignity and drank great bowls of coffee. Then they returned to the front room and Silverbird said, as they gazed upon the helpless bridal party:

"The *señora* was cross to me for no cause. Now we give a good reason to be mad." Stooping, they drew the guests into a pattern, arranging them in pairs. With lips parted and a timid frown upon his face, Domingo lay beside his mother-in-law, La Chiquita, who was like a fat monk wrapped in her shawl. The bride was beside her father-in-law, her brown hands folded on her white sash, her face looking slightly vacant, and that little man wore a fierce look, even in his slumber. All through the company they went, mixing husbands and wives. In couples, like enemies made friends by death, the bridal party lay sleeping.

Silverbird went to the door, and, facing the east, seemed to speak a few words into the sky.

"Come, friends," he said to Eaglestar and Stonepath, "the sun will wake them by and by. I have told him to do it. Now we go and leave them to be cross with each other and not with Silverbird."

Chapter Eighteen

MORE and more, I felt that my real home was in the Pueblo. All through the spring, I hurried out there every morning, and it was like entering into another and a new dimension.

I spent part of the time in Tony's house, and part in other houses near by his. Next door, an old man named John Archuleta lived, married to Tony's sister. There were a lot of children in that house, but none in Tony's. These nephews and nieces used to gather round us when I sat next to Candelaria and, hands on hers, directed the ivory needles into the tangled wool.

Tony's wife didn't like his sister and his old mother. They never came into her house, though the young relatives did, but they watched everything that went on next door, to the best of their ability. Candelaria often stood in her doorway, looking haughty and smiling—a beautiful woman, always spick and span in her clean calico and shawl—and ignoring her in-laws, standing in the doorway next to hers. Only a wall separated their houses, but a world of different feeling kept them apart. Candelaria's house was always orderly and shining, and she had a slightly malicious, sharp humor, but not real warmth; while in John Archuleta's house there was a confused and crowded atmosphere, many children, much love, and warm tenderness.

A woman named Stephanita lived on the second floor of a house a few doors away, near the entrance to the Pueblo, and she beckoned me from the roof one morning and I went up the ladder. She was a round, comely woman with large, liquid eyes and a slightly undershot jaw, and she held her chin in, so her hair, tied with bright worsted in a double loop, stuck out from the back of her smooth head.

"Teach me?" she asked, in a cooing voice. So I sat there, too, alongside her on the mattress rolled against the wall and covered with a clean sheet. From the open door, one looked across the brown Pueblo to the mysterious green canyon in the east where I had never been. Once in a while, her sons, Manuel and Telesfor, came in, smiling, to watch us. They were gentle boys, eighteen or twenty years old. A small red fire always burned in the white-washed chimney place; and from all the pueblo chimneys, blue smoke from sweet piñon wood was rising merrily.

It was nice to be in such a clean, empty room, where things did not sap and absorb the human emanations. These rooms were full of an active, living satisfaction, so one could rest in them and feel replenished. Each morning I hurried out, hungry, to the Pueblo; each noon I returned with some contentment in my heart.

Tony was not always in his house. Sometimes he was sitting outside with some friends, and he would wave me in with a large, round gesture. Once he strode into the room with a great heavy white sack on his back, and threw me a funny look as he went by, half prideful and half rueful. He disappeared through a rear door and Candelaria laughed as though it were a joke, and said, "Wheat!" in the low, tuneful, Indian voice.

One Sunday morning I was sitting there, knitting, when Tony came into the house wrapped to the eyes in a white sheet. He came and stood before me, looking down for a while, and I didn't know why. His eyes showed deep and dark under the visor of the white folds. Finally he said, in a faraway, dream-like voice:

"Ni-i-i-ce color!" He was looking at my purple ribbon, and I knew he saw more in it than I did. Whatever he saw that day made a lasting impression in his mind, for it has remained until now his favorite color.

Soon he sat down beside the fire on a little wooden stool and, staring into the flames, he began to sing in a low voice while he beat upon a small metal water drum. A queer magic that opened windows in my imagination soon filled the room and I drifted upon it, leaving my regular life, my known, circumscribed, real life—the understandable, rational kind of living which was all I had known, except for occasional strange hours of unstability when things turned queer and frightened me by their alteration.

But Tony did not turn things queer. Instead of that, he was deepening the reality of life by his present magic and his sing-ing. The limitations of the senses were spreading out and lift-ing higher, so that I suddenly saw, too, what purple could be, though there are no words to tell it here. And I heard his voice joined to other sounds that had been unheard or unnoticed before now, the actuality in the crackling fire, the voice of the wind outside; and the life inherent in these common sounds was shown to me so I heard them like new voices speaking. There is a live hearing and a deaf one. We are mostly deaf all our lives long, and blind to real seeing.

I didn't know Tony was absent from us that day in the world *peyote* opens to those who have eaten it. I didn't find out about that until some months later. But somehow he was able to take me with him where he went. Was it any wonder he drew me to the Pueblo day after day? He shared with me more than the magnified and enhanced sense impressions that he experienced. It was the Indian life I was entering, very slowly, a step at a time. I was becoming acquainted with a kind of living I didn't know existed anywhere. I had heard, of course, of the Golden Age, and of the Elysian Fields, but they had been only words to me. Now I found out what they meant.

There was a broken wall around the Pueblo, and it enclosed a most lovely and potent way of living. I rarely heard any angry or harsh-toned voices there, never anything but courteous and dignified exchange between neighbors whose houses joined wall to wall. They must have evolved politeness, I thought, as a necessary protection from contacts so close and intimate, for were there not some guarantee of privacy, they would end by killing each other from sheer exasperation.

But maybe I was mistaken. Perhaps there is a relatedness I could not conceive of that needs no protection, that is held together in a happy combination of stimulating strains, that is positive, life-giving and taking, like that of bees in a hive. Certainly there was a honey sweetness in their daily bread that I never knew in mine.

When I trudged back home, down the road past the close-cropped, community meadows, where the horses grazed on the fresh green just appearing, down the road and over the two little bridges that crossed the gay, small, sparkling Pueblo creek that came tumbling from the sacred mountain, my heart was not so full of anticipation as on my journey out, and I was reluctant to arrive. Down through the avenue of big cottonwood trees Mr. Manby had planted and which made a village street as lovely as those in New England, I plodded past the three or four houses set back from the road, until I came to our arched adobe entrance.

I ran in, always just in time for lunch, but with none to

spare. I assumed a bright, noncommittal expression which I
supposed was the way Indians looked. I wanted to be like
them and felt, in an obscure way, that if I looked and acted
the way they did, I would be. The family were usually either
gathered in the living room or washing up: Maurice with a
cloud on his face, Andrew with a frown on his face, John
with a frown on his face. Why did all these men frown so
much?

Where I had come from, they did not frown or grumble
or ask questions. I think nobody in the Pueblo ever asked a
question; it almost seemed to be against their code. What was
their code? My companions began to ask me questions as soon
as I arrived. We sat down at the table and I kept my eyes on
my plate as I had seen Tony do.

"Mother, why do you have to go out to the Pueblo every
day? Do you think the Indians like that? I bet they wonder
about it."

"Really, da-a-r-rling, are you teaching those girls anything? I
am afraid you are wasting your time!"

And Andrew! "Why don't you come along with me, sometimes. I have an entirely new location to explore, now—over
towards the north where you used to wish you could drive, a
month ago."

Mr. McKenzie usually just watched and listened. I hated all
this interference, and my impatience would begin to rise in a
very un-Indian fashion, and I would soon be frowning like
the rest of them! As soon as I had eaten, I would excuse myself
and wrap my shawl around me and throw myself on the couch
in the alcove—for I had a shawl by this time. Oh, yes. It was
a purple shawl with long silk fringe, just the color Tony had
stared at in my ribbon.

Lying on the couch, I tried to exclude my companions from

my consciousness, and to remain in the other world I had left behind me, in that Pueblo where the women sat quietly in full, starched calico dresses, or silently walked down to the river with shawls over them, to fetch water which they carried home in round, clay pots balanced upon their heads, one arm stretched up with the long shawl-line falling straight down in lovely folds. The Indian women were sheltered in their shawls, seeming so comfortable and encompassed within them, so that their whole being was contained, not escaping to be wasted in the air, but held close and protected from encroachments. How exposed we live, I thought, so revealed and open! I longed for the insulation of the shawl and wore mine whenever I could.

Chapter Nineteen

JOHN ARCHULETA'S oldest daughter, Marina, was a beautiful girl with soft, black eyes and thick hair as soft and black as a raven's breast. Her short nose jutted out like a young eagle's, and her hands were beautiful. She had the same look in her eyes her father had, a steady, faithful, glowing gaze, and I came to know she was Tony's favorite niece. She was always helping Christina, her mother, to take care of the numerous smaller children that tumbled over each other in the family room, and who gave it the aspect of warm disorder that Candelaria's neat, childless room never had.

Tony's mother lived in the room between his and his sister's, and the children of her dead daughter lived with her, and there were a number of rooms adjoining, with others built on top, all occupied by different members of the same family, for this was how the two Pueblo community houses were made up—of different family groups.

There was a little dark room next to the Archuleta family living room, where Christina, fat and shapeless and full of mother love, often ground cornmeal on the *petate,* while her old mother cooked in the open fireplace. There was always a great deal of cooking going on in that house, and a constant odor of weak coffee, chili, stew, or boiling beans, for the old mother and her grandchildren ate together with the Archuletas.

The simultaneity of Pueblo life was always a mystery to me. They told the time by the sun and they were not dominated by clocks and watches the way we are, and they did not try to have meals at regular hours like us. "Indians eat when they hungry," Tony told me. But then they all got hungry at once at the same times of the day, so that of a sudden, all over the Pueblo, there would be a quickening in the fireplaces where people were throwing on fresh wood, and out of every chimney, with one accord, fresh, new, blue smoke would come pouring merrily, long furling waves from the blazing piñon sticks.

One morning Tony took me in to see Marina, who was lying down beside the fireplace on her mattress which was usually rolled up when I got out there. Her face looked swollen and her eyes were too bright.

"He catch cold," her father said, laughing. I saw what short, hard breaths she took, and I thought she looked very uneasy.

"Why don't you have the doctor?" I asked him.

"The doctor don't come to the house," he replied in an informing tone, as though I ought to know better. "He go to the school house twice a week and if the Indians want medicine, they can go get it. We got our own Indian doctor. She coming to see Marina pretty soon."

I thought something had better be done and I told Tony so when he went outside.

"Yes, he get too wet going out to the corral in the night-time with bare feet; then he get sick." I knew what that meant, for I had learned how, in winter nights in the snow, as well as in the summertime, the Indians went outside the Pueblo wall whenever they had to relieve themselves, for that was the custom. That was why there were never any bad odors in the village.

I sat in Tony's house beside the fire all morning. I missed Marina, for she generally came in there. But no one else seemed to notice she was absent. It was as if she were forgotten. Though I did not forget her I didn't say anything more, for it wasn't my business, I thought.

When I came back next day, Tony and a couple of Indians were sitting in the sun with their backs to the house wall.

"How is Marina?" I asked him.

He got up, looking at me with a closed face.

"He *sick,*" he said. "Come inside."

She lay in the same place, and she was breathing like someone who has been running a race. Her head turned from side to side, and her eyes searched the corners of the room with a frenzied look in them. She did not see us. Her mother sat on one side of her, looking very sorry, and Tony's mother sat on the other side of her favorite grandchild and patted her tenderly once in a while. The fire burned brightly, but she did not need it. I touched her forehead and it scorched my fingers.

"The doctor *must* come and see her!" I exclaimed to Tony in a whisper. "I'm going over to the school house and telephone him."

Tony didn't look as though he were with me in this, but he walked over across the creek with me, through the south side of the Pueblo, and up to the school house where it stood beyond the Indian life, a grim, gray building that didn't belong there.

Outside in the cluttered yard of the teachers' house, a big, coarse-looking fat man was standing, a cap pulled down over his face, watching some Indian boys piling wood.

"Get that damned wood piled even," I heard him say, crossly, as we came up.

"This lady want to telephone," Tony said to him, coldly.

He gave me a suspicious look, as much as to say, "What are *you* doing around here?"

"There's a girl very sick in the Pueblo," I explained. "I'd like to get the doctor to come and see her."

"Dr. Bergman's inside the house there," he answered, ungraciously, and then I saw there was an automobile standing outside the gate with a woman peering out of the window at us.

We went and knocked on the door and it was opened by a worried American person who had on a soiled apron.

"Can I speak to the doctor?" I asked her.

Tony waited outside while I followed her into the house, through the untidy kitchen to a small back room where there were shelves with a collection of bottles and bundles. I saw some old familiar labels: Castor Oil, Camphor, Cascara.

A tall, blue-eyed man, who looked very surprised at my invasion, was pouring something from one bottle to another smaller one, and a little Indian girl waited beside him.

"Dr. Bergman, can you come over and see John Archuleta's daughter? She seems very sick."

"Well," he hesitated, "when I get through here, I'll run over."

"Please come as soon as you can. I'd like to hear what you think before I go home."

We walked back to the Pueblo and Tony said, "I don't think them American doctors know anything for Indians. They give very rough medicine."

"But you have to do *some*thing for Marina," I exclaimed, impatiently. "What did *your* doctor say?"

"Well, he give her some sage to drink, and he rub him. What for the Indians get cold all the time, after they been to school? That not natcherel. I never cold when I been young. Maybe that because I don't go to school much."

The doctor finally knocked at the door and came in with a self-conscious look, as though he were unaccustomed to visiting in the Pueblo, as of course he was, and he acted very professional. He felt Marina's pulse and counted it and murmured, "Hum-m-m . . ." in a surprised tone; then he opened a black bag and took out a stethoscope and listened to her heart.

The women sat back against the wall on the rolled mattresses with blank faces and with the warmth wiped out of their eyes, and several nephews crowded round the door. Of course a number of small children were collected in the room as usual.

Dr. Bergman took out a bottle marked Aspirin and rolled some tablets into a piece of paper. He gave instructions when she should have those, then he gave some directions that sounded like some kind of ritual. He told the whole room, since he didn't know to whom he should address himself. He said they had to give her a complete bath every four hours, and they must bathe the right arm, then the left leg, then the right leg and the left arm. Tony looked unconvinced and I am sure he thought it was some form of religious ceremony that belonged to the white people and not to Indians.

I went outside with the doctor when he left, and asked him what the matter was, and he told me she had double pneumonia. He drove away with the woman who waited in his car and he never came back. Marina died that night towards morning.

I didn't know it until I reached the Pueblo, but already she was laid out on the floor and her face looked beautiful again. She lay with her feet in brand-new moccasins made for her in a hurry, and they pointed west where her journey would take her. She who had faced the east, waking and sleeping, all her life long, was turned towards the Indian death

IN THE PUEBLO   *by Ansel Adams*

road now. Dressed in her best, she lay upon the gifts the whole family had provided for her, their blankets, shawls, silk dresses, and turquoise jewelry which would go with her.

The women sat around the sides of the room with black shawls over their heads: "Ai-ai-ai-i-i," they cried, and groaned in a loud, rhythmical chorus. All the relatives were there, aunts and uncles and cousins from other parts of the Pueblo. Men, anonymous in blankets that covered their heads, crouched together on their haunches. I did not know which Tony was.

An old man got up and stood at her head, looking down upon her upturned face, and began to make a long address to her, and it sounded as though he were giving her directions. He spoke directly to her, intimately, but in a loud voice as though he had to penetrate her sleep, and he made gestures downward, over westward, and up to the sky. He told her a great many things and she seemed to listen, while all the time the women cried in the loud Indian formula for grief and the men kept terribly silent.

Finally he was through, and Joe Lujan, Tony's uncle, who had been to Carlisle and spoke what was supposed to be good English, came up to me and took me by the arm:

"Now you must go," he said. "They have their own doin's."

I went out into the bright sunlight and everything looked very sad, and I didn't know what to do with myself. I saw Stephanita sitting on her roof, so I climbed up the ladder and joined her. She shook her head and gave a sympathetic gasp. Many people sat as she did on their roofs, and watched.

After a while, a little procession came along the road below the house and we looked down upon the slim package they had made of Marina, wrapped round and round in silks and blankets, swathed like a mummy, completely covered and bound with ropes. All her relatives followed the young men who carried her high and over to the graveyard that lay west of the Pueblo, and they laid her deep in the hole in the ground directly onto the earth, with her feet still pointing to where the sun would set.

After she was buried, the family went back to the house to have a feast; but before the young men joined them, they went down to the river, took off their moccasins, and strode into the icy water that came down from Blue Lake. They took off their blankets and quickly dipped them vigorously into the stream, and then quickly shook off the sparkling drops before they soaked in. Then they dipped up handfuls of water and smoothed their hair and faces, purifying themselves from the corruption of death. Replacing their moccasins, they returned to the house to eat the fresh baked bread and funeral meat.

I went home and wrote a letter that noon to the Indian Bureau in Washington and told them the doctor had neglected a girl whose case he had diagnosed to me as double pneumonia; that anyone with any knowledge and humanity would have worked over her a little, would have stayed with her that night. Presently they sent out an inspector who called upon me and to whom I told more details. He looked sympathetic, but he said:

"This man can be removed to somewhere else, but the chances are the same kind of man would replace him. They can't get any better for the salaries they pay."

In the late afternoon, I took a walk along the road to Placita and I met Tony coming towards me with his blanket over his bowed head. The sun shone behind him and made him look tall and broad and like a Biblical figure. He stopped and I saw how haggard he was.

"I been walking a long time," he told me. "I feel so bad."

I didn't know what to say to him. What can one say? So I walked along beside him in silence.

Dr. Martin drove past us slowly in his old car. He called out genially: "You trying to get some red blood in you? That's right," and was gone.

Tony looked at me strangely.

"What she mean?" he asked.

"Oh, he thought I was too pale when I came to Taos. He's been telling me all winter I ought to stay outdoors more!"

"Funny," he mused.

Chapter Twenty

WHILE we waited for spring to deepen, Tony told me of places he would show me, and I could hardly wait until the roads dried up so we could go. Finally, one morning, he came for us in his two-seated buggy to drive over to the Hot Spring. Pete, Maurice's model, sat beside him, and Maurice and I sat behind. I wore my purple shawl over my head and I wished I sat with Tony.

It took the whole morning to drive northwest across the desert, passing through some scattered hamlets. Tony told us their names: Placita, Prado.

Tony and Pete talked together in the murmuring Indian language, talked of what they saw along the way, seeing everything, alive to everything. But Maurice and I were different. He clung with one hand to the rail of the buggy seat and frowned when it lurched in the ruts of the road. He did not look out around him, and his eyes were not fed. As for me, I was in retreat within the folds of my purple shawl, and all I saw was the back of Tony's head in front of me. Once in a while, a faint perfume blew back to me from him.

By this time the stream of my life was flowing towards Tony. I had never been alone with him for even a moment, but he called to me constantly with irresistible persuasion, and I went out to him. I had learned to watch for the quick look he gave me when, even with a number of people around, he saw a chance to exchange a glance, to give me his face, as he called it once, later on.

For Indians had to learn to talk with their eyes, their fingers, and even with the folds of the blanket. Since they were always in company, they had devised a kind of super-privacy, within which they exchanged glances, gestures, and semi-tones between the current, flowing patterns of intercourse and conversation, little signs for lovers, some traditional and belonging to them all, but others invented on the spot, instantaneous subterfuges as rapid as the flicker of sunlight and lost if one were not as quick. I learned, in time, to be alert.

The desert spread out all around us after an hour, no more houses except the little Indian country houses, empty in the fields—the adobe rectangles that looked like lost notes of music. How sweet the sage smelt when we crushed it under the wagon wheels, and how the birds were singing!

We had turned left off the main road and wound up and down over some hilly places until we came to the road down into the Rio Grande Canyon, and there it plunged right downwards, looking terribly steep. Maurice hung on more than ever, and so did I, now, for the wagon tipped forward and lurched from side to side on the rocks that it hit, but Tony shoved on the brake and drove down unhesitatingly, singing a glad song with Pete. We seemed to be entering a region no one had ever been in before. The mountain rose on the left side of the road, and on the right, dropped to the river away down below us. Across the chasm rose another dark hillside and in the sunny gulf between, wild birds swooped and screamed, startled from their solitude. Midway down the incline, a tall evergreen stood silhouetted against the background of river and mountain and it seemed to me I never saw anything so quiet and distinct as it looked, so completely manifested in the light that shows things up in this country.

We reached the bottom after a mile of curving descent,

and there was a stone house built along the brink of the stream that was no curling ribbon, now, but a broad, brown, turbulent river.

"Mr. Manby built that," said Tony, pointing to the house; and he showed us inside it. We crossed a rickety, narrow bridge to enter the door which seemed to be in the top of it, for the slope from the river edge was still steep up the hill. Under the loose boards of the floor, we glimpsed water, gleaming below through the cracks. Very dark and sinister it seemed in there, while from the open door we saw the startled birds outside, still swirling and calling to each other in the bright sunshine.

"My God!" exclaimed Maurice, "do we bathe down there?"

"Look," Tony told him, "you go down this and you find very nice water."

And we found there was an old, shaky staircase leading down below.

Maurice and the two Indians went out and left me, pulling the door to; so I undressed and climbed down into the black, waiting pool. A slight steam came off it and moistened the black stones that were piled around the sides and built into walls, and a window high up let in a beam of light that bored through the misty air and showed me where I was. It was like an archaic bath in the earliest days of the Greeks.

I stepped into the water and gave a great breath of delight. "Oh, it's wonderful!" And it was, so hot and enveloping and having, besides, some mysterious properties that I had never known before and could not define, but that my flesh and bones accepted, not bothering to name them.

The water gave one a new feeling of content. It solaced and satisfied the restless, questing nerves and blood, and when I came out into the world again, I felt made over, and newly put together. I laughed and shook my wet hair in the sunshine.

"Hurry up, Maurice! It's marvelous!"

He and the others went in, then, and I sat beside the fire that was lighted on a little level patch of sand, white among the lava boulders, and waited for them. My heart was light and I was full of gladness and every cell in my body turned expectantly towards Tony hidden behind the stone walls of that house. I was without thought or desire, living completely in the continuous flow of being that entered and passed through me towards him. I didn't want anything more than to be alive like this.

When they came from bathing, they all looked refreshed and serene. "I feel all smoothened out," Maurice said.

We cooked coffee and beefsteaks on long crotched sticks over the fire, and Tony washed the coffee pot in the river afterwards. I watched him. His smooth, hairless face was under his own control and he didn't show his thoughts unless he wished. If he was tired, he looked tired, but if he didn't want to look tired, he looked rested. Sometimes his life seemed to sink down, way down in him, and leave his face empty and without significance. Often he looked perfectly uninteresting. Then again his soul rose up in him and informed him. It never left him completely, though it disappeared sometimes. He did not worry about the tides in him. He permitted the ebb and flow of being, unless he had a wish to be all there for some reason, then he was at his own command in an instant. There was a constant flux, a come and go about his intensity. His brow shone and his sensitive, plucked eyebrows had beautiful modeling. He had the kindest face I ever saw.

He showed us some markings on the rocks. Behind the

house, a huge flat stone lay near the edge of the river, and when it was moistened, it showed a large, dim, blunted fragment of carved decoration: a band of the Greek key pattern. How had it ever come to be there? Another rock bore some straggling marks, "turkey tracks," Tony said, and the small, childish representation of a man.

"Long time ago, the Spanish people was looking for this spring," Tony told us. "They knew the Indians had some nice water some place along the river. This is the Indian sign to show the Indian people where it is. Another one over by the side of the house. And I show you one halfway up the mountain when we go."

He led us, clambering over the rocks, around the house and pointed to a faint carved sign on the face of a granite boulder: a circle with a dot in the center of it.

"That is the name of the spring," said Tony. "Means you always live, always be young."

I found a place in the sand and lay down, and we looked at the carving on the rock, and I was wondering. . . . Tony came up to me where I was, and all of a sudden a small flash of red passed from him to my hand, where it lay open. Alas! I was not quick enough. It rolled away and fell down over the rock ledge several feet below. Maurice, turning at that instant, espied it, picked it up. When it was in his hand, I had a chance to see what it was: a little round bag of something in red silk.

His face had an expression on it I never saw before, of surprise, as though he could not believe his eyes. He flashed a look at me, who pretended not to see it, and at Tony, who, apparently oblivious, was shaking the sand out of one of the rugs. Maurice continued to stare for an instant at the object in his hand, and then he dropped it into his pocket, and the two ends of time joined together, before this had happened and after he had put it out of sight, and it was as though it had been effaced from experience and had never happened, so far as we showed. But none of us, I think, forgot it for a moment. I, at least, could not wait to get it, and I hated Maurice because he had it.

In a little while we climbed slowly up the long, steep hill, the horses stretching out their necks with the effort, and halfway up Tony pointed to some carvings we had not noticed when we passed down in the morning. Little markings of birdtracks, a sun, a tiny man . . . things for another kind of mankind than we were, to read and understand.

Suddenly I felt afraid. I had a strange sensation of dislocation, as though I were swinging like a pendulum over the gulf of the canyon, between the two poles of mankind, between Maurice and Tony; and Maurice seemed old and spent and tragic, while Tony was whole and young in the cells of his body, with his power unbroken and hard like the carved granite rock, yet older than the Germanic Russian whom the modern world had destroyed.

When we reached the top of the canyon, the sun was getting low in the west, so our wagon made a long shadow beside us on the desert and the two Indians were singing softly in a quiet, evening tone, now. When we came to the fenced fields, where some green was pricking brightly through the earth, I asked Tony what it was, for I knew nothing about farming, though I had lived on a farm in Croton.

"That winter wheat," he said, pointing his whip at it. "The Padres gave us that."

"Padres?" asked Maurice, in an irritated voice. I could see he was angered by his thoughts.

"Yes, when they first come, long time ago. Then we had

just corn. Now we got wheat, too." He went on singing.

We drove along beside the darkening fields and pretty soon he said to me, turning around in his seat and smiling a pleasant, social smile for anyone to see:

"I got an Indian name for you."

"What is it?" I asked, as polite as himself.

"White Hawk. You like it?"

"Why, yes. It's a nice name." I wondered if it was!

Presently I noticed a small bird that was flying along beside us, alighting on fence posts, then flying on ahead to wait till we caught up. I didn't know how long it had been with us before I saw it. I had seen that kind of bird doing so several times before this.

"What is that bird?" I asked him.

"Oh, that? That chicken hawk," he answered, cheerfully. "Huntin'."

"Oh!" I murmured.

We drove up to our house in the dusk and got out stiff from the long drive. I stood back against the adobe wall and waited while Maurice dug the basket and rugs out of the bottom of the buggy. My eyes were on Tony. He stood up in his buggy and stretched out his arms with his blanket in his hands as if to wrap it around him; but he bent a quick look down upon me and with a mysterious smile in his eyes, he made a motion that quickly enveloped me in it, folded me inside it close to him. One gesture and one look, and he had done this in his imagination; but it was completely realized, shared, and over in a flash. I felt drawn out of myself—and I trembled when I walked into the garden.

I couldn't stay with the others that evening. I went to bed early and tried to read, but Tony's face kept coming before me as it had in my dream in New York. When Maurice came to bed, I pretended to be asleep until I knew he slept, and then I got up and went through his clothes that lay on a chair in the dark room. I found the little bundle by its perfume. It was a rose-sweet bag of scent of some kind I had never known except when a breeze blew it off Tony. I slept with it under my pillow.

Maurice missed it from his pocket when he was dressing the next morning, and I saw an expression of annoyance on his face as I sat up in bed drinking my coffee. I watched him plan his attack upon me in a silent and unconscious rehearsal of his forthcoming conversation. When he was dressed, he stood beside me and he said, raising his dark eyebrows:

"Did you take that thing out of my pocket?" His voice was cold and he was trying to act authoritative, but he was not used to it, so he seemed merely nervous.

"Yes, I did," I answered him.

"Is that a *love token* that Indian was giving you?" he demanded, menacingly.

Upon this, I burst out laughing.

"Oh, Maurice! What a word! Love token!" He flushed darkly at my ridicule.

"You'd better be careful," he threatened, though he did not say of what.

I didn't answer him and he went out to his breakfast.

I wore it inside my dress for a long time—until Tony gave me another one, late in the summer.

Chapter Twenty-one

IN OUR house, from that time on, a new strain was apparent. I walked up to the Pueblo as usual every morning, for the sake of sitting in that happy neighborhood, and to share its warmth and gaiety, but my heart sank a little when I reached home, for Maurice just glowered at me, now, when I came in. He did not actually take up the issue with me, nor did he hide his feelings until we were alone. No, he brought them to table, and with his strong personality he spoiled our meals, sitting there frowning and not speaking to anyone.

I did not care, really. I was truly content inside myself, not thinking of present or future, or of those around me. It was as though my old self had ceased to be, or had run away and hidden and left the place open to another. I did not feel myself or feel like myself, yet I seemed to feel more alive than I ever had, and in a different way; and I seemed to understand things I never had before. I remembered how Mrs. Hopkins had used to tell Maurice I was an "Atlantean," and I thought to myself that maybe that was true, and that only now it was coming out! But what it would be, and what really would come out, I had no idea, nor did I speculate much about it, for I was too occupied with being real for once in my life.

It was at this time that I began to open my hands and let things slip away. Things! One sunny day I was looking at the white-washed wall in Tony's house: it was perfectly bare, one whole side of the room, except for the sunlight that moved upon it.

"How nice an empty wall is!" I exclaimed.

"Indian houses are empty," he answered, "because God said Indians cannot have *things*. White people have *things,* but God give the Indians just what grows on the mountain."

Candelaria laughed a silver, ringing laugh, and said something that made Tony smile, so I asked him what she said.

"He say God give white people things and Indians watch them go under them. You know. Wheel turning." He made a large, round gesture. "So many things carry the wheel down, with the white people underneath. Pretty soon Indians come up again. Indians' turn next."

Right from the beginning, I had had the power to see into his mind and catch the pictures he saw, and so now I saw the huge wheel turning slowly, weighted down with all the accretions of our civilization: the buildings and machinery, the multitudinous objects we had invented and collected about us, and ourselves fairly buried under the heavy load, muffled, stifled, going under. On the other side of the wheel, rising bare-limbed and free, heads up bound with green leaves, sheaves of corn and wheat across their shoulders, this dark race mounting.

"The time to come is his," I thought, "and he knows it." And I felt he was right. Well, for years I had had the belief that the Oriental nations would join together and spread across Europe, entering through the gate of Russia. But they were great in number. What could a handful of Indians accomplish against millions of Americans? When I thought of Indians, I thought of the pueblos along the Rio Grande and forgot the Indian populations of Mexico, Yucatan—all the Central and South Americans!

1 5

I grew careless with my few possessions, and gave Anita many of my clothes and things. The little sack of perfume had a greater value for me than jewels. My own belongings seemed meaningless, now, and without association; but when Tony brought me a branch of evergreen, I treasured it.

He drove Julia and Agnes up to a cave in the side of the mountain, once. I was watching for them beside the picket fence of the garden in the late afternoon, and they came along quietly, the horse's hooves muffled, and they looked vague and dream-like in the twilight. When they all got down, Tony did, too, and came up to the fence and handed me a small branch of spruce with long needles, the kind that grows only at some distance higher than we lived in in this valley. It was a sign to show me where they had been. I hung it in my room and let it speak to me of mountainsides.

I had no opportunity to speak to him alone and he did not seem to make one. I knew we were flowing back and forth to each other, and I knew he was as aware of it as I was. But he made no effort to carry anything further so far as I could see. He proceeded slowly forward upon the road we had to travel, and I followed him, taking no initiative for once!

We did not have much talk together, and when we did there were always others there. But I slowly learned something about the Indian point of view in the occasional moments when we were sitting in his house or driving somewhere in the two-seated buggy. I remember once he gave us a dissertation when he was driving us up to Glorieta, an old sacred grove of cottonwoods up the canyon beyond the Pueblo. Perhaps it was because we saw so many birds that day, larks singing, bluebirds dipping among the leaves, black and white magpies in pairs, all kinds of birds singing and chirping and fluttering.

Anyway, he started to talk, saying: "You know, God put all the little and big animals on the earth each in his own place and with his own way. The birds, and the fishes, and the ones on the land. And they all stayed where he told them to stay. Everything wants to stay in itself. God told them not to change.

"Then after the animals, God put the Indians on the earth, and after that the white people. But they were separated by something. By time. Indians have no time. They have never had no time. Now the white people, God He told them to change. And so changing began when the white people came in the world. But He told the Indians to stay themselves; not to change. He never put change in the Indians. The white people have to change, that is their way. So they have to try and change everything. They take God's animals and change them from one thing to another. Now, only a bad witch Indian work this change, and go into a coyote sometimes and out again or be something different. Good people among Indians never work changes. But good white people do because God put it in them to do it. So even they want to change people and nations and will not let them be. Their religion is in machinery to change things and now they come to want to change the Indians though God told them to stay Indian."

"Well, what is the religion of the Indians?" I asked.

"Life," he answered.

Natalie Curtis and Paul Burlin came to Taos and found a little house to rent in Cañon; and Maurice joined up with them now for a large part of the time. They had a guest, a large, gray-eyed, rather solemn girl whom Maurice fixed his gaze upon and fascinated. He sometimes tried to get me to go with him to see them, or to join them at the movie, but I said, pleading with him, "But I didn't come here to know Americans!"

The moving-picture house was in Miramon's dance hall a little way down the street across from us, and the pictures were so bad and the air so thick with dust from all the muddy feet that I went only once, and didn't stay. I walked half the length of it in the dark and out again, another time, to make sure that Maurice was in there with that girl, for I wanted to know if he had lied to me. He had.

My awareness of the people around me in our house had grown so dim by late spring that I cannot remember who was there and who was not; but I think Andrew and Bobby had gone away, and that Julia had returned from Chicago where she had been spending the winter with her brother.

In the queer, unconscious way people have sympathy for each other, she understood my feeling for Tony. She appreciated him, too, and she used to like to give him little things, silk handkerchiefs, knives, and anything she could think of to please him, which was difficult because, though he liked getting presents, there was very little he wanted.

She invited him down to dinner with us and when he came, Maurice would hardly speak to him; and only Tony's ease and dignity at the table carried us through an unpleasant meal.

One night she had a vivid dream that she told me about in the morning: In a foreign country, somewhere in the Orient, a great crowd of people were celebrating an event. They rushed in with arms raised, crying jubilantly in a half-foreign language: *"La cha est mort! Est morto la cha!"* And then a bier was rolled in and on it was Maurice's corpse!

Julia said she wanted to ride horseback and Tony must take her. I had been out riding once or twice on one of Mr. Manby's horses, and he had taken me back through his fields towards the eastern hills, past two or three Mexican houses on the raised ground at the edge of the desert Indian land. I remember he stopped under a great cottonwood tree and showed me the wide circle of the valley from there.

"Some day," he had said, waving his crop, "some day I shall build my wide boulevard that will go around through here for miles, that will circle the whole valley as far as the Hot Spring over there and back. I have shown you the plan for my big hotel? Well, I will have another one at the top of the canyon above the Baths. This is one of the gardens of the world and it will be known one day."

When we rode through the sage and cedar up to the hills and on to a projecting knoll that gave one an open view of the whole valley rolled out, so fair and lovely, swimming in light, I had felt a momentary fear of the old man, he looked at me so strangely, with a glare in his eyes and a chuckle bubbling from his lips.

"This is all Indian land," he said, pointing down where we had ridden through, "but it will not always be."

Tony brought two horses saddled, so I went riding with them. When he and I rode, side by side, forgetting Julia for a moment, behind us, it was the first time we had ever spoken alone.

He said, "I saw you before you came. I dreamed you, but you had long hair."

"Yes. John cut it off the first night I was here."

"Too bad. You look nice with your hair, here on each side." He touched his ears in the place where I had coiled the two strands of long hair for years.

"I saw you in a dream, too," I told him, "before I left New York. It made me come here."

1 5 ★

"Yes," he agreed, simply.

At this point, Julia struck her horse a smart blow with the branch Tony had given her. All we knew was a sudden clatter of hooves and the horse streaking past at a gallop, with her bobbing up and down while she clung to the pummel.

Tony burst into sudden laughter, dug his heels in and dashed after her. The two of them galloped down the road until he caught up with her, then the two horses engaged in a race; but finally he reached her bridle rein and stopped them. When I reached them, her hair was hanging down her back and she looked angrily at me, as though it had all been my fault.

"I've got to go back to the house; I don't like this horse at all; besides, I never meant to gallop like that my first ride in years," she chattered.

That night I cut her hair off. I persuaded her it was more comfortable; but when she went home her family was furious and her friends never ceased joking about it.

One day, Tony said he wanted to try and drive our Ford, so I got McKenzie to take us out that afternoon. He drove us towards Arroyo Secco and then let Tony try, sitting beside him and telling him things. All seemed to go well as far as I could see, for I didn't know a thing about cars or driving them; but all of a sudden there was a frightful noise and we stopped in the middle of the road!

We sat there a long time while Tony walked off and finally came back with a pair of horses that pulled us very slowly into town. It was dark when we reached the house and I ran in to see if they were worried.

Maurice met me at the door with a black face, and in the entry way, where no one could see him, he struck me across the face with his hand, in a complete silence.

It was the first time such a thing had ever happened to me. He had thrown a book at me once in Croton, but he had never touched me. I had sometimes wished he would; that he would beat me, give me something to fight, to resist, to come up against. Now that he had, it was without significance for me. Like his sculpture! I had worked so hard and long to make him into a sculptor. Now, apparently, he was one, and it did not seem to matter.

John came upon us at that instant. He was close behind Maurice, but he hadn't seen him hit me. I went in to supper with them all, and they told me how worried they had been, but it didn't seem to mean a thing. Often things happen in me and I don't know it until quite a long time afterwards. Something happened that night that was not finished until August. I didn't think Maurice's blow had meant anything to me, but apparently it had. The next morning I was sick in bed and unable to get up. My head ached with a strange bursting pain; my throat ached; everything in me hurt. I could only lie in my dark, adobe-colored room and give up to it. Julia had made friends in the town and went out to see them, and I was all alone.

I lay there wishing I could see Tony, for I knew that, and only that, would help me. I longed for him. About four o'clock I heard a low singing outside in the garden, and there he was, sitting on the old garden bench under the apple tree. He sat there quietly singing in an undertone and I watched him through the iron bars that were fastened over the window. His face was grave and still and his expression withdrawn, his eyes lowered. He sang for nearly an hour, and then he stood up and went away out of the garden, and all my aches and pains were gone and I felt light-hearted; so I got up and bathed and was ready to face the world again at supper time.

Now I knew I could call him when I needed him, and he would come, and for the first time in my life I had a feeling of security and safety in this world that I have never lost— the realization of a real connection with another human being, an experience I had not known until that day.

Chapter Twenty-two

THE DAY came when Julia had to return to New York, and she had the idea of taking Tony with her. She said she knew her brother would like him, and it would be so interesting to show him New York; and maybe she could take him to Washington to meet the President.

Tony wanted to go, particularly for the last reason. It is in the Indian tradition to go and see the President, for there is an ancient hope surviving still in Indian hearts that he will help them. Abraham Lincoln had impressed his image upon Indians forever as a man of fairness and loyalty. He had confirmed the land grants the Spanish King had allowed them, and, to the office of each of the pueblo governors, he gave a silver-headed cane to be held as a kind of scepter by successive rulers. His name was engraved upon the silver knob and his words of presentation, and each governor in his turn has always cherished it.

Lincoln's sad, rugged face was to be seen hanging in quite a number of the pueblo houses, and his was the presidential picture that they had in their minds when they thought of "government" and protection. Perhaps Tony saw him in his mind when he agreed to go with Julia.

The evening before he went away, he walked down the road and stopped beside the house. It was the loveliest hour. The sun was just setting and the air was full of golden light and birds were singing quietly and calling to each other. The mountain had deep purple shadows upon it, and there was a bell tolling down in the village. I was out in the garden when Tony came up to me.

"I bring you these," he said in a low voice. He brought out two pale pink wild roses from somewhere within the folds of his blanket.

"How *sweet* they smell!" I sniffed with amazement at the strong fragrance. I was learning step by step through this new year all the deep flavors and scents that came out of the earth here in this place.

"They the first ones," Tony said in a low voice. He had walked those miles to bring them.

"Oh, I wish you were not going away tomorrow!" I exclaimed.

John and McKenzie drove up in the Ford and I suddenly felt nervous and walked out to meet them, dropping the roses heedlessly as I went.

"We've been over to the Hot Spring," John explained, bundling out. "Can't you stay for supper, Tony?"

"No. I got to go," he answered. He had the frail little flowers in his hand as he turned up the glowing road towards the Pueblo and he did not give me his face.

The next morning several members of his family drove down with him to see him off on the stage with Julia. Candelaria sat beside him; the shawl over her small, neat head was her best black one. In the back, nephews and nieces were crowded together.

At eight o'clock there was quite an unusual hustle and bustle in our quiet street. The stage drove up with Oscar at the wheel. It was an open touring car and Julia and Tony were its sole passengers. Our household were all out to see them off, and Mr. Manby stood at one side with a sardonic expression on his lowered face. Doc Martin came out of his office and joined us all, too. Across the street, I noticed Mr. Phillips was watching from behind his window curtains.

The bags were packed behind. Julia always had a great number of things when she traveled, especially to come to Taos. Upon her last arrival, she had brought a roasted leg of lamb in a black silk bag, cooked by her maid Martha, for upon her previous visit we still had Anita, who never gave us anything but beefsteak!

There were innumerable combinations of farewell. Tony pressed his wife's cheeks with his own, right and left, clasping her somewhat slackly; and he did the same with each of his relatives in turn while we all shook Julia by the hand and kissed her. She was dressed in a brown, tailor-made suit with a kind of a brown poke-bonnet for a hat. She had several scarfs wound around her neck, and two or three bags on her wrist. Now that she was really going off alone with Tony, she looked rather nervous.

He had new ribbon tapes winding his long braids, a pair of new beaded moccasins, and a bright, striped blanket of purple and blue. He looked very grave and handsome and distant. He did not meet my eyes as he shook my hand in a loose grasp, toneless and unresponsive. I felt I could hardly stand having him go off like that, without re-establishing the life between us. It was as if he had turned off the current.

They were in—the car was driving away.

"Good-by, good-by, good-by—"

"Be good, Tony!" shouted Doc Martin—and they were gone.

"He's going to see the President," I remarked brightly to Doctor, above the sad thud of my heart that ached already.

"Not a chance," he answered as he turned back into his house.

From the moment the car drove away, the light faded

right out of everything. Until he left, was gone where I could not reach him, I hadn't known how completely I lived through him now, and through him alone. When your whole life is planted in another, and he leaves, you go with him. There wasn't any of me left behind in Taos in my empty body.

This absence was the most complete one I had ever known. It was not just defrauded nerves—as I had suffered when Maurice had left me in Croton, or Reed, before that, when he stayed behind in Paris—this was like dying altogether. As soon as he was gone, I longed to find him, to speak to him, to return to happy being. But how could I? He could not read, if I wrote, and I didn't want Julia to read my letters to him. There was no known way to communicate, except in the silent calling of one heart to another. All that day I wandered, lost in empty space.

"He who loves with passion, lives on the edge of the desert!" I thought I was going crazy, because I found out how little the real life around me meant. I sat in the garden and scarcely knew when the others spoke; yet I do not think they noticed anything strange in me.

Only when I was in my bed in the dark, I found my way to him. There is One within who will guide the soul into another dimension, into a place where one may find what one will, or whoever one wishes to reach. Utter need seeks the impossible guide, supplicates or commands, first in anguish, but soon in calm certainty.

"Give me Tony! Give me Tony!" I cried silently, and presently, reaching inward, where inside turns outward like a bubbling spring, we met somewhere else in complete recognition and fulfillment. We were together. Ever since then, we have found each other in that other elsewhere. This was peace for the night, but it did not last through the next day. The days were empty, empty, though we came together for those few instants of reality every night while he was gone.

The days are blank, when I look back: nothing at all written on them . . . yes . . . the wild roses grew plentiful in the lanes and hedgerows, and every day I gathered them and put them in water in jelly-glasses. They always reminded me of my stupid thoughtlessness towards the first ones Tony had brought me, and I wanted to make amends. How an odor can make the heart ache!

One day I got a letter from him. It was a scrawl of unaccustomed, barely formed hieroglyphics, put together in broken fragments; meaningless phrases that he had tried to recover from the meager schooling he had received, and never used before.

There was not a word in it of actual meaning from himself to me, yet there was carried in those imprints some of his essential self, as though the flow of his loving heart had struck through the pencil that faltered across the cold page and been registered there. This was so evident, he spoke in so direct a way to me behind the masking symbols of words written in lead, that I recognized for the first time in my life there is a mystery in the transmission of feeling across wide space; the fact that individual essence may be poured out of one and carried on a sheet of paper faithfully to its goal, may run through the living fingers, a stream of vital energy, possibly ponderable, anyway effectual, speaking to one of what it will, and that one receives messages with some receptive organ besides the elementary ones of eye and ear. Every written word is embued with a portion of the writer's total being; the properties of the blood, bones and nerves have flowed into the electrical stream that charges the page. Every signature con-

tains the whole creature in miniature, and is a complete picture of him at that instant of his outpouring life.

We are all so differently conditioned that we do not see the
same aspect of any human creature that our neighbor sees.
When Julia arrived in Chicago with Tony, her brother was
horrified, seeing only his bright, striped blanket and his brown
skin!

And Julia, as I gathered from her account afterwards, had
a sudden awakening, and made one of those painful transi-
tions from one point of view to another, that uncertain people
sometimes experience who, goat-like, leap from crag to crag,
where one moment a thing looks one way and the next instant quite otherwise. For a little while, in Taos, she had seen
Tony as himself, a creature in space, endowed with certain
attributes and qualities, having a dignity and an authority that
were incontestable, seeming a sure thing with an unbroken
integrity, and giving out a gentle radiance and a sense of protection and security. There had been a moment on the train
when she had wavered about him, for once when Tony came
back from the wash-room, he had looked a little cold and
more reserved, and he had said something in his limited
English about a cross man in there. But she had shut out this
momentary surging suspicion, this possibility of antagonism.
She had rejected it, holding fast to his point of view, remaining safely within his vision of life, which seemed so valid and
so true. Through his eyes, the earth looked fair, and living
was a rich and easeful thing; there was no friction or mean-
ness possible in his outlook—so there she chose to remain.

But she seemed to awaken from a dream in Chicago. Or
was it that she had been for a brief time really awake to the
truth of things, and then been clubbed back to unconsciousness by the impact of her brother's dynamic negation? Any-

way, all of a sudden, she saw things from his angle, and Tony changed in the twinkling of an eye into an Indian in a garish blanket at whom the curious crowd was staring. So, quickly, she allied herself with her own blood, deserted in spirit the embarrassing object and walked rapidly along beside her brother, leaving Tony to follow as best he could.

By the time Julia had deserted Tony, her companion had managed to accept him. There he was; something had to be done about it. They were in a taxi, now, and he stopped it in front of a large store and gave his sister a roll of bills.

"I think it would be better if you get him a suit of clothes and a hat," he said, kindly.

So Julia, wishing she'd never gotten into this, led Tony to the men's department and let him select what he wanted.

"It was terrible, Mabel!" she told me. "He picked out a kind of light green suit, and a blue shirt—and the hat! Well! The clerk took him off to put them on, and when he came back, I wouldn't have known him."

So she had no more pleasure out of him. But he enjoyed the new clothes until the thick, smoky air of Chicago got the better of him and made him feel weak and sick. Added to that, he had a constant longing to return to Taos, and a feeling he had never known before, about a woman. He told me:

"I never miss anyone in my life. I like a woman when I see him, but I don't think about it, 'cept as I would about a nice saddle. But when I leave you there, seems like my heart cryin' all the time." And he said, "At night and mornin' I pray, then I find you again, so I know I got to go back soon."

Julia didn't stay but a day or two in Chicago, then they went to New York, stopping off for a day in Buffalo. She thought the Carys would like Tony, because they were sup-

posed to have Indian blood; they looked like Indians, and their
mother had been taken into the Iroquois tribe in Batavia. But
when she arrived at the ivy-covered house down on Delaware
Avenue, she with bobbed hair, and Tony in a green suit with
long, black braids, the Carys had nearly died laughing at the
strange pair. So she got no comfort there.

When she was home again, with her maid Martha, who had
been with her so long, it was no better. Martha grew more
and more English the longer she stayed away from England,
and when Julia arrived with an Indian, she became a replica
of Queen Victoria with red hair, though she pursed up her
lips and did her duty.

So Julia didn't know what to do with him. It was summer
in New York and already the pavements were smoking hot.
She lived down near Washington Square where there was less
air than uptown, so she thought a ride on top of a bus might
make him feel better, for he seemed very sad. So they sat up
in front and plowed their way through the traffic and all the
carbon monoxide gas from the exhaust pipes of the cars below
them rose in blue clouds to their nostrils.

Tony looked more and more stoical and heroic and sad as
they slowly made the long journey—fifty, sixty, seventy blocks
of suffocation and burning lungs! When they reached the
Metropolitan Museum, Julia thought she ought to take him
in there and show it to him, so they got off the bus and
climbed up the long stairs and entered the hall that is filled
with huge statuary.

That was Tony's limit. Statuary might be the saving of
Maurice, but it was deadly for Tony. He looked about him
at the great, motionless figures, and Julia said he turned a
pale gray color and he began to sway. He said:

"All dead. No life anywhere," and she thought he was

going to faint; so she quickly led him to a marble bench where they sat for a little while, and then drove home in a taxi.

Of course she gave up the idea of taking him or even of sending him to Washington. She saw he couldn't exist away from home, that he grew more tragic-looking every hour; so she decided to send him home right away.

Before he left, someone (was it Agnes, back in New York too by this time?) took him to Jimmy Fraser's studio, and Jimmy photographed him in his blanket, looking very down in the mouth and ill, really. Julia sent me a copy of that picture. I have never seen him as they saw him there at that time.

When he came home, he got out of the stage in the plaza and walked up to our house. I was there when he came in.

"I back," he said, and held out his hand and made a little bow. He had on the green trousers and a white shirt and his blanket hung over one shoulder like a toga.

With him, life flooded back into the room, into every corner of it, into the chairs and tables, into the bowl of wild roses, and into me, too. I didn't say anything, but I looked at him and he returned the look and gave a nod and sat down.

"Home," he said, "be better. What for I leave here?"

"To see the President," I answered, laughing.

"Good air!" he went on, taking a deep breath. "I don't see how them people *stand* it like that! *Why?* What *for?*"

I felt so light-hearted in the flowing stream he opened in me, I could only laugh and be young and gay.

"Oh, they don't know any better!"

"But you know better, now?"

"I'm afraid I can never leave here, now," I said—but jokingly, of course.

1 6

"That good. That right. Here is more power, here is more powerful. You know that nice piece of land I show you? You fix the little house on it . . . you goin' to be happy there."

Then he looked at the flowers on the table and said:

"You threw away the roses I bring you."

Chapter Twenty-three

WHEN I saw Tony was hurt, something happened. I felt for the first time in my life another person's pain and perhaps this was the instant of birth, certainly the awakening of a heart asleep since childhood.

Before that day I had only *seen* things going on in other people and been able to feel only my own sorrow or discontent. Was it heredity or was it environment that had conditioned me so that I had gone all through the years like one cut off from life and other human beings? I had been something like an octopus with many arms, a psychic belly, and a highly developed pair of eyes, for I could see everything with my mind, though I felt nothing of what I saw. I could reach out and grab practically anything I thought I wanted, stuff it into what Edwin used to call, ruefully, my "insatiable maw," and assimilate it, if assimilation is a blotting out of extrinsic values by "understanding" them.

I had been grabbing things for years, to try and satisfy an unnameable hunger. I had been trying to understand others for years so that I could find out what was the matter with myself, and I had always thought that understanding came from seeing. I comforted myself by believing that my capacity to be unhappy, and to feel my own misery acutely, was a sign of superiority. I had been proud of an adolescent *grande passion* lived through and, as I believed, survived in Buffalo years ago and I often quoted to myself: *"Rien ne nous rends si grand qu'une grande douleur,"* and though I had been rather dissatisfied at times with a sense of sterility in my sorrows, I had blamed the poverty of human nature for that.

Now, over this little matter of a couple of wild roses there occurred in the tight, hard heart a stirring that I can only liken to the first surprising involuntary orgasm that Karl caused to break in me on the hardwood floor of my mother's house, how many years ago. Since that, actually nothing real had happened to me or in me. I had been merely repeating that experience or repressing it, and I was as immature as I had been at eighteen.

No wonder some middle-aged women have that childish look! No one has taught them how to live. Their inheritance has been meager, their surroundings unnourishing.

Once I had bought some incubator chickens. They had been hatched by machinery from Rhode Island eggs of the finest stock it was possible to secure. They were brought to me when they were about a month old and they were magnificent. Great, tall developed chicks that would have looked three months old had they their full regalia of feathers on.

They came in crates and we set them down one by one in a pleasant, shady, wired yard with their house at hand with its new roosts ready and waiting for them.

And then what? Then nothing! They just stood there rolling their wild eyes. The afternoon waned and night fell but did they go in to roost? No. They didn't know enough to do that. They didn't know enough to go in out of the rain which began to fall after sundown. Someone had to go and pick up every last one and set it on the roost by hand, and when it fell foolishly off, had to set it up again.

The next day they had to be taken off their perches and put down on the ground outside. I thought: "Surely now they will begin to scratch around like all chickens do!" But not at all!

They had to be taught to scratch! How? no matter. They had to be taught every single thing that chickens are supposed to do by instinct because they had never had a mother to show them how to behave. I found out then that a mother is everything in a young chick's life. It doesn't matter what fine breed they are, how well grown, how handsome, or how edible. Without a mother they are as nothing, or at least without some instruction. If someone had not been there to teach them I dare not think what would have become of them. And once was not enough either. They had to be shown until they formed the habit of scratching, roosting, and finally of laying! They learned to peck but unless there was something right there to peck at on the ground, what did they do? They started to peck at each other in an automatic sort of way, and they pecked until the insides fell out of those being pecked at, who didn't even know enough to move on. We had to have a boy with a long stick to poke them to keep them from devouring each other. Carnivorous? Instinct? Heredity? I found out those words don't mean a thing! Teaching, training, education are the most significant words in our poor language. Example— emulation—persuasion are important ones too.

What a different story is the one about Mister! Mister was a large Tom-cat that belonged to Emma. He had had a splendid early training from the day he was born, first at the hands of his mother, a gentle tortoise-shell named Miss, and later from Emma's mother, who introduced him to his "box," when he was still a kitten. The "box" was always ready for him in the kitchen and as he grew older he preferred it to the wide open spaces of the garden and so he used to come inside whenever he needed to relieve himself.

As he outlived Miss, Emma's mother asked a neighbor for a kitten to keep him company and a small black one joined

him in that house. The very first day, after examining it carefully for some time, Mister began to walk toward the "box"
and back to the kitten who crouched under the stove, trying
to get its bearings. He kept this up for two or three trips and
then he reached under the stove and gave it a smart tap on the
side of its head to bring it to its senses. Having really secured
the young one's attention now, Mister walked to the "box,"
entered it, looked sternly over at the amazed kitten who was
observing him with the most satisfactory interest; then he
crouched down in the customary attitude for an instant but
without really doing anything except to show How. He followed this regulation by the usual kicking but greatly exag-
gerated it so the loose dirt in the "box" flew all over the
kitchen, a really unmistakable lesson.

Mister was satisfied after he had fulfilled this obligation to
teach the young. He got out of the box and seemed to forget
all about the whole thing as he sprang up onto the windowsill, and looked out and washed his paws between whiles.

The kitten moved cautiously over to the "box" on tiptoe,
got in and tried it. It worked. After that Emma's mother knew
she need have no fear of the mistakes most kittens make. Instinct? Environment? No! Instruction is more important than
either and can overcome both. It is a biological necessity to
pass on what has been taught to one. This is the basis of culture—any culture.

After the first cold years of childhood there came into my
life a number of people who taught me about several of the
human faculties, that is to say, they awakened some potentiali-
ties in me, and there were a few people who tried to help and
who did help me, but Tony was the first one I ever knew who
broke open in me the capacity to actually share the feeling of
another person.

When he spoke of that careless, insensitive action of mine—that abandonment of his gift—the roses dropped in the dusty road and I trampling them to reach John, and when I looked into his face and saw how he felt about it, then for the first time I more than saw. I more than knew what went on in another person; I felt in myself what he was feeling and at the same time I had an unfamiliar disinterested respect for it; and strange, strange to me, this small pain of his was more poignant to my unaccustomed heart than anything I had ever suffered, or thought I suffered, in my own solitary experiences. The pang of it and the dissolving, the flooding into the blood of the realization of how another feels, has felt before, and will feel again, was both terrible and desirable to me: terrible to know that until that instant I had been so insulated from others; desirable, oh, desirable, to come alive to them at last.

How new, how fresh, how vivid, life might be, no matter if it did hurt like this, if one were always aware of it all instead of isolated portions of it in oneself. As I stood there facing Tony when he spoke to me, perhaps it was only an instant in time, yet I was by grace born in that flash as I should have been years, years ago; inducted into the new world. For there is a new world here, though few seem to have the luck to penetrate it. I must assert that what I am telling of myself is not a single strange case of one egotist isolated in the crowd. It is the story of many, it is the familiar, the usual, the accepted. Who reads this knows it to be true. The world is an alien place to nine-tenths of those who live in it or who appear to live in it but who merely go through the motions. Adaptation! It is called adaptation to act *as though*. As though one were alive throughout. As though one liked what is going on around one. As though one felt the way one pretends to. As though one were good, beautiful and true when the reverse is the case and one can't help it.

As a matter of fact, hardly anyone likes "the" environment. It does not draw one out or let one live. It dominates the essential living. The environment has gotten away from man, from him who is supposed to have created it. When will he dominate it again and relieve his buried nature from its constraints? Perhaps only when he learns to be so objective he can see it and himself in it, not just man the individual but all men. Possibly the gradual cracking and breaking of forms all over the world today comes from men's inability to hold together the environment they loathe, and that crushes them in its great civilized patterns, and codes, and false values; and perhaps these mistaken, false attitudes will slowly shatter themselves against each other and go up in a great cloud of dust from dry rot.

But for the individual to be transported to the new world in the twinkling of an eye—who can say how that is brought about except to call it luck even while believing in an underlying plan?

Was it not strange that I, who was nobody in myself, and in whom instinct had never been awakened, should have been brought so far to one who was all good instinct and who, besides that, possessed a magical power of Being? This was the true *participation mystique* I had read about and understood in a way, yet never realized before. Now I found it was one of education's most powerful and mysterious instruments.

"Oh, Tony," I cried, throwing my hands out to him, "excuse me."

He bowed his head gravely. "That's all right," he answered. There was dignity and generosity in him, and always from that moment to this the faint air of a teacher's authority, to which I have submitted with recognition and gratitude. No one has taught me as he has, no one else but Tony has modified or helped me to modify the crooked, strangled, stupid results of environment, though to be sure it will take more than a lifetime to eradicate them completely, just as perhaps it will take ages to change such environments as produced me and the others whose story I tell here as well as my own. It is true that two other influences came into my life afterwards, two men who must be called teachers, for they also opened up new channels for me, but if I had not been broken-down and made over first by Tony, they would have passed me by as I would have passed them by, without knowing them.

To start life all over, to start living at last, to give up all the old ways, the old adapted way of enduring this existence without being truly a part of it that I had achieved for myself for so long, and to endure the consequences of being feebly awake at last—I wonder I had the courage for it, when I look back and see what I came through. But of course it was because only a step at a time was ever shown ahead that I could take each one of them.

In the same hour of which I am telling, the hour of Tony's return, there quickly followed two other realizations that were also momentous and radical, and were obviously the consequence of the birth of feeling. One was that I was his forever and he was mine, and the other was that I could leave the world I had been so false in, where I had always been trying to play a part and always feeling unrelated, a world that was on a decline so rapid one could see people one knew dropping to pieces day by day, a dying world with no one appearing who would save it, a decadent unhappy world, where the bright, hot, rainbow flashes of corruption were the only light high spots. Oh, I thought, to leave it, to leave it all, the whole world of it and not to be alone. To be with someone real at last, alive at last, unendingly true and untarnished.

These quick thoughts went through me as feelings, so they were changes in the blood, and I turned to see if he were going through it, too.

"I comin' with you," he said, nodding his head, gravely. We were in that dark house but all around us there were flying clear light waves of good feeling so that it seemed as fresh as a dawn in the room. A moment, no, a flicker of pain:

"Can you leave your people and can I really leave mine?" I asked.

"Perhaps we help more when we go back, leavin' for a little while," he said.

I had not meant that. I had not felt any moral or ethical responsibility towards *my* people. I had meant was it possible for me to get away from them, throw them off, lose them, lose their influence, get out from under, and wash away from myself the taint of them, the odor of their sickness and their death? Could I, who was of these, ever be other than they? I hated them in myself and myself in them, and I longed to blot them out in this other. But, as a matter of fact, his answer answered my question, as I found out later.

Those who have followed this story up to this time must come upon a change of values now, and in consequence a change of attitude because I cannot continue to write about Tony and the Indians as I have written of others. In the other volumes of these memories I have written more like an anthropologist than like a human being. I wrote observantly and coldly like one recording his findings, having returned from an unknown island, telling about an undocumented race of beings. In that manner, revisiting them in memory, I have told of the habits and customs of myself and my own people. With the passionate curiosity of the hunting anthropologist and with his single-minded willingness to throw away honor, loyalty, and integrity, if only he can get to know and tell about them, I have studied and sacrificed my people and myself in order to tell about us. And as the true anthropologist is driven by pure scientific fervor of knowing and understanding and adding something to the knowledge of the human family by his sacrifices, so have I been.

But I am not an anthropologist where Tony and his people are concerned! Where my scientific brother takes it up I leave off! That I could "write a book about Indians" is the least that might be said: that I may not write one is the most.

Yet for my purpose in this work, it is not necessary to be unreticent about ourselves. If I can get any part of the truth out to others it will not depend upon the intimate details of Tony's life and mine together. But if only I can translate into words something of all I have learned from him! For I have a deep conviction that we were brought together for this purpose, and that my reason for living is to show how life may be, must be, lived.

Chapter Twenty-four

THE INDIAN fields were divided by bands of thorny white plum blossom. Wheat and corn, emerald green, pricked up through the rich dark earth and the valley was full of perfume from the blossoms. The flowering wild plum has a smell so bitter-sweet it causes the heart fairly to fall open in an aching bliss.

When I walked in the deep lanes between the Indian pastureland and the desert, I met Indians singing, sometimes on their ponies, sometimes walking, or working in the fields and I always looked for Tony but I did not often find him, for I did not know yet which fields were his.

The Indians were working now all over the wide country that was theirs and sometimes they bound their heads with thick wreaths of cottonwood leaves to keep off the hot sun, or wound the white sheet round and round in coils like a huge turban, so their dark faces became Asiatic. But I never believed they were Mongolian as the scientists insisted they were. It seemed to me more likely the Far Eastern peoples and themselves had descended from a common stock; that from one of the great continents sinking in the oceans, parts of those earlier races had migrated east and others west. Why should not the Indians have dwelt on this continent as long as the Orientals upon theirs? I can never think otherwise.

I could close my eyes and see them on this side of the earth, stretching all the way across North America, and down over Mexico, Central and South America. Hunting tribes living in the open, agricultural peoples living in villages of earth shaped like pyramids, worshiping the sun and growing things; then the stone-cutting people, artists worshiping imagery, building great temples, and more pyramids, and carving serpentine creations, all the way to the heated zones; and these miles of continent were permeated with the Indian psyche as the Far East is saturated with the Indian psyche, that there too has its mountain tribes, its high magnetic centers, its stone-carven temples, engraved with symbols of creation. Only scattered and isolated groups of Indian influence are left up north here in these states which we Nordics have swarmed over and fought to own and call united, but below us millions upon millions of undamaged Indian souls wait the moment of awakening; they wait until the European element has worn off. Their five hundred years of quiescence has been like a twilight sleep in which their forces accumulate in the great racial reservoir. They are sleeping while their brothers here in these mountains keep the true fire burning and alive till the morning of emergence.

Now our paths were outlined with bands of purple iris and Mr. Manby worked in the garden every day planting flower-seed, pruning the lilac bushes into neat shapes, and digging, digging, digging. He was a great one for that. He believed as much in digging and loosening the earth as he did in irrigation, but he irrigated too, from the old Indian irrigation ditch, and once a week the water ran along the little channels so systematized and mathematical that every plant received its share and the trees were watered, and the apples, plums, and apricots soaked in what they needed.

It was one day after lunch when the round, low apple tree outside my black-barred window was still all white with blossoms and full of bees, and a heavenly scent was filling the house that I said to Maurice: "Well, I'm going to buy a piece of land over next to Jack Young-Hunter's and fix up a place to work."

What did I know about work? I didn't think this, I just said it because I was moved to do so, without calculation or realization or any conscious process.

Maurice looked rather airy and nervous at the same time. We were sitting under the apple tree.

He said, "But—here it is nearly June, darling! I want to do a head of that Indian girl, and go back to New York in August."

"Well, you go," I said, and I was as surprised as he was to find it all settled.

"You really wouldn't let me go without you?" he asked, looking incredulous.

"Yes, I would," I answered, gently, and that was all there was to it. No explanations or discussion. I just got up and went in the house and found my hat, and then I started to walk to the Pueblo to find Tony, to tell him. I almost ran, I was so happy and excited and glad to be able to tell him, but when I got there he wasn't home. I rested a little in Candelaria's house and ate a pueblo cake. They are made like our pale flour and vanilla cookies, only they are thicker. They have gritty sugar on them, too, like ours, and they have a pale, delicate, thick taste.

I liked to look at Candelaria, she was so buxom and yet so fine. Her little head was proud and her face very subtle and full of knowing. Her father had been one of the most wizard-ish of the old men, Mr. Manby told me. He had made a sanguine drawing of that eminent head, enlarging it from a snapshot, and how cunning he looked and what power in the brow. "There's no mind that can equal his anywhere around here," said Mr. Manby, "unless it be mine," he added.

On the way back to town, at the corner of the Mexican graveyard, I met Tony driving home in his wagon, and I stopped him.

"I was looking for you," I said. "I'm going to buy that piece of land and fix up the house."

He nodded. A light came into his face, and brightened his eyes.

"Get up," he said, moving to one side of the high seat.

I climbed up beside him and he turned the horses round and I balanced there, bracing my feet against the dashboard while he drove back towards the village of Taos.

"I take you home and then I go make the deal," he said. "Better I go alone 'cause if you come you going to mix it up," he told me.

Of course I wanted to go with him, but from the first I never disputed his decisions. It was as though I couldn't impose my will against his, he always seeming stronger than I, and his judgment better than mine. It was certainly a rare thing for me to recognize the authority in a man, and a great satisfaction. I'd always wanted to have that submissive feeling but I never really could; though I had occasionally pretended I knew less than the other with whom I had a relationship I always actually felt I was wiser and stronger than he. Perhaps, as Mrs. Hopkins used to say, I had been "unlucky in men," or perhaps something in me had engaged me only with those men with whom I could successfully contend.

On that high spring seat beside Tony I felt full of my own life which was different from his, and it was as though I could let go and just be, and feel ample and protected and free to be myself, because he would cope and act and determine things. This gave me a most comfortable freedom of feeling, unworried by thinking, scheming, planning, trying, or being efficient and practical.

So it was as though my life was unimpeded and could rise richly in me and flow roundly about us both, while I just sat there and let it, and he, holding the reins, would drive us along taking all the responsibility. Nothing could happen to us so long as he was in charge, I felt, and this was a wonderful and luxurious feeling. I glanced sideways at him, and I saw how he was at home in the universe and with me, balanced and strong, and able to do anything. Step by step we had come to each other until the moment I climbed up into his wagon-seat and drove along beside him, and then we reached an equilibrium together that sustained itself, and that we did not have to bother about.

We drove down along the broad avenue under the cotton-woods Mr. Manby and he had planted years ago and the sun was at five o'clock on a late May afternoon. Everything looked right, not only beautiful as I had often known it, but composed and essential, and we fitted in; we were not on the outside looking at it, nor shoved into a corner where we didn't belong. Nor were we hanging on to a whirling planet in fear of falling. For almost the first time I had an experience of location, and of being where I belonged. Tony seemed to give me the earth; that is to say, he gave me what I had always missed, a relatedness with my surroundings and I could breathe in peace with no need to struggle. For this, then, I would have to exchange everything in the world that I had known, and that had been far too little to keep alive on.

For a long time I had been pretending a kind of deference to Maurice. Pretending to myself as well as to him that he had authority, because I wished to respect him, to believe him "stronger" than myself. For as long as I lived with him I had to try and look up to him, but it was an effort that constantly failed. Inwardly I was almost always critical and disparaging of his complex, indecisive character, and what seemed to me to be his lack of nobility. I don't know why I expected him to be noble when I was scarcely that myself. Perhaps just because I was not! Possibly the qualities I lacked seemed adorable and desirable to me and I sought them in others instead of bringing them into being in myself, for all criticism of others is unconscious self-criticism. It had been very degrading, really, to hold to Maurice and use him as I had all this time when I thought as little of him as I did. Making a sculptor of him had been my subterfuge, I discovered, the high motive to justify me for keeping hold of him. No wonder he had felt restive at times and longed to get away!

But I had put so much effort into my justification that here he was, a sculptor, and, by some curious metamorphosis, a husband. Now, at the time I came to a realization of this, he didn't want to leave me. Forgotten his restlessness and his doubt. As he wrote me afterwards, he had never realized how much he had unconsciously loved me.

He started a head of Albidia Marcus. She was a beautiful young girl with eyes that were large and dark like those of a doe, and her head was well balanced on her little shoulders, with its coil of hair wound round with worsted so it fanned out above and below and hung separate, leaving the outline of her neck clear.

Every day she came down and posed for Maurice and he laid hot black wax onto the armature with a brush, little by little, and I used to go down the street to the studio once in a while and wonder if he would ever be finished with it.

I had imperceptibly taken over the deciding tone about his

departure and now I was saying, "You must be gone by the first of August." I hadn't any explanation to give him, for I didn't know it myself then. I only knew I wanted to be alone and away from him. He was aggrieved at first. He didn't want to go without me, he was nervous at the thought of it, and he found he was fond of me.

I wanted to be fair, and not to hustle him out in too much of a hurry, and that was why I gave him until the first of August so he could finish the head of Albidia and take it away with the head of Pete. He himself had always named August for departure, but he was a slow workman, retarded and unable to speed himself along. I was determined to be patient with him, though I wanted him gone. Now it was May, and Jack Young-Hunter had begun to remodel and add to his little adobe house, and Tony had charge of the work. Jack was adding two studios for Mary and himself, and two little bedrooms above them.

Tony had several Indians working there, Tomas, Candelaria's brother, Luis Suazo, and a very good adobe man named Antonio Martinez. Jack was so happy among them! He loved being with Indians. They worked happily, singing and joking all day long, so it was more like a game than building usually is. Jack worked with them and it all went rapidly.

So now I bought the place Tony wanted me to have and no purchase ever gave me such a feeling of satisfaction. Edwin had secured the villa and the *podere* in Florence while all I did there was to hunt for chairs and tables, velvets and brocades and all kinds of little boxes, and *objets d'art,* so I never really felt the house and the land were mine, and the other years of my life since I left my mother's house I had lived in rented houses.

Here was a big field and a lovely old orchard, an adobe

box on the upper edge of the place, and it was my own, bought with the money that had accumulated in the bank since we had been in Taos, for living was so simple we had had practically no expenses except the rent of Manby's place, and our food. When I moved to my first very own house, all I had to take to it were my Santos!

I could not help a feeling of unfairness at buying those acres and orchards and the home of a family for so little money but Tony told me old "Chimayo" was satisfied. Besides, he said, they were going to build another house outside on the lane, and they would like to work for me when I needed extra men. There were three brothers and several daughters in the family—one of the nicest families in the valley. Very soon José was helping us, and he has worked here ever since. Palmists had always looked somewhat puzzled at the life line in my left hand because it broke in half right in the middle, and now I can see from this distance of the years that the second half of my life began when Tony made me buy that piece of land. For the first time I ceased hovering over the earth where I had only landed from time to time to taste and try a flavor of neighborhood or of race, of person, place, or thing. I had lived like a dilettante; like a visitor to this planet and nothing had been more real to me than food in new places is to travelers.

But when I bought the Taos place my feeling for Tony made me take root in it and I began to live in a way that was new to me.

This does not mean that I stopped putting out feelers, or that I was through with curiosities, for one does not really change, one only develops. I will always be trying to penetrate into the mysterious varieties of human nature, though with perhaps a different motive. Self-preservation had been the greatest need, and what I had called love the tool to draw out of the human material at hand the various mysterious savors of life. In order to lose the sense of death and isolation that was my solitary mode of being, how often I had flung myself into fictitious relationships in order to escape the conviction that I was nothing in myself! I had called it love, when at its best it had been a certain chemical magnetism motivated by curiosity, the curiosity of the damned seeking the chance of salvation. This combination of magnetism and curiosity was a potent one. It had enabled me to know and understand people. It had been a kind of searchlight fastened on my head as I groped through a dark world. Whereas a person like Andrew concentrates upon an idea, or on an occupation like collecting or painting, all his attention upon it until every secret part of it is revealed to him, so I had done with people and always will, I suppose, though much blame has been put upon me for it at one time and another, and still is sometimes now. Never mind. Never mind the blame and the shame, the hurts and the regrets, the burned fingers and the angry looks. I know what I know. I know what it cost us all and I know what it has been worth. Particularly I know that it was a preliminary exercise for an eventual self-realization.

Of course acquiring a piece of this land here was a symbolic move, a picture of what was happening inside me. I had to have a place of my own to live on where I could take root and make a life in a home. This earth and Tony were identical in my imagination and his, and I wanted to become a part of them, and the day the place became mine, it was as though I had been accepted by the universe. In that day I became centered and ceased the lonesome pilgrimage forever.

Of course in the first awakening to real life there is always

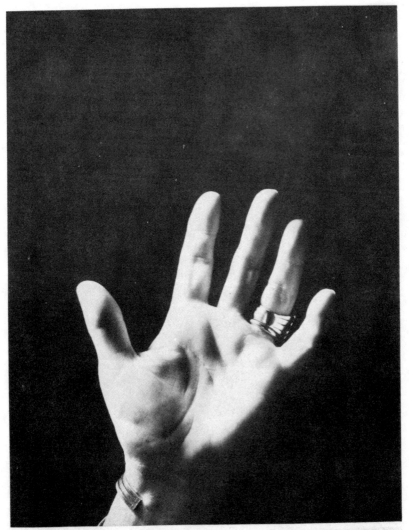

THE HAND WITH THE BROKEN LIFE LINE   *by Ernest Knee*

so great a relief in the mere opening of dark sealed channels that there is little room for any other experience. So now every day, every hour, was just a feeling of life unfolding, a sense of perpetual, river-flowing, pleasurable being.

It was a period of respite between the misery of an insane and fractious immaturity, of non-existence, and the strong, inescapable suffering of reality. God was kind and let me rest awhile before I had to take up the duties and responsibilities, and the dangerous hazards and problems of life. The previous years of amateur experience were shown soon enough to be the pretenses of nursery firesides. When I learned what it really was to love and be loved, to suffer and to cause another to suffer, I found that to be accepted by the universe, and let no one doubt this, is the test of human strength.

I did not start work immediately on my "studio," for Tony wanted to get Jack's place finished first. The days were beautiful now, strong leaves covered the big trees, and the water ran cold and strong in the *acequia madre* that bordered and circled our properties. My old orchard was solid with white blossoms, and there was another little orchard of young trees across the fields. At one end of this new orchard grew two wild olive trees like the one I remembered on the roof of Francesca's palace in Florence.

Through April and May the wind had been a torment a great deal of the time, sweeping up from the south across the desert and filling all the air with dust so one had to run into the house and stay there with all the windows closed, and afterwards find a film of adobe on everything so the whole place would have to be cleaned. But now just before June the days were quiet and the wind had shaken the cottonwood leaves out until they were fully formed and it had brought the big leaves of the hollyhocks open, and purple flowers bloomed on the alfalfa.

I don't believe Maurice ever came over to see my place. He ignored the whole thing, and I never spoke of it to him. He just went to his studio and spent the whole day laying film on film of black wax.

Chapter Twenty-five

WHEN Elizabeth Duncan's School was over, she came out to visit us.

In her long, soft, white draperies, she sat in the garden and breathed in the lovely, refreshing air. She loved Taos. Its funny, innocent ways and its crystal-clear, untouched quality of beauty revived her, for she was a little tired of the castle on the Hudson to which she had attained. It was just as well for her that she did not realize she was doomed to occupy several of these great piles of masonry along that river before she would get back to Austria and move into the same pompous outlived type of dwelling there.

Max Merz was always responsible for the Duncan School being quartered in these more or less abandoned strongholds of the rich—where high, wrought-iron gates shut them all in with old-fashioned plumbing and a defective lighting system. Elizabeth did the best she could with them. She would get out her strings of beads and colored scarves and hang them on ponderous dressing tables in the high-ceilinged, dreary chambers of those static estates and I suppose she did the same in the Schloss Klessheim, to which Merz led them back. I never saw it, but in the pictures of it, the wrought-iron gates were there, and high stone castle walls rose behind them. Elizabeth was never one to care for castles though her practical mind gauged correctly their influence upon parents; castles still signified success and rightness of judgment in spite of their increasing vacancy throughout the world, so that parents could be counted upon to like to have their children living in them while they were learning a way of life and the point of view of "the long line" acquired by the Duncans upon Hymettus.

When she came to Taos there must have been a reminder of the Grecian days that had marked her forever, in the dark mountain against the blue-black sky, and in the smiling splendor of the dewy jeweled mornings. She became blithesome and like a girl again, and ever after that first visit she would come back to Taos to breathe freely after too long an imprisonment in those so-called "country places."

In looking back now, I cannot tell what she did all the time. We were all of us engrossed in our own interests. Maurice spent the whole day in his studio and later moved up to a deserted mountain mining camp named Twining, where there was a long, empty, white frame hotel and several log cabins. There was a wonderful-looking old miner still sitting on his claim up there. His name was Jack Bidwell. Tall and slender, with wide shoulders and narrow hips, to watch him walk down a trail was to know what a delight may be in motion. He had a ruddy complexion, burning blue eyes, and thick snow-white hair and a heavy white mustache.

Twining had once been a feverishly active spot. Nine miles up the winding and twining rough road, across nine rickety bridges, over the ice-cold mountain stream, into the high altitude of aspens and pine trees, men struck gold, and built a kind of village consisting of the one-story hotel, cabins hewn from logs, machine shops and saloons.

There was still, when we saw it, the massive decaying machinery of the principal mine, and there were several thousands of cords of pine wood stacked, unused or rotting, to operate it with—but of the fever and the gold there were no traces at all. Large pack rats with angora tails, chipmunks

and squirrels ran in and out of the empty cabins. And Jack
was the king of it all. He never failed to go up and dig in
his hole in the ground. Every morning up the mountain, every
evening home at sundown.

Sometimes he would be alone for six months at a time,
shut in with the long winter, and then he would talk to himself out loud so as not to forget speech. His life story was
simple, brief, and clear-cut. Gold hunting in the mountains
under the uncomplicated code of rights and claims, long
years influenced by luck and perseverance and the discipline of
his own laws of living had made a man of him, for no matter what the activity, a pattern of life chosen and adhered to
enforces a discipline that will form a man as no industrial or
governmental machine can ever do. It will develop judgment
and initiative, develop self-possession, and among pine trees
high in the hills, it will give a kind of stern, authoritative,
almost god-like trust in his own rightness. Nothing on earth
could have made Jack Bidwell doubt himself.

When his one-time partner drove up in a buggy one still
morning and Jack, from the shadow inside his cabin, saw
him lean over and take up his gun, Jack did not hesitate an
instant; he picked up his own gun and when the man stepped
inside the door, Jack shot first. Because the man stood there
swaying slightly, he thought he had missed, so he raised his
gun once more, but the other said, "Don't shoot again, Jack.
You've killed me," and then fell.

Jack took the buggy and drove down to the court-house
and told the sheriff what he had done. Two days later he
was acquitted and carried out around the plaza on the shoulders of a cheering crowd, with the dead man's widow among
them enthusiastically waving a handkerchief.

Jack didn't linger in the village. He went back to his claim and his cabin and started out next day with his pick.

He told us about this incident one evening when several of us were up there. Tears came into his eyes at the end, when he said, "It was a kind of hard thing to have to do." There wasn't a shadow of remorse or self-doubt in him, however; he had simply acted as a man is sometimes forced to act in this life.

Sometimes people would go up and camp in the old cabins and that was what Maurice did. He took Albidia and her brother with him and they had a fine time. The Indian boy hunted while Albidia was posing and Maurice was brushing on the wax, thin black layer upon layer. When noon and darkness came she cooked their meals and in the evening Maurice would go over and sit on Jack's porch, and they would smoke together while the boy beat softly on his drum where he sat at the foot of a big tree with his sister, and they all watched the large moon cross between the ranges and swim over the sky from Wheeler's Peak, twelve miles over to the east.

John was living his own life, too. He had several boys and girls whom he spent his time with, Ralph and Margaret Phillips across the street, Everett and Lowell Cheetham, Dot and Charley Berninghaus and the Hawks up at Del Monte Ranch.

This ranch was a large cleared acreage up on the north side of the valley on the side of a mountain called Lobo. It was a lovely place to go and all the young people used to like to be invited up there by Betty and her sister Bobby and Bill the brother. They were beautiful, clear-skinned children and Bill looked exactly like someone out of one of Thomas Hardy's stories, he had such a beaming light in his deep blue eyes, such a ruddy complexion, and a natural radiation of goodness and kindness.

The Hawks lived in a large, unalluring square house with the lower half of adobe and the upper part of wood. The rooms inside were without any trace of charm or proportion. They were just large, ungainly, rather echoing rooms, but the house did not matter. From the porch one looked down miles over miles of the tawny valley, and over to the jagged black crack through it that was the Rio Grande Canyon, and beyond it to the mountains far away.

The house stood on a level, empty space, and below it and to the sides grew apple trees, and there were many acres planted in alfalfa and hay, so there was always a great deal of work to be done there in the spring, summer, and fall, and the boys from Taos would sometimes go up and help, but not one of them knew how to work like Bill Hawk.

Behind the house, Lobo Mountain shielded them from the north, and the canyon had a fine trail to go up to reach the ridge and the twin peaks that, from down below in the valley where we lived, looked like two sharp pyramids high up in the sky.

From up on the tiptop of this range one could go over to Twining or on to Wheeler's Peak, or to Gold Hill, or down the other side slopes into Red River Valley.

It was beautiful country up there at the foot of the big mountains, sweet with the smell of pine all the year round. The sunsets that spread over the sky from that vantage point, slightly raised above the whole world of the valley and looking over to the east, south, and west, were almost terrifying in their great spread and sweep of color. The sky has so much significance in a wide landscape like this. It is on a scale where the mountains can tower right up ten thousand feet and still the heavens go surging illimitably up beyond. And in these blue regions, rise and tower and sweep across each other such immense and almost solid-seeming white clouds that they diminish the great dark mountains and make them huddled and companionable like a home place, and the big, ungainly house turns into a cracker box under the gigantic sky, and one is reduced oneself to the scale of an ant or any other minutest living thing.

The tallest tower in New York would be lost in these generous heights and depths of ether and space where the children played and made hay and went on picnics.

There was one such picnic I remember when they went, stayed ten days at Twining with Margaret and Albert Gusdorf looking after them, and did they have fun! They ran the hotel, they ran the Post Office, had a Post-Mistress, wrote each other letters, made stamps and called for the mail every night, and Mr. Gusdorf made up packages of peanuts and candy and mailed them to each of the kids as long as the provisions lasted. And the number of hot cakes Jack made in ten days!

And, of course, the initials they cut in the tempting soft, white trunks of the aspens! These hearts entwined have climbed irrevocably up the trees until now they are far overhead!

Besides these, John also had his adopted Indian brother Eliseo. They were of the same age and they had had from the first day one of those strange everlasting friendships. They opened veins and exchanged their blood to make them truly brothers but this was not necessary. They were friends and brothers first by affinity and they always will be.

By the time Elizabeth came, the work on my new place had begun. At the end where there was only a plain adobe house of three little rooms, Tony wanted to add a large room.

That was all at first. Just one large room. At the east end it would reach to the edge of the desert Indian land. We could not cross or touch the Reservation boundary line, in fact, the Trujillos, from whom I had bought the property, had gone nearly to the border but had not quite reached the iron peg in the ground that showed the Indian line, but we meant to go all the way, a few feet more; in the front we could go almost to the ditch but we would leave enough space for a wagon and horses to drive around. This would make a wing and we decided to build a long porch to join it and shelter the other rooms, and we began to build it with old seasoned wood that was of a pale dry powdery gray color. Tony found old long-cut trees for the columns, and Luis cut the corbels to support the roof beams out of the pieces we had left. The curves and points of these corbels looked raw on the inside when they were hacked out, so I invented a mess of wood ashes mixed with kerosene oil to rub on them and it made a perfect match, and blended with the dry weathered outside surface.

I walked across the fields every morning, through the curving avenue of locust trees, lindens, and cottonwoods that Manby had planted and that led over to his great land project upon which I was building now without his knowledge. It was strange that he did not know but it has often been so in Taos Valley that people go their own separate ways and know little of what way their nearest neighbors go. It seemed to me there was never a place with less *esprit de corps,* or group spirit, outside the Pueblo, while out there it was only a tribal or group life. These two extremes so close together but not touching were, perhaps, destined to exchange their modes some day, the Indians to individuate, the valley folk to unite in some new group form, but neither suspected this nor even analyzed their differences.

It did occur to me that, where individualism had arrived at the peculiar development that it had here—where *everyone* was entirely different from everyone else, in taste, activity, and interest, so that everyone seemed queer to all the others and everyone was deeply lonely and negative in loneliness, it was almost the moment for falling into a pattern together. They could scarcely go farther than they had in the development of parts, and to go forward they surely must get together or go over the edge into madness.

Manby's avenue stopped abruptly at a fence, and the fence was mine now. He had intended to buy the property some day from old Chimayo, but Tony had picked it out for Jack Young-Hunter and me and now it was ours.

There was a head gate at a point on the *acequia madre* where the Indian land reached the public land, and this, open, furnished water into a small ditch around the outside western edge of the place, to the old orchard, the alfalfa fields and to the new orchard.

I loved the two little wild olive trees from Manby's that grew in this small orchard. They had a fragrance that was bitter and sweet when they were covered with flowers at the end of May. The trees all did well because there has always been a good quantity of water here, with the mother ditch running in a curve between the upper level of the land where the old house was and the new addition was going, and the lower part where the fields spread out in a dip. There was a lovely slow sweep of field to be seen sloping from across here and rising to the terrace, and on it that enormous cottonwood tree stood drooping over the stream.

On early mornings and late afternoons this big tree cast a

large, black shadow on the green below, and from across the way it looked massy and compact like a Corot painting.

Sometimes Tony came to meet me, for he would get down to the work with the other Indians a couple of hours before I would go over there. We walked through the winding avenue where the trees were growing near enough almost to touch across the top. We didn't talk much. We never have talked much. But we were glad to be together.

I still wore the white dresses I had had since I first knew Elizabeth Duncan, and Tony wore white moccasins and white leggings and a white sheet wrapped around his waist. He had a fine carriage and walked with great poise and dignity. One morning an Indian came along from where he had been changing the water at the head-gate, and he laughed and nodded with a benevolent look and said something in the Indian language.

"What did he say?" I asked, curiously.

"He said, 'Like a bride,'" Tony answered in a matter-of-fact voice, and walking right along.

My heart gave a jump and missed a beat and from that time on it has been missing beats for twenty years. The morning was fresh and lovely and everything looked brand-new, sparkling and as though just made. We reached the upper level where Manuel was making adobes and laying them out in the sun in straight rows and Luis was astride one of the long, gray tree trunks, sawing it. The big man named Antonio Martinez had just driven in from the back with a wagon load of stones, and the horses stood there, hanging their heads and sweating.

"Come on. I going to show you the new room now," Tony told me, walking up to a bare place.

Antonio Martinez came along. He was to be the adobe layer.

1 8

He had built several houses in the village and Tony and he had worked together on the Harwoods' big house and Tony admired his work and had engaged him. Of course, all Indians know how to make adobes and how to lay them, but there is as much difference in the way they mix mud and straw so the bricks will become as solid as stone, and in the way they lay them with the binding of wet mud between, straight and precise and pounded down to get the air bubbles out, as there is in the execution of any work of art or science, and Tony and Antonio Martinez were both fine builders, conscientious and interested in the job.

Tony took a stick now and broke it into several pieces and whittled points onto them, and with one piece he began to draw the length and breadth of the new room in the earth. It looked pretty large to me. At the corners he hammered the pointed stakes into the ground. At the west end of the room he drew an alcove that jutted out about six feet.

"Here," he said to us in the same voice he used for telling about doors and windows, "here I want a place big enough to put a big bed in. This nice place to sleep."

Antonio nodded. He saw that it would be, for Indians can see everything in their imaginations—just a fraction of something is enough to give them the completed whole in the mind's eye. But a flash of lightning struck through me. There seemed such portent and importance in that simple instruction. I walked away and sat down under the cottonwood tree beside the stream.

Chapter Twenty-six

IT IS impossible to tell adequately what surprises came to me in this new life. For instance, there was not the high, exciting exaltation I had often enough known before, when after a dismal interval, during which I had been submerged in a twilight depression I emerged like a rocket into another stimulation.

No, this time it was as though a gentle organic growth was taking place, and actually in my heart I felt small, imperceptible movements, like tiny leaves unfurling; a wonderful evenness marked my days and nights so that waking or sleeping I felt a sweet balance that was delicate and strong.

To know this equilibrium was such a positive experience that every hour I renewed my consciousness of it, turning to it, feeling it in wonder and humility.

When I was with Tony, I was in tune with all outdoors and with myself as well, for the first time in my life. I felt real at last, not a pretended reality such as one may feel when one blots out pain against another and loses the sadness of one's own cravings. No, a true reality of my own was coming into being within me.

Not since I had been pregnant with John had I known this blessed fullness of being. Now, as then, I could sit in the window and look out on the world and know that I was part of it. I remembered once Mrs. Hopkins and I were talking of heart's ease and I had said to her:

"I don't see how you stand your life—so alone except for

all these people who come to you for help. Alone here in these two rooms in the Iroquois Hotel!"

And her face had beamed as she said tenderly: "Oh, it is wonderful to be alone and feel your oneness with everything outside you! My child, don't you ever feel that?"

I shook my head, puzzled and sad. All I knew when I was alone was a horrible emptiness and a fear of absolute immobility.

She went on: "Sometimes when I am waiting for a student I go in my room and draw the curtains, and I lie down on my bed and draw the blanket over me, and I have the most delicious moments."

I was burning with envy at her words and at her evident sincerity, for what she was capable of was not for me. The nearest I had ever come to it, and that was only a frail suspicion of a relatedness that she possessed strongly always, was the time between living through men, when at the Sharkey cottage in Croton I had known a kind of impersonal content through something that I had called Nature. But that was nothing compared to this living responsiveness to life. That had been an escape down into the depths of nature within one, a rather cold if solacing separation from life, more of a denial of it than a going through it.

But now I came up out of every depth—up to the surface at last ready to meet life and I found it so good!

Reality was acceptable, naked and sensitive, and I went right on to meet it closer. As always at first sight it was irresistibly attractive; luring one deeper into knowledge one could not and would not draw back. Had I known what that wedding is for one who finally accepts life and faces truth, and for whom there is no turning back, would I have run away while there was still a chance? No, I do not believe it. So I embraced Truth and Truth embraced me and I went along into joy and sorrow and it seemed that day by day I was ceasing to be an amateur after so many years of the pretense of living.

One morning I started out along the curving path behind our garden and it was one of the most lovely days I had ever seen, so still and mellow and fragrant, and every leaf and every flower petal seemed new and as though they had opened within the hour and were breathing quietly and deeply in the silent gold and blue day. I hummed a song as I went silently along on the soft, shady, wide path, and then I laughed when suddenly I heard it myself:

"Rejoice! Rejoice!
Ema-a-an-u-el shall ransom captive Is-r-a-a-el!"

Tony did not come to meet me so I reached the terrace alone, and then I saw him sitting on a log a short distance from where the other Indians were working. As he didn't get up when he saw me, I went over to him and then I found his face was averted from me and he did not raise his eyes. He had a discouraged expression and his face was so plastic that everything showed deeper on it than on other people's. I have never seen anyone whose flesh is a mirror of what takes place within as his is.

When he was with someone he was used to and liked, his features were unconscious and free, though he had a capacity for drawing down the shades of his eyes so they concealed his inner motions. This concealment was like a mask over his face, assumed at will, leaving it firmly impersonal and set in a bronze impassivity. As time passed I came to know that there were friends of mine who never saw Tony as I saw him and

1 8 *

perhaps some of these could not understand what I saw in him because he had never let them see what I did.

Not only Tony but all the other Indians had this faculty of controlling their expressions of thought and feeling and they gave to most people the blank, noncommittal front that has grown to be called their reserve.

I do not mean they are face-fixers, like many among us. They will never be seen through the curtains assuming suitable faces as they approach, they do not pretend one thing when they feel another, for they are not socially sly and deceitful.

They are exactly as they appear to be, either open and expressive, or closed and sealed against one another or against us. They burn continuously with a hard, gem-like flame but they know how to bank their fires.

"What's the matter?" I asked him. "What is wrong?"

"I was sittin' here this morning early, I don't know if I sleep or be awake, but I see you goin' by, goin' by, just like water." He moved his hand to show how it was, like a river flowing away, swift and smooth.

From the first I have known what Tony meant as though I could see the pictures of his thoughts, for he did not speak much English, and truth to tell, I have sometimes thought he speaks less and less English as the years pass by, possibly to protect himself against losing his Indian identity and becoming Europeanized by those who are always coming and going in our life. Yet that is not the truth because I and others have been amazed at unexpected moments to hear a flood of most accomplished English flow out of him. Is it perhaps that he does not care to talk to most people?

I saw instantly what he meant, and how did I know it was not a true picture he saw? How could either of us know? Unstable as water, unstable as water, went through my mind.

TONY

Had I not always passed on and would I not forever depart from everyone and every place?

I saw the pain in him, the doubt and the uncertainty. He was so firm and sound himself, was it not a terribly unsuitable attraction that had drawn us together? He was one who knew himself for what he was, deep, permanent, and true. I? What was I but one of the less fortunate products of civilization, one without roots, continuity, or conviction, a mass of nervous sensibilities but without feeling, one who had spent her years cut off from her source. How could I know I would ever be different? Can one be born again so late? As every word he spoke always fell hot on my heart, stirring it, melting it anew, so now.

"Oh, Tony," I cried, "that is how I have always been—like water, shallow water running away fast, but maybe I don't have to be so any more."

He got up, smiling, and bending a very kind look upon me.

"Come on," he said, "we won't worry about that. Come see what Antonio Martinez has done since you were here."

Chapter Twenty-seven

SO WITH all of us in the house occupied in our different ways, I wonder what Elizabeth did?

She was one who liked to sit in a garden, cross-legged on the grass, and do nothing, watch the big clouds roam over the deep blue sky and chew a blade of grass and I think she passed many hours out under the apple tree.

Julia, too, was there again on one of her trips back and forth across the continent and Elizabeth and she turned to each other, I think. William, who had left us in the spring, had started a little restaurant down in the town and they liked to go down there and sit and gossip with him once in a while.

I have a feeling our own food had grown very sketchy by this time, for I think I had decided to do all the housework and I knew only how to do the most elementary cooking. I could make good coffee and broil a steak, fry potatoes, and open a can. Beyond these camping requirements I am afraid my knowledge stopped. Oh, yes! I could make pancakes, if I had Aunt Jemima's pancake mixture, and fry bacon. My life now was certainly growing more and more simplified. I remember it reached the extreme of elimination of inessentials the time we drove over to Ute Park to put Julia on a train.

Tony came for us in his two-seated buggy and we left one early morning. We had to cross the mountains behind us, and we drove eastwards to the village of Cañon, that was built at the opening of the long range, and from there we followed the creek that came down into the valley and irrigated the east side of it. We climbed and climbed and as the sun went higher in the sky the horses went slower and the sweat oozed out of them.

It was a beautiful narrow canyon and the little river wriggled along in close-cropped, grassy meadows that looked like parklands, and the mountains rose on either side, one Christmas tree above another, dark and symmetrical.

"Good fishin'," Tony said, pointing with his whip, and we saw it would be heavenly to meander along in the soft, close turf and trail a line—if one liked fishing, which I didn't, any more than I liked gambling, or games.

Further along, the stream was bordered on either side by beautiful trees, large, healthy cedars black among the light green of aspens and cottonwoods, and it was so orderly and ample and tended-looking it resembled an old beloved park more and more, yet it was new and fresh and untouched and showed no faintest corruption of the enjoyment of people, such as had nearly every natural place in the world that I had previously seen. This seemed untrodden by feet, unscarred, and unhandled by men. It had not the dimmed and dusty appearance of the nature I had always known. This was really a new world, for only man makes natural things old and shabby; time does not seem to tarnish organic life, not in the passing of thousands of years.

The road was only a rutted wagon track that was still full of holes from the spring thaws, so we went very slowly, but finally we crossed over the top of the ridge and Tony told us it was called Palo Flechao. Later I saw this name written and it was spelled Flechado which seemed odd.

We began to drop down into a wide valley and here the mountains suddenly lost their primeval appearance and resembled the Massachusetts Berkshires. They were wide and round and green, and vast cultivated fields swung away on each side of the road and slowly climbed the moderate hillsides.

Tony said, "Different kind of people here called Swede. Very good farmers though."

Down along this broad Merino Valley a big wind was booming and blowing at our backs, so it tipped our hats over our faces and dust came up into our eyes. The wind started Tony singing and I heard the two women on the back seat murmur together under the song. They were saying this was nice —this was fun.

We traversed the valley at a brisk clip, the wind helping the horses, and it seemed a large, empty place, for there were only occasional small one-story houses dropped about among the fields at the feet of the rolling hills, and somehow, though it was a rich countryside, there was a lonely feeling in it, a bland, featureless look that nature can take on sometimes, and that seems inexpressive.

"What's the matter over here?" I asked Tony. "It feels so different from Taos Valley just the other side of those mountains."

" 'Cause no Indians here, I guess. Indians put life in Taos, don't you know that? Why you think the water so sweet over there, and the sun so good? People call it 'climate' but I guess they don't know any better."

We met several pale-eyed blond men whose faces were burned darker than their hair. They rode horses whose tails and manes were blown straight out behind them, and they looked like folks asleep and dreaming; and we met two or three men driving wagons slowly, who looked at us as we passed and murmured a greeting but gave no smiles.

We came to a long, low, log building on the left side of the road and Tony pointed to it with his whip and instructed us. "School house," he said. "Children come on horseback from all over the valley all winter long."

Finally we came to a shining lake and the wind was blowing it into ruffles and we could see the shadows of clouds pass rapidly over it, darkening it in some places.

"Oh, what a lovely lake!" Elizabeth cried from behind me. "It looks like a little mountain tarn up in Scotland!"

"That's no tahn!" Tony corrected her gravely. "That's a lake some men made. It's Eagle Nest Lake and it has a dam between the mountains over there."

"Are there lots of eagles?" Julia asked, peering into the sky over the side of the buggy.

"Lots," replied Tony.

"When are we going to eat?" I inquired. We had been driving for hours and for the last of them my thoughts had continually turned to the basket under the seat.

In my imagination I had rehearsed several times how I would cook those steaks and boil the coffee in the clean lard pail, as Tony had already taught me to do. How fixed and firm I felt sitting beside him waiting to cook our dinner! I had had to pack a generous supply, for we would have to pass the night somewhere and return the next day and he had told me there was no place to eat. Well, I thought, I have plenty of meat and bread. That is really all one needs. Besides, I had brought some Indian yellow cornmeal to cook mush for breakfast, for I knew Indians generally had that—the hand-ground coarse meal that is so delicious and really tastes like corn.

"We going to eat up in that canyon," Tony answered, pointing west straight across the valley and up the mountain where we saw the road winding over the hill. "There's a nice place I know over there."

I think we all sighed, for we were already stiff and tired but we knew we could do nothing about it.

However, it wasn't so very much longer to wait when we entered Cimarron Canyon and trotted along after we got over the hill. It was quite another kind of canyon here, narrow, with thick deciduous trees of many shades of green; the pines were climbing farther up on the hillsides. The brook ran rapidly beside the road, brown and clear, and I was thirsty as soon as we came close.

"Oh, let's stop and drink!" I begged.

"Pretty soon. Over there." Tony kept on pointing.

There was a curve in the road and the low brow of the hill turned and was outlined across the higher mountain beyond, and suddenly we saw smoke rising over the edge of the near curving greenery. It rose very blue and it smelled delicious as the wind brought it to us.

"Indians," announced Tony, succinctly.

Sure enough. When we went around the bed, there they were, four or five of them, sitting around a fire on a grassy knoll.

Tony drew up and flung the reins around the whip, and we all climbed out. The Indians turned to us and gave a greeting in warm, low voices. At least they greeted Tony. They really did not seem to see the rest of us. Not that they excluded us but all their feeling went to Tony, and they were all joking and murmuring together in their language which is like a soft humming intonation up and down and not crisp or clear-cut. It has a very affectionate sound and never seems suitable for anger, or for harsh imperatives. Even in an argument, there is never a sound of clash or clamor.

Once upon a time, a little later than these days I am telling of, Tony took me out to the Pueblo with him when he had to go to a council meeting and I had my first chance to hear their speech over a space of some hours.

The councilmen were meeting in the governor's house to talk about a door.

Now, Taos Pueblo builds up irregularly in block houses and forms two great community houses of pyramidal shape with the river coming down the mountain and running between them. The Indians used to cross from one side to the other over two foot-bridges made of logs thrown across, and on one very good wagon-bridge.

These low, rambling houses look like pyramids from whichever direction one sees them. They rise five stories high and spread out a good deal at the bottom. From a distance of five miles or more out in the desert, they point up like two breasts —and looking down upon them from the steep side of the Pueblo mountain, they draw up like two of its foothills, earthcolored. They were reared there out of the land that forms them, and there they endure unchanging. That they have kept their pyramid shape through thousands of years, with the Indians living and dying and being born again and building more rooms on every year as old ones fall down, is a thing that everyone wonders about; but I don't wonder about it any more after this night I spent out there listening to the old men.

I was waiting there outside because Tony was in the council meeting. The door the Indians were meeting to talk about was in the neighbor's house next to his mother's, so he had to be there, too. All I knew about it was that this neighbor wanted to move his door from the east side of his house to the north side. To do this he needed the consideration and approval of the governor and his whole council of old men:

the Cacique, who has, by heredity, almost unlimited power, and the war-chief with his lieutenants. No one in the Pueblo is able to add to his house or build a new house or even build an oven outside somewhere without all these people meeting together to talk it over and pass judgment on it—maintaining the form.

Why do they want to keep the pyramid form, anyway? I don't know why. And maybe they don't know, either, for it was judged necessary to build it that way so very long ago that perhaps the reason is forgotten. Well, they do it. Passionately, persistently, and with the fire of the spirit. When this fire of spirit is still in men to preserve something, it endures.

This night that I was out there was one of those still moonlit evenings when everything seems changed into something else and one loses one's customary sense of things, and yet the reality before one is no less intense than the one at home in the fire-lit room—is perhaps more intense for not being so familiar, yet seeming so crystal-clear and full of significance.

The governor's house has one small window without glass, for there is no glass in pueblo windows except in the church. Once I asked Tony why they allowed glass there if not in their houses, and he replied: "But that is a different religion, you see." The governor's door was narrow, and from where I was I could watch it swing open and let in one shrouded figure after another, passing into the broad beam of light thrown out by the unshaded oil lamp and the fire.

The moonlight fell so that half the house was in black shadow, including the door corner; and the rest of the adobe walls were softly glowing. The window cut out a high yellow square from the blackness. It was very simple, that picture, with hardly any detail. A square house jutting out from the dark mass of the whole structure, the little yellow lighted

THE GOVERNOR

THE SUN PRIEST

window and the moon-lit wall, the door opening and shutting in the shadow, throwing out a path of warm light as, one after another, the Indians silently opened it and passed within, an air of serious celebration and a something withdrawn, inwardly concentrated, about each figure. They wear their blankets until they are soft with repeated washings so that they mold the body easily, clinging to the head, and flowing back over the left shoulder. Some wear white and some pale gray, and a few of the blankets are brilliant and patterned.

The room filled. They gathered there quickly after the governor and his officers called them from the roof of his house, their voices reaching all through the Pueblo into dim out-of-the-way rooms and farthest corners. The Indians always hear these calls, announcements, summons, no matter where they are in the Pueblo. They don't stop talking and listen or stop in their work, but they all hear and understand, and obey. And the criers on the house know how to throw their voices so that it will reach the one who hides as easily as the one next door.

Soon all the old men were gathered within. The door was left open and their voices flowed out gentle and vibrant like the beam of light. At first they were merely chatting together as they assembled, seating themselves on low, white-covered couches around the walls, smoking and laughing a little.

But when they were all there a silence came. Then a single voice in some kind of prayer arose, calm, contained, a majesty in it; and after that all the voices, murmuring. Then the young men came, singly and in twos and threes, padding on quiet moccasins out of the gloom, swathed in white wrappings, only their eyes showing. They stopped below the window to overhear what was going on inside. There is no secret diplomacy in the Pueblo regime. Everything is open.

The light from the window fell on the white figures. They know instinctively how to move, how to stand. Their attitudes at that hour and in that light seemed to betoken a mysterious participation in some ceremony unknown to me. Anyway, beautiful, beautiful, the whole atmosphere beautiful and strange and significant beyond usual things, and a queer chill crept over me as I watched.

Inside the room the old men's voices murmured together, rising and falling in a cosmic sound. Sometimes one voice would rise over the others in a priestly note of exhortation or warning, but it was always measured, rhythmic.

The white figures in the group below would melt away, others would take their places. These spoke no word to each other but, approaching, would stare in silence into each other's quiet eyes trying to fathom the identity, not touching, not moving, as each searched the soul confronting him. Then satisfied that he had penetrated the personality in the other's eyes, one would make way. They respect, utterly, the anonymity of the night.

The old men's voices flowed on, a river of sound, and the rhythm emerged. This was, somehow, cosmic music. Over on the bridges the young boys sang happy songs in the moonlight. Against the wise and secure old men's voices, the young voices soared like lark-music. Contrapuntal. And how enhanced by the river water! How many thousands of years have the Indians known that voices over water make their songs lovelier?

The night was very quiet, as if it listened, too. The moon sailed on, smiling, and the old men wove their spell. Once I went to the window and looked in and I saw on Tony's face a look of exaltation. It was vivid and illumined, his eyes raised to the wall opposite him.

The hours crept by and yet they did not seem long. They did not seem like hours, anyway. Time was unbound. And from that roomful of old men a revivifying spirit issued, refreshing and restoring one.

Sometime near midnight there was a pause. Several Indians came out, and Tony came up to the place where I sat. "Are you all right? Not cold?" he asked.

"No, but Tony, what *are* they talking about?" I whispered eagerly.

"About that door," he answered, and returned to the house.

Again that cosmic murmur filled the air and passed into one's consciousness and did something good for one. Then all at once I had a realization. It's not that door that it's all about," I said to myself. "That's only a point of focus. But there's something else underlying what they are doing. This is a tribal expression, they are making something, continuing something that is alive. They themselves live by their creation. This is their kind of 'creative work.' Altogether they are projecting some essential life-giving energy and each one gives and each one receives of it."

A council meeting? Then I thought of our council meetings, our committee meetings, our Leagues of Nations, and I wondered if they, too, have an underlying life of their own that is spun out all unconsciously, while we think we're meeting to carry on grave discussions of this and that. But our meetings don't animate us and refresh us. Why not?

At about two o'clock I gave in to a feeling for sleep and I slept till Tony came out in the early morning and waked me.

"Well, did they decide to move that door from east to north?" I asked him.

"Oh, yes," he said, "the meeting was to decide that."

Now in Cimarron Canyon we all sat down on the ground together and Tony brought the lunch basket out of the buggy, and he and I unpacked it.

"Have they eaten, do you suppose?" I asked him in a low voice.

"Maybe they brought some bread and they eat that," he answered.

"What are they doing—where are they *going?*" I asked, wondering, and he told me that they had walked over the mountains above the Pueblo and crossed Merino Valley and were on their way to the same place we were, to Ute Park, to get something.

"Something?" I exclaimed. "Something at the railroad station?" I know my voice had that rude American sound in it then that is so completely unsympathetic to anything uncomprehended.

Tony dropped his beautiful eyelids over his eyes and his face seemed veiled from me.

"Indians don't get things at railroad stations," he answered with dignity.

His voice and his face and his manner rebuked me and set up a nervous flurry of dismay in me.

"Oh, dear!" I murmured and I raked his face and tried to find a crevice in him where I could penetrate and be at home again, but there was no opening for me.

I lifted the brown paper bundle of steaks out of the basket and opened it. Eight nice, big, juicy steaks for our lunch today and tomorrow, and here we were, nine people sitting around a fire. I handed them to Tony, saying:

"I guess we'd better share these now and maybe we will find some more somewhere." This somewhere was an utter void in my imagination, for I had no idea what was ahead of us:

whether it was all a leafy canyon with a brown stream running in it, what Ute Park amounted to, or what kind of place we would sleep in. Tony seemed to live so completely in the here and now that I had already learned not to question him about what the future held. I never knew what the next hour would have for us and still I do not know, except to know that it will be all right. The thing I discovered quite soon was that the hours took care of each other, and if one lived wholly and well at present the future could truly be left to itself. Though even now I cannot always remember to give up to this fact.

Tony laid the bundle of steaks down on the grass and went over to the stream and washed his hands and face, and then he lifted water in both hands and smoothed it over his black head. He stood up beside the stream and called to the Indians: "An-n-n-g yuh—An-n-n-g yuh." Come on, come and wash.

And they sprang up and joined him beside the water and bathed themselves and they all had a wet, pleased, and happy light in their eyes.

When they returned to us they brought knives out of hidden recesses in their clothes and they cut branches and whittled sharp points onto them.

Tony handed us each a steak. Emulating the Indians, we laid them on the grass and hastened to the stream to wash, but I fear we had not a careless ease and familiarity with running brooks. Julia was dabbling her face with three fingers and wiping it on a wisp of handkerchief.

Elizabeth stood on the bank with raised eyebrows and laughed with her lips pursed out: "Who-o-o ohoo!" Everything amused her except herself. She did not know how sweet and funny she looked standing there in her flowing white

Greek draperies with a broad-brimmed haymaker's straw hat on her head.

The lunch tasted wonderful. The steaks were finally cooked to a turn, crisp on the outside and pink within, and eaten without benefit of forks or knives. The coffee was good, the bread came from the Pueblo and was made into small, crusty loaves out of whole-wheat flour, and oh, it was satisfying!

After we had cooked and eaten, we sat still under the trees. That is to say, we women sat still and watched while the Indians talked together in low voices. Their conversation always seemed to have a narrative form. They would speak in turn for several minutes at a time, and often they gestured with their hands, drawing maps upon the sky, or picturing with extended forefinger long trails across the mountains above us, and always their voices were low and musical, having a kind of courtesy to the ear and a benevolent refinement in them. I am sure we three women listened very differently. To the others, all this was like an entertainment to be watched: by Julia, like a traveler; by Elizabeth, to compare with ancient Greece; for me, to find a way in, to belong, and not to be the outsider that I so obviously was.

Finally, with one accord, like birds, the Indians rose to their feet and smiled over at me under my tree.

"Ta-a-a," they murmured, and one of them raised his thumb and forefinger to his throat and waved them off into space, laughing.

"What did he mean?" I asked Tony, who stood beside me.

"He said thanks. Full up," Tony told me with a smile. "Everybody had a nice dinner today—feelin' good. I guess we all go on now."

The horses had been taken out of the buggy and left to browse, so he harnessed them and we started up Cimarron

Canyon again. We soon overtook the Indians, who had gone on ahead. They were walking lightly along, singing, and they had gathered the supple twigs of cottonwood and willow and bound them into wreaths to keep their heads cool in the afternoon sun. It was comforting to see them moving along, carefree and happy, with the high trees and the canyon walls protecting them on either side. Why did one feel this solid comfort in Indian life?

The shadows were long when we reached a narrow railroad track that ended in front of our eyes.

"Ute Park," announced Tony, whipping up the tired horses.

The canyon opened out broad here and we came to a raised platform beside the track and that was all there was to it as far as I could see. But Tony pointed out some piles of lumber and a sawmill, one or two shacks, and a road leading at right angles off the highway.

At the end of this road, outlined against the black mountainside, we saw a long, low, white building.

"You all goin' to sleep in there tonight," he announced in a tone of finality.

We had turned now and were trotting up to the hotel or whatever it was.

"Where are you going to sleep?" I inquired, wondering if we were going to be deserted.

He pointed up beyond at the left side of the building.

"I sleep with the Indians up there." He sounded reserved and uncommunicative and as I was just beginning to learn it was no use asking questions, I didn't. He drew up at the ramshackle, dingy, one-story house. It had a black-screened porch that ran around the front and sides.

None of us made a move. We didn't want to go in there at all. However, Tony climbed down and began to lift suitcases out of the bottom of the buggy and stand them on the ground.

"Come on," he said, in his kind voice. "This place all right. You rest yourself and pretty soon the Indians come and we fish and get you trout for supper."

So the three unenthusiastic ladies descended unwillingly.

I hastened into the building to look for someone to show us rooms but I looked in vain. There were a lot of closed doors and a terrible coughing going on behind one of them, so I came out of the front door and went around to the back to another unattractive screened porch. In here I found a girl with her hair done up in curl papers.

"Could we get some rooms here for the night?"

"I guess so, but the lady isn't here right now," she replied with a strong, unfamiliar accent.

"Well, can you show us some place to put our bags?" I demanded with the authoritative tone of travel.

She looked somewhat surprised but led me back to the front of the house. When she saw Elizabeth all in floating white, Julia very stylish in her tailored suit and brown chiffon veil for traveling, and Tony, standing beside the drooping horses, her mouth opened and she only just succeeded in snapping it shut upon some exclamation.

She led me to the back of the hall and opened the door upon a room that had four sagging beds in it.

"These do?" she asked.

"Yes, I suppose so. But we only need *three* beds," I explained.

"Well, you can just let the other be," she replied, flinging the window up.

There were two frail metal affairs that supported thick, white bowls and pitchers, three straight chairs and the four beds, and that was all the room contained.

"I'll go and bring in the suitcases. How much is this room?"
She hesitated. "Fifty cents apiece."

"Any supper or breakfast?"

"Oh, no! No eats."

When I saw Tony lead the buggy away behind the hotel, leaving me alone with my friends and our bags, I felt desolated. The world was too sad and lonesome with these dreary beds and chairs in it and my two friends, who had no consolation to offer, who themselves needed all the consolation they could get after the lives they had lived through.

Never mind. As usual we smiled and joked and covered up our real thoughts. We stretched ourselves on the thin mattresses to rest, for we were stiff from long hours jolting over the rough wagon road.

We lay and stared up at the ceiling and refrained from conversation for a long time, and the light faded out of the room. The sun must have set already behind the high mountain to the west of us.

In the dusk Elizabeth murmured in a childish voice after a while, "Do you really think he will come back and give us our supper?"

"Certainly. Of course, he will. What do you *think?*"

"Well, I was just *wondering. . . .*"

Finally it was pitch dark and I got up and lighted a match and looked for the electric light.

There was none. But I found a meager glass oil lamp standing on the floor and when I got it going I said to Julia coldly, "Have you your wrist-watch on?"

Julia was lying there winking very fast as she always did when she was nervous.

"Yes, I have," and she turned it to me.

"Mercy! Eight o'clock!" My heart began to beat fast and I felt perfectly furious. Was this any way to treat us?

"Just you wait," I cried, hustling around, looking for my powder, my comb, smoothing down my crumpled gingham dress.

The others raised themselves out of the dips in their beds and dangled their feet over the edges and Elizabeth began to giggle. "Who-o-o-o whoo!" she murmured. "What do we do now?"

"Don't whinny like that," I said harshly. "Just you wait. I'll find some supper for us! I just hope those Indians haven't eaten up all I had left in the basket!" As I took hold of the door handle, someone knocked on the door and it opened upon the girl who had closed us in there some three hours ago.

"That Indian says come on," she told me.

When we met Tony outside he was standing in the moonlight, smiling.

"Supper ready," he said, and we all felt comforted once more by the warm, friendly radiation that came from him.

He led across the grass and away from that ugly house where we saw a rosy firelight ahead of us.

Tony was beaming with satisfaction; he made us happy for his good feeling was strong and contagious and when we reached the campfire we saw why he felt so pleased. There was a big can of coffee bubbling beside the fire; there were two stakes driven into the ground, and suspended upon them there were some long willow branches strung with many hot crisp trout in rows, dozens of them, all ready to eat!

The Indians stood on one side waiting for us and laughing with pleasure at what they had done. It didn't matter that they had been walking up and down mountains all day since before sunrise. They had not been too tired to catch all those fish and clean them!

"Oh, Tony!" Julia cried, "how heavenly! We're starved."

"I thought you'd forgotten us," I confessed. I was feeling ashamed.

"I never forget nobody," Tony replied with a good deal of pride. "I carry ever'body and ever'thing here, in my little box," he went on, tapping his breast with a wide smile. He had a way of bending his smile down upon one that was like laying a kind hand on the shoulder.

We sat down as fast as we could and the nine of us ate up all those fish in no time.

The moonlight and the firelight blended together and there was a faint half-familiar perfume all around us. After supper was over, the Indians sat shoulder to shoulder and sang for a long time. It must have been late, for the moon was about to follow the sun over the western rim of the mountains when Tony got up and stretched and said, "Come on. Time you people go to sleep."

He was always herding us around like that because we were so new to the country we never knew the next move to make. It was a fine feeling, too, to have him take all the responsibility of us. It made one feel unburdened.

We said good night all around and I added haltingly, a trifle embarrassed, to the fishermen, "Ta-a-a—"

"Han! Han!" They nodded, flashing their teeth in the flickering light. "Yes, yes, we understand, you like our fish, and you want to be a friend. All right. We are all friends together." All this and more they communicated in their few syllables.

Tony led us back to our dismal hospice and when we came to the steps, he put his hand on my arm to detain me while Julia and Elizabeth went on ahead.

"I'll be right along," I told them.

When they closed the door on us, Tony drew something out of the front of his shirt: a small, round ball of something wrapped in a scrap of cotton, and handed it to me.

"What? The perfume?" I cried.

He nodded.

"That's what the Indians come walkin' over here to gather."

"Does it grow *here?*" I was pressing it to my nose—the delicious, subtle Indian perfume perhaps more like attar of roses than anything else.

"He grow up there beyond where we camp. He fresh and green now."

"Oh, thank you! I am so glad to have it." It had a tremendous value and significance for me. For Tony to prepare it and give it to me made it important. Any stone he would have bestowed upon me would have been precious, as the green, high mountain, pine twigs he had brought me a while ago had been precious to me.

"That Indian perfume very very good medicine," Tony told me earnestly. "He help you, lots."

"I am sure it is," I answered, and knew that it was so.

"Good night, now. You sleep," he said, and patted my shoulder, and it felt kindly, like his bending smile.

So I went into our room and there were Julia and Elizabeth sitting up in adjoining beds, each one with a white handkerchief tied over her head.

"My goodness!" I cried. "This looks just like an old ladies' home." I was rippling with laughter, for I felt so happy.

After we put Julia (or was it Elizabeth?) on the train in the morning, we turned back for our long day's drive. We had had a good, early breakfast of bread, coffee, bacon, and mush in the woods so we did not dwell upon the thought that there was nothing left in the basket but cornmeal! We were learning, perhaps, to live in the moment.

However, towards noon those inevitable rumblings and questionings began, those signals as universal as death.

"I am getting hungry again. What a nuisance," I exclaimed.

Tony looked down at me and laughed. "That's not a nuisance. That's nice. Natcherel."

"But what are we going to eat?"

"We got cornmeal, ain't we? We don't need any more. We got salt for it, water to boil it in." And he waved to the stream beside the road. I heard a faint sniff behind me.

"Well, let's stop and boil it then," I said ungraciously.

Tony cooked the cornmeal mush with care and a kind of reverence. Everything he did was done with thoughtful attention, and in silence if there were things to consider concerning the act, and I had learned already that there was a great deal to ponder upon when he handled cornmeal, or meat, or fish. Associations crowded upon him, the whole life of the corn was living in his mind when he stirred the bubbling mush. If he was handling meat there was somewhat the same concentration upon it, though naturally it was not so colored and intense in his memory. For corn, the corn he sifted through his fingers into the water, was his brother. It had its long ancestry side by side with his own in the Pueblo. The fathers and grandfathers of this very same corn had been reared beside his grandfathers since time everlasting.

When we three sat under a shady tree with saucers of plain, thick mush in our hands, it may be seen that what it was for one of us was not anywhere near the same for the others.

Tony looked wonderfully satisfied and appeased but I only knew a need for milk or cream or something to dilute it with and we had finished the can of condensed milk at breakfast. Elizabeth—I think it *was* Elizabeth—ate small amounts off the tip of her spoon and said nothing.

Presently a fine-looking countryman drove along and stopped his buggy and got out. He examined us carefully as he walked up to us, and said:

"*Buenos días, Antonio. Para donde vas?*"

"Taos," Tony answered laconically. The man was agreeable. He stood a moment and examined us thoughtfully, then when he turned to go he said something to Tony in a very authoritative voice and Tony smiled swiftly and slyly when his back was to us.

"What did he say?" I asked curiously, as he drove on.

"He say you are a very nice lady and I am to take much care of you. I guess he think maybe I scalp you." Tony said, with a beaming smile.

Elizabeth giggled. "What did you tell him?" she inquired.

"Oh, I tell him I take good care both of you," he answered.

When sundown came we were only on the top of Palo Flechao because we had lost time waiting for the train to leave in the morning.

We hadn't eaten since the noon-day mush and there we were hungry again. So we stopped on the top of the pass and Tony cooked up the last handful of meal which we ate in grim silence, and then we went on.

It had rained the other side of the mountains that afternoon and the road was full of mud holes; the poor horses slid around in the slick wet clay, and the buggy lurched and swung. It was not so bad, though, until it grew really dark and the moon not risen above the mountain behind us.

Then it seemed to Elizabeth and me that we were simply trusting to luck. Tony didn't seem to be guiding the horses, but just letting them pick their own way down the slippery mountainside in the pitch-black night.

"How are you getting on?" I asked Elizabeth, turning around and trying to see her.

"Oh, I'm hanging onto both sides. Do you think these horses are going to fall down or go over the edge or anything like that?" She giggled in a high-pitched voice.

"No-o-o-o! No-o-o-o!" Tony soothed in a sweet singsong. "Don't you be scared! I takin' care of you. Listen! I make you a dark-night song . . ." and he began to chant a little tune over and over. It was very reassuring and sure somehow, and it put us both in an easy frame of mind, so we relaxed and just lurched around in the buggy and didn't try to resist and sit straight any more.

So Tony sang us all the way home and it was midnight before we reached the house, but of course the moon had come up long before that and made it easier for horses and driver.

He left us at the garden gate, saying:

"Well, I guess I take good care of you. We had a nice trip, didn't we?"

2 0

Chapter Twenty-eight

IN THE years gone by, yearning and unsatisfied in Italy, I had had preoccupations that had absorbed all my thoughts and I had called them love. Then in New York I had learned to use the name of sex for that strong autonomous serpent in the blood that once unleashed took full possession of all my other activities, and rode me unmercifully.

Here in Taos I was awake to a new experience of sex and love, more mature and more civilized than any I had known before. It is difficult to define the difference but here Tony was providing me with an enveloping kindness that was of the very nature of security and protectiveness, a warmth that relaxed one, delivering one from the anxiety and the tension of life even while it stimulated and made one more aware of living. The feeling that came to me from Tony and that in return grew stronger daily in me, made me more wide awake than I had ever been before in my most conscious moments, but with this difference: that there was growing in my awareness of all about me, a tenderness, a sensitiveness to things outside myself, that had been peculiarly reserved before now for my own quandaries. I had been keenly aware of myself and I had been sorry for myself often enough, and perhaps there had been plenty to feel sorry for in my repressed and injured existence; I had also been very alert and intuitive about other people and what went on in them. But I had been a cold observer.

Then the men I had known had been of the same material

as I, of the same environment and social system. They, like I, had been in various ways competitive, restless go-getters. Of course, they thought of themselves as dynamic, for they went so far and so fast in their efforts to escape themselves.

Everything they did took them away from the contemplation of the inner man. They would create new art forms, they would re-make the world, but they would never come to grips with their own solid crystallized deformities. This world of escapists I had lived among, this crowd of reformers, artists, writers, labor leaders, philosophers, and scientists, they had been terribly busy all the time "doing the job" as they were wont to call it, the job, in fact, of avoiding the responsibility of themselves, and of getting onto themselves, and their activities had not left them time or leisure to be: for merely being. They reasoned and they rationalized, they fed themselves and they made love, they wrote, painted, telephoned, and talked at a furious rate—but they never radiated. They had not the time *to be:* to be anything much, and never the time to be kind, kind, as, I was learning now, a man could be.

Evidently it took time and leisure for one to well up perpetually from the source as the water from a spring, and to color and enrich the space around one, and to warm and console those near one as Tony did, in his static fashion, unconcerned and whole. It was like sunshine falling. The essence of his mode of being was kindness, disinterested, involuntary, and unceasing. But it takes time to be kind and my other friends and I had never had that, just as we had never had any culture in the real sense of the word and for the same reason, for kindness and culture are closely related and require the same soil.

Yes, we had all been too busy for the kind of love I was learning to know in Taos.

Too repressed and unhappy and busy to be kind, to be loving, living on substitutes for love, trying to blot oneself out in
another person as lacking in essentials as oneself—how desperate an undertaking that had been!

The need to be lost in activity had driven us around and
around in endless haste, so as never to sit still alone and know
our emptiness. Were we empty, and frightened at our frustra-
tion? Did something wait for us there at the center of being
ready to touch us if we paused? Surely that was true for very
many of my nearest companions. But what was there in our
environment to restore us to ourselves? What to uphold and
feed our spirits? What vision did we share in common, to
what end did we look forward? Why, the very fact of the
ever-recurrent discussion one was always hearing about progress and whether there was any or not was one of the signs
of our great need. And what was there to meet the need that
grew in us? Competition, self-assertion, the feeling of personal
influence, was probably the greatest enhancement my genera-
tion knew. Personal influence for good, of course, "a construc-
tive influence," a reformer's ideal!

Social standards had altered since the days of Grandpa
Cook and the ideal of making great fortunes. ("Do you know
what that is? It's a Silver Dollar!" he had said to me porten-
tously one day on the big dark staircase in his house.)

The love of money was still there in everybody but it had
been camouflaged under a new mask. Talk! Talk! Talk! How
that had increased since Grandpa Cook's youth, but did it accomplish anything? Did it get anyone anywhere? Rather it dissipated the remaining spiritual energy, thinning it out the
more!

No wonder Hutch, observing our society and its far-gone
reaching into error, had dreamed of somehow "subtly under-

mining the community," breaking it down, opening it up, and smashing the rigidities of false values.

Now here in this new world, knowing Tony, realizing day by day his rich, deep, self-contained nature, feeling day by day his goodness and wholeness, I grew ashamed, more and more ashamed and humble, and it seemed to me I hardly knew how to act. My responses belonged to an entirely different world. They had been imposed upon me from outside by theaters, books, and the conventions of that other world, and here they did not fit at all.

I was speechless most of the time when I was with him but he did not seem to mind. Talking was not the most significant, the only, way to communicate. His whole being spoke continually.

So I found I was in contact with a culture impregnated with realities I had scarcely dreamed of and that were foreign to my own social structure. These realities are difficult to name, and anyway, I am barred from naming them. They were basic, true, and natural, and they produced a courtesy that came from the heart and not from expedience.

Not a day passed that Tony did not make me realize how rough and insensitive I was, and that all my past sensitiveness had been employed in self-feeling and never in fellow-feeling. When he saw I suffered from this dawning awareness of myself as an isolated egotist, he consoled me. There did not seem to be anything he did not understand. He was unresponsive, becoming faintly aloof and disapproving at any appearance of self-assertion, of snappy authoritativeness, and he disliked cocksureness. But at the smallest sign of embarrassment or mortification at a blundering break that I made, he was right there with a helping hand to lift me up and comfort me. It was as though he gauged all the handicaps of my past

2 0 ★

years and what they had done to condition me, and wanted to help me disentangle myself from their effects.

He was patient in a way that I had never imagined anyone could be, a patience unending and constant—never having failed these twenty years.

His judgment appeared to me very different from the intellectual and trained opinion I had known in other men. It was immediate and unreasoning and I always found it sound, though it had no need to be run through his mind and be mentally tested, and it was never mistaken. He had a kind of direct knowledge, unhindered by the need to think out things. He was intuitive, as was I, but his heart was alive while mine was out of kilter.

Tony never spoke of love. He seemed to have no urgencies or emotional fevers in him, nor any slave-driver in his nature. But he loved and his love awakened love for the first time in one who encountered him in her eleventh hour, almost at the end of her rope.

What I say cannot be illustrated by incident or recorded conversation. It must be taken as I tell it or rejected. I am only able to tell a small part of this experience because it was real. I can more easily describe what I was discovering about the former years of my life, for somehow they were not life itself but only the subterfuges I had known in its place. For instance, I began to understand something very piteous and it surprised me enormously: It was that what I had heretofore taken for love in myself and others had been a succession of neuroses with their various fixations, compulsions, and the many complex sensations of vice. That's all that vice is—the pitiful neurotic escape from reality and from the inner self. How many people are vicious? Just as many as try to hide themselves in others, and, in relationships based on sensation, never feeling *real* except when lost and oblivious in some "love-affair"; or else in drink or drugs, trying to find the stimulation that doesn't arise naturally in one's own depths.

How many of us had depended upon our vicious satisfactions, going from one stimulant to another, never daring to be alone because nothing happened inside one, escaping the horrible stillness and emptiness and immobility of the soul?

How many of those I had known were like myself? I had been constantly under the influence of external stimulants and unable to get along without them! Dependent upon them. That was what made them vices.

And even those, like friends close to me, who had not been of the vacillating, inconstant, changeable type, who had been wedded to one, true to one, unable to get away, bound hand and foot, surely they had been no less vicious persons than those whose solutions seemed to lie in new excitements. It was neurosis just the same, servitude, the infantilism that prevailed and prevented them from coming to ripeness, to freedom in maturity.

Now then, I relinquished my favorite imperative grafted upon me by dear Hutch—"the inevitable!" I began to see it as a rationalization of some inherent weakness, just as many philosophies have been the strong and stubborn expression of conditioned natures building thought-systems to dignify their imperfections, and making a virtue of necessity.

There did not seem to be that kind of habitual and inevitable weakness in Tony.

He wasn't enslaved. He belonged to a subjugated race but somehow he was free in himself, and his people were free in comparison with their conquerors.

Chapter Twenty-nine

THE VERY first time I saw Tony when he sat on a hassock in his house and sang a little song for us, there had been a strangeness about him that I had taken for part of his Indian difference from us. Again when he stopped in front of me when I was sitting in Candelaria's house teaching her to knit, and he gazed at my violet ribbon, musing deeply upon its color, I had felt no particular strangeness in him because everything about all the Indians seemed so different from us. But as time went on through the spring until the summer and I knew him better, I gradually discovered he really seemed different from himself at certain times. My realization of this crept upon me imperceptibly, and the reason it took a long time for me to notice it was because I rarely saw him on Sundays. The work on the house stopped Saturday afternoon and he seldom came to town on Sunday, so I did not see him again until Monday morning when I found him as I had left him. I missed seeing him those Sundays, and I wandered restlessly about the house, trying to occupy myself with Elizabeth or John, but the hours passed slowly.

It was on Sundays I came back, as for a short visit, to the people of the village, and sometimes I would have one or two of them in for tea, or I would go and call upon them. In these unoccupied hours I grew to know Lee Witt—the one-armed sheriff.

Lee Witt was a natural, a shrewd, sensitive, red-headed man, very slim and graceful, with twinkling, dark-blue eyes. He knew many of the old folksongs of the cowboys and the adventurers of early days here, and he sang them gaily, with his head on one side. We had never heard these songs before, they were not either on the air then, nor on records, and they were new and fascinating to people from the eastern states because they had in them the very essence of an unfamiliar environment; as all folksongs do, they contained the life of people.

Lee was apparently a member of the Penitente group, too, and he knew their strange songs and chants and he would sing them for us when we asked him. He was full to the brim of all there was to be known about this countryside, with the exception of the Indians and their ways. No one knew anything about them, though those outside the Pueblo deduced a great deal from the few slight signs of another mode of existence than their own, that they occasionally came upon unexpectedly. Little by little I found out that every interpretation of Indian life by a white person, from the most ignorant villager up to the most learned archeologist or anthropologist was rationalized from a false premise, from the standpoint of his own white psyche, a psyche without any affiliation or any slightest relationship to this other race, being more different from it in kind than from the Aryan East Indians. As different, in fact, as the Chinese, though of course totally unrelated to them as well, in spite of all the Mongolians-across-the-Bering Straits explanations to the contrary.

There has never been written any true version of the so-called American Indian life, or any valid interpretation of the Indian spirit. These people, one race from North America down through Mexico, Yucatan, Peru to South America, have never been known by any of the white people, nor yet by the yellow or black. They are other than these, possessing their own other powers and approaches to the mystery of life, and there has been no Wilhelm come to live among them and, by *communio spiritus* or projection, lose himself temporarily in order to find their essence. It was through his long years of identification with the Chinese that Wilhelm was able to understand them, and to deliver up the secret of their racial spirit when he returned to himself. That schizophrenic genius finally returned to his own kind after having been Chinese in thinking, feeling, and being, after having been one with the Chinese soul. Jung calls his reversion to his German nationality and the German mode enantiodromia. To my mind he does not realize why, when Wilhelm returned to Germany, snapping back with elasticity into his own skin and spirit and rendering up the soul of his hosts in a logical, though to us a well-nigh unintelligible, literary form, he developed a resistance to them that was followed by a dimming and forgetfulness of his experience and finally by his death. There is a warning in this rare example of the penetration of mysteries not one's own, of the great mysteries of race and being, and in the attempt to bridge these depths and make the world one through understanding. There is possibly a necessity for certain unknown factors in life to remain unknown so as to maintain a true balance of power. I learned very early from the Indians that they believe the power goes out of a truth as soon as it is told, spoken, or written down, and when I applied this lesson they taught me to what I saw happening in my own people through the years, I learned how it may be so.

It has always been true that the hermetic religions preserved the life-forces of the people. In our own environment we know we are losing certain values through the violations of our incorrigible and over-curious scientists and we are not learning anything more valuable to take the place of what we lose.

Truth will continue to elude as long as the pursuit goes on. The more we discover or uncover, the less we know. The more we communicate the less we live. Life itself depends upon its mystery for its enhancement and its enlivening stimulation, and if vision and wonder have forsaken our people it is because, cracking the nut we worshiped, we have found it apparently empty.

I learned first from Tony to respect the inviolate unspoken mysteries but I did not learn all at once. I had to knock my head against the stone wall of his silence for a long time before I could accept it, and all during that hard time he did not try to make submission easy for me. His attitude was "take it or leave it" and I could not go away, so I finally gave up and resigned myself. When Lorenzo came, years after, I was already schooled and ready for his passionate doctrine of the "dark gods." I knew what he meant, for Tony had taught me to respect the unseen and undisclosed gods, dark in their dark inviolate mystery. Lorenzo's doctrine had always been: let the unknown remain unknown.

It may be imagined that for one as avid of life and experience and mystery as I was, the Indian cosmos never ceased to fascinate and attract me. Whenever I was with Tony or when I was in the Pueblo, I felt I was up against an indefinable organization of physical and spiritual faculties that couldn't be explained even if one succeeded in defining them. They couldn't be proved as any sum in arithmetic can be; cause and effect did not work out according to the usual simple logical formulas. Nothing made sense as I recognized sense, for there were different laws at work all the time.

Had I not seen Tony, in the earliest days we were together, call Indians down to the house where he was working—call them so they arrived smiling, on horseback, in the time it takes for a person to get a telephone message and saddle a horse? It was enough for me to say to him, "I wish we had Romero here today—" for Romero to come cantering along; or for Tony to say, "We need another plaster man—" to have an obedient boy come down with his trowel stuck in his belt.

Of course I exclaimed over it. "Now how did you do that, Tony?" I would plead. But he would smile and shake his head, or else he would nod and say, "Just call him," and presently I began to wonder if he knew himself how he did it, so familiar a faculty it was, like the unconscious bodily functions.

I was dying to know, to know, to know. To know How. Was that not the absolute destiny of my race, to know just how everything was done? Creation must be solved!

So at first I pestered him a good deal with my questions and he was very patient with me but absolutely unshakeable. He didn't seem to be able to answer a direct question for one thing, he couldn't answer my questions about how things were done, for another, and he wouldn't tell anything about anything even if he could, so from the start I was stumped.

That peculiarity about Indians never seeming able or willing to answer any direct question got on my nerves at first until I realized that it was unintentional. They were not putting one off, dodging an issue, being contrary, or trying to hide anything. They were that way about the simplest interrogation, and I finally understood that that mode of question and answer does not even exist in their system. They do not use such means as that for *finding out* anything.

When I came to that realization, I began to surmise faintly what our type of education must have done to the makeup of Indian children sent to the schools as they have been these many last years at a very early age, for our method of teaching is based altogether on question and answer. Theirs, I knew later, is founded upon suggestion, example, divining, drawing out, showing.

Tony, luckily for himself, had for the most part escaped the school training. He was Indian, whole, uninjured, and un-split by the torture of combining in himself two opposing modes. What made him so patient with me? I have never known, unless it was that he accepted the bitter with the good in a situation that from the beginning he recognized as ar-ranged by God for a purpose hidden from us both. There was always that deep conviction in it for us both and possibly we did, after all, have our sense of inevitability.

Well, I questioned him and pestered him, and never got any answers except about unimportant things. When it came to himself it was as though he said, like Lohengrin: "Never will you ask me, nor be concerned to know, from whence I came to you, nor what my name and race."

One Sunday morning when I grew impatient, missing him so much, and walked out to the Pueblo, I found a curious at-mosphere around his house.

The walk along the road between the green fields had been so lightsome and full of a splendor of high blue skies and soft west wind, with skylarks trilling up above in the clear air! It was my road and I was at home upon it. I was all aflame with confident happiness when I reached the Pueblo.

I saw three or four Indians sitting on the ground, leaning against the wall of his house, and they were wrapped to the eyes in dazzling white sheets so that only a dark triangle across the eyes showed a glitter. They did not move nor appear to recognize me, they were lost in the precious anonymity of the blanket, so dear to these people, and I hadn't any idea who they were.

I had to step to the door between them, they motionless and

indifferent, I feeling a trifle embarrassed and my good feeling sinking down in me. I knocked on the blank, closed door and no one came. I knocked a second time, and still no slightest sound or answer, and this appalled me, for I felt completely helpless and thrown back upon myself. I could not have tried the door handle and entered that house even if it were unlocked, if I had had to save my life by doing so. There was something invulnerable about it, a feeling of "Thou shalt not pass" that struck me in the face. I was dumbfounded at the silence all around me, no children, no people save the Indians under my eyes wrapped in their sheets. The Pueblo was empty and I was up against that terrible immobility that had pursued me in my inner life since childhood. To find it externalized here was like a nightmare.

In confusion and alarm I made my way home down that road so different-seeming now, without the sweet intimacy and friendliness I had felt along there so short a time ago, and forlorn and abandoned, I returned to the Manby house where all that day I suffered a feeling of dislocation and unrest, being neither here nor there and not any more at home on this earth as I had been lately with such great relief and gratitude.

But that day passed somehow and likewise the night, bringing the tender morning sunshine of Monday and I set out to meet Tony on the curving path leading from our garden to the little wilderness we worked upon together.

As I saw him coming towards me under the trees, I was struck once more, as I have been every time anew since then, with his dignified bearing, in which one perceived a certain impressive and royal poise and movement. There was no nervous unbalance nor any hustle and hurry in his flowing stride. With one end of his serape hanging from the right shoulder, the other end of it twisted around his waist, he came along towards me with great self-possession and as though he carried within him a satisfying world.

For he gave an impression of bearing with ease a whole cosmic universe and this lent him his weight and balance, and his appearance of strength and fullness of being was strikingly unlike the shifting uncertain demeanor of many white men who seem unballasted and empty and uncertain when they come hurrying along on their unconvincing errands.

Tony was a part of the fine sunny morning; he matched the mountain and the trees and the authoritative sun that marched like him with a measured stride and I, suddenly breaking into a faltering run to reach him quickly, I was all out of the rhythm of his universe and like an accident in an otherwise harmonious picture.

"What's the matter?" he asked me when I reached him. "Why you like that?"

His voice was kind and yet it was undisturbed, as though there was nothing to worry about, and if I thought there was, he would reassure me. It is true that one of the irresistible effects his grave attention always had upon me came from a parental attitude that I had never encountered before and that I had perhaps always intensely wanted and needed. So now I felt I could throw my burden of nervousness and uncertainty upon him and he would take it for me and transform it into sense of some kind.

He took my hand and drew me down in the shade of a flowering locust tree and we sat on the damp ground where the dew still twinkled in the grass, and leaned against the tree trunk.

"What happened?" he queried.

"Oh—I was so frightened yesterday. I wanted to see you, and I walked out to the Pueblo. It was so queer there . . . no one around . . . some Indians sitting against your house and not speaking to me, and when I knocked at the door, no one answered."

His hands were clasped loosely together between his bent-up knees and he bowed his head back and forth and gazed down at the earth between them with the expression of gravity and consideration that was comforting. He said briefly:

"I asleep."

"Asleep, Tony? Asleep at eleven o'clock in the morning?"

He was silent for nearly a minute, thinking. Then he moved and stood up.

"Listen," he said, "I goin' to tell you something now. White people don't know anything about these things but you—I goin' to tell you because maybe you got a little bit Indian blood in you. Sometimes I feel like that—that you got some Indian in you; other times it's lost, sink away down, gone."

He stood there looking at me, considering, and I looked up at him and the relation between us became that of pupil and teacher.

He slid his hand into the folds of his clothes and brought out a small object wrapped in a scrap of silk which he untied as he knelt down beside me. A dried, round, wrinkled button of *peyote*.

"*Peyote!*" I exclaimed with a quiver of fear.

"You know Him?" he asked me.

It lay on the palm of his hand and he gazed down at it intensely, concentratedly, seeing something into it, deep into it, past its dry, unrevealing exterior.

"Yes, I know something about it. I am afraid of it."

"The God is in the Peyote," he told me. "The Peyote is a big chief among the weeds."

"Do you Indians out here eat *peyote*?" I asked tremulously.

This was very upsetting. I would never forget the night in New York we had experimented with it, and the consequences of that to one of our group.

"Eat It?" he repeated. "We not eat It just to eat It." He paused, feeling a difficulty in telling in words, in English words, what was perhaps incommunicable in any language.

"I goin' to tell you about Peyote." He tried once more. He raised his head and stared up between the branches where the sky burned so blue against the gray-green leaves.

"This Peyote . . . He not *ours*. The Plains Indians gave Him to us. Maybe He belong to all Indians long time ago but not now. Now He come up from the south and He go among a few tribes. He make a big trip to come up to there in Oklahoma. Maybe long ago in passin' time He made His home in Oklahoma like He still make it in south. This is Montezuma's medicine. You know Montezuma?" he broke off his difficult narrative to ask.

"Well, I have read something . . ." I began.

"*Read?*" he murmured, with a small, affectionate, contemptuous smile. "Well—we got to talk. I tryin' to tell you. We go visit Oklahoma tribes and there they have their church for Peyote every Saturday night. Seems like this their whole religion now 'cept Sun Dance and Ghost Dance and some. Sure they used to have other religion like we do here but they lost it maybe, or maybe they mix it all into the Peyote religion."

I interrupted him here. "But *peyote* isn't your religion, is it?" I didn't want it to be. I was still frightened of it.

" 'Course not. Think I tell you my religious? Never. I only tellin' you about Peyote 'cause it not my religious, so I can tell you. We just *borrow* the Peyote. But He is a God just the same," he hastened to give it full credit.

"Now I goin' to say: maybe long long time ago the Peyote

2 1

was in our customs but not since the old men remember in their blood. So now it is just like a vis'tor."

I saw he felt pretty satisfied with this analogy.

"You know. A vis'tor like some others." He did not explain who he meant and I didn't ask. I was anxious to get on with the meaning and use of *peyote* in the Taos Pueblo because it seemed to be a terribly important issue between us, perhaps actually the most important adjustment we had to make.

"Now nearly ever'body in our village has tried the Peyote sometimes," Tony continued. "He is so powerful! He cure the sick people, He give us songs, He show us wonderful things like colors we never see before. And some people see God. Once Enrique see Jesus. It was the first time he came to the meetin', for he been against Him. Then he come, laughin' at Him, just for fun, he said. Then he see Jesus. He cry."

Tony stared at the little god in the palm of his hand.

"Well—what do you do at the meeting?" I persisted.

"You should see that! All the boys bathe in the river first and put on their best things, all their nice feathers. They don't eat before. Then they come and sit in a circle around a nice fire, and the Head Man, the Peyote Chief, he put the Peyote in the center and the Fire-Chief take care the fire all night. One boy sing and another play on the water drum. Every meetin' they tie the drum fresh with fresh water. The singer stop and the drummer pass the drum to the next, and so they sing and drum all night. Haven't you heard the drummin' in your house Saturday nights?"

"Yes—I have—a faraway fast drumming like a bee buzzing."

"That's the Peyote drum," Tony said, nodding his head. "Sometimes they bring a sick person in, maybe someone *very* sick, burnin' up, or can't walk, and then they boil the Peyote in fresh water and give it to drink. That sick person get up well in the morning. I see it many times. I see the lame one get up and walk home, and I see the fever get out of the burnin' body and that person all cool and damp. Wonderful."

"Tony," I forced myself to say, "I'm scared of the *peyote*. I have seen it once in New York. It made someone crazy."

He looked at me in mild surprise and said, "Tell me," and I tried to describe that evening at 23 Fifth Avenue, and I did feel how tawdry it had been when I told him about the fire simulated by my red shawl and the path made by a sheet and the mountain of the moon, for he knew this experience so differently.

"You got to do it right," he said, "or perhaps the Peyote get mad. Just think," he said, "how beautiful the singin' when the Peyote Himself give the songs! Then it get better and better all night till the mornin' star rise over the mountain and we can see him come. Then the Water Chief bring us fresh water to drink, and we finished the meetin'. Everyone feel good. Light. Then we eat and our food is better than ever. All we know is how good, how happy, the life is. We been prayin' all night, prayin' to the God in the Peyote, and He is with us now. So we go home and sleep, rememberin' what we saw.

"You came to see me; I sleepin'. Happy. Why you have to be scared?"

"Oh, Tony! I am still scared. It seems to me you go away from yourself when you eat *peyote;* you lose yourself. That frightens me."

"And seem to me I find myself more and more," he contradicted gently.

He looked at my troubled face and soon he showed his

careful justice, that fairness to the other that had been noticeable in him from the first day I saw him.

"I tell you," he began. "I know you right in one way. I
myself have seen people crazy from Peyote, but that not the
Peyote's fault. That the fault of the way He been used. He
get mad if He not used *right*. Got to be very nice and not just
eat; but must pray, too, and sing all night long. Else go *wrong*.
Certain is some people treat Him too easy, and He powerful."

"Well, do they do it better in Oklahoma than here?" I
asked, because it seemed a danger indeed if it was not truly
understood.

"They got their real church for Him there. Here it too easy,
carry around Peyote, and eat Him and not pray and sing. Yes.
That bad. That make bad too. Now many of our old men get-
tin' mad at the boys for usin' Peyote here. They see it go wrong
and they say: 'That really not our custom, we goin' to stop it.'
Too bad. Not Peyote's fault at all."

"Do you *have* to go on using it, Tony?" I begged.

"I don't have to do anythin' I don't want to," he answered.
"But this a good thing. I always goin' to believe It a good
thing." He began to wrap the silk around it and knot it up.

He rose and held out his hand to pull me up and said,
smiling:

"We talk too long. We got to watch the work. Come on."
So we went over to the new house that was growing higher
day by day.

Chapter Thirty

THERE was a pleasant ease in the way the Indians worked and it took me a long time to get accustomed to it, for I was used to another kind of labor. I had seen other houses in construction. I had watched Italians working on the Villa Curonia with a foreman dogging them, and all my life I had been half aware of an unpleasant atmosphere in the areas where workmen were engaged.

In Buffalo, in New York, wherever I had lived, there were always islands of confusion in the midst of orderly living. Houses being torn down, streets being torn up, new buildings arising upon old sites, and everywhere this activity was taken for granted by most people as a miserable necessity that had to be accepted along with the antagonistic, cut-off feeling in the men engaged in it; the unfriendliness and the sullenness of workmen was an element in everyday life everywhere encountered and everywhere side-stepped, especially by women. Ladies walking down Fifth Avenue often daintily picked their way with averted eyes through the dirt and disorder of alterations but those miserable creatures of another world who were carrying on these labors felt no need to turn away their gaze. They stared boldly at a class from which they were separated forever except for the improvements they were making for it in the standard of living. In the eyes of day-laborers there was usually to be seen a mixture of apathy and endurance for their lot, and a crude rough curiosity and contempt for those who did not share it and who were spiritually removed from them

by every chance of environment and training, although physically they passed so close, skirts sometimes brushing the muddy
wheelbarrows, pretending they were not there.

Men, however, gathered in silent groups to watch the de-
molishment of old walls, the tremendous excavations for new
foundations and cellars, the perilous operations of monstrous
machinery swinging steel beams upwards, long-necked cranes
and complicated pulleys operated by a race so mysterious the
watchers frequently forgot they too were men like themselves.

Sometimes, when the laborers were still young, there would
be a pair of lively eyes, a tune whistled, or a flash of teeth
between lips that had not forgotten how to smile, and these
had to be strong and imperious enough to penetrate the dirt
and the grime, the clumsy work clothes and all the indignities
that accompany labor in our world, strong like a flash of lightning across a city dump.

But here in Taos it was delightful to be with these workmen,
for there was no indignity in raising a house, and nothing
sordid in either the materials or in their use of them. Mud was
mud, yes, but mud was earth, something living and precious
to be handled with understanding and care. Mud was earth and
somehow it was not dirt. It was clean and kind and possessing
an importance. Working with earth was a noble occupation.
To loosen it and make the adobe bricks, mixing the wheat
straw from last year's harvest with it thoughtfully, laying them
in rows to dry while the rock foundation is being built, and
then fitting them carefully upon each other with the rich dark
mud between that will turn as hard as stone, all of it is a
sacred matter, for the wonder of creation is in it, the wonder of
transformation which always seems of greatest significance to
Indians. To take the living earth from under their feet, undif-
ferentiated and unformed, and shape it into a house, with

length and breadth and height, each person's house different, yet always basically the same as others, to bring the trees from the mountain and spread the long, round beams across the walls, to cut the young saplings and lay them close and even, either straight or in the ancient herringbone design, and with more earth and mud to form the roof and so have a shelter that will last forever if it be taken care of, this, it must be admitted, is wonderful.

One can see that it is pleasant to straddle the wall under a summer sky, and hammer down the adobe brick with the end of the trowel, and lift up the bucket of mud from the helper and spread it along in a thick, moist ooze ready to take the next dry brick. Singing comes out of this pleasant work, and there was always the sound of it going on, and the sound of funmaking and laughter.

When noontime came, the sun telling them, the Indians went down to the stream and washed. They removed the remnants of dried mud from themselves, and they smoothed their black heads over and over with their clean, wet palms, and then seated themselves upon the bank beneath the big cottonwood tree to eat.

Sometimes one of them, returning from the desert on the other side of the house, would bring a bunch of fresh sage smelling so sweet and good, and lay it on the ground among them, or one would bring a branch of flowering plum blossom, now it was in bloom, and it would perfume the air they breathed.

The lunch hour was always happy, always full of fellow feeling, for the Indians continually joked among themselves, and though I could not understand their language, I could understand their affectionate interchange that was never sly or suggestive in its fun, never accompanied by the unmistakable twinkle of obscenity. Apparently they were too happy to be obscene, or possibly had regulated outlets for it.

In the late afternoon they stopped work at five o'clock as I knew by my wrist watch and as they knew by the sun or by the Padre's bell, on the days we could hear it up on the hill. But if they had a piece to finish they finished it, whether the hour was five or after five. I never saw an Indian throw down his tool and stop work because a bell rang!

Money had very little to do with all this. Although the Indians were working there because Tony had engaged them for me to build the house, their thoughts were not on their paychecks but on the job itself which they enjoyed and did well.

The wages for it would seem small to builders from elsewhere, and the materials cost hardly anything. For instance, a dollar apiece for the long trees that formed the beams of the ceiling, yet a house was going up there that would last forever if it got good care, like the Pueblo itself, earth delicately piled up and constantly cared for through the thousands of years it has been lived in, first on its present location and before that on the space a little above it on the creek.

When one thinks of the continuous occupation of these piles of adobe earth lasting for so many years that it goes back to a prehistoric antiquity that makes the birth of Christ seem to be recent in comparison, it is not difficult to accept the visit of Montezuma that the Indians recount and which was only a few hundred years ago. Carried in a litter by relays of runners, their visitor came up from the south and gave them his dance, and he asked them to keep it until he came again; he also gave them his fire, the fire that burned for fifty-two years among his people, and then was extinguished and re-created anew. He told the Indians to keep his fire burning until he came again and undoubtedly he intended to return.

They kept it alive and it still lives, I have heard, though I have heard this only by rumor outside the Pueblo and never from an Indian. Cortez came over the sea and Montezuma did not come back here, though possibly the Indians are right to expect him and to wait for him. It is not impossible to believe that the fire that burned in him still lives upon this earth and has never perished and that it will come up again from the south to mingle with a living flame in these United States, joining with those who have waited and kept alive, in more ways than in the literal one, his fire and his essence. In the legend of the first great flood it needed only a survival of a handful to make a new world. Comparing this unfamiliar Indian cosmos with what I had known, how soon after leaving my old sad world and coming here to learn new values and new ways did I begin to whisper to myself, not daring to say aloud the words: the future of these continents lies with the Indian Americas?

When the plum blossom darkened on the branches, fading into fruit, and the wild roses dropped their petals and ripened into the hips and haws of the sterile rose fruit, then the sturdy wild flowers succeeded them, goldenrod·and Queen Anne's lace, yellow daisies, pentstemon, purple lupin, and many others. In the hills the chaste cold Mariposa lily swayed in the tall grass and Tony told me the big blue columbines were blooming higher up in the mountains.

All the winter and spring I had waited for the time to go up to the Blue Lake somewhere behind the sacred mountain, for Tony had told me about it and made me see it from the Indian viewpoint, fathomless deep and cradled in the bosom of the highest peaks in this country, the birthplace of the sun, the holiest spot in all the Taos Indian geography.

Now, one morning, he said: "We can make our trip to Blue

Lake some these days. Maybe soon. There is only a little while it's dry up there; after the snow is melted and before the new snow comes."

"When do the Indians go up for their ceremony?" I asked.

"I guess we go next week," he replied, if one can call his part in our conversations replies. "We can go all we want to in July," he continued.

Here we were in July and Maurice was leaving on the first of August without a word about it passing between us. Tony and I waited for that departure. He knew that we would belong to each other then and I knew it too. It seemed necessary for me to have the change absolute and clear-cut, and for Maurice to be gone completely out of my life before I could take this next inevitable step, and that no faintest overlapping of these two people should occur.

So, though day by day the intimacy between Tony and myself had grown deeper and we had become ever more sensitive to each other's thoughts and feelings, our closeness was psychic; physically we remained strictly apart. It was like a period of probation and preparation. Possibly these probationary intervals are essential for the growth of inner awarenesses so the radiation from the center outwards towards the object of devotion will find its direction and its goal, and perhaps that is why they exist in every religious mystical marriage system and in all the organized human marriage customs the world over.

So before we ever knew each other in the ultimate outward relationship, Tony and I had grown together inwardly, and in our daily companionship we had already accomplished a union of our utterly opposite characteristics.

It only remained to set the seal upon it—the seal that can

never be broken, since it is made (for so it is claimed by those who know) in heaven.

This narrative about Tony and me grows more and more difficult to tell, for I feel increasingly obliged to leave most of it unwritten, not only the secret aspects of his religious life and experience, but the secret intimacies of our own personal life together.

Was it I who had believed so short a time ago there are no secrets, no privacies? Were all my beliefs to be made over in this new world? Not only my beliefs but the actual soil in which they had grown must be turned over and over, fertilized and cultivated.

Let no one believe that a rebirth takes place in one bright convulsive flash. It is a slow, dark passage in time accomplished with blood and sweat, and not only by one's own but these vital juices of another, who loves one enough to work upon this creation, are wrung from him too, in patient agony.

It is a consoling paradox to realize that the extreme sufferings undertaken by lovers for some cosmic purpose unknown to themselves, the intensity and the endurance of suffering, the pain they cause each other, becomes in the end the source of their happiness and satisfaction and that they reach heights equal to the depths they sometimes plunge each other into.

I went forward and I learned that the mills of the gods really do grind very, very slowly, and I found that to learn the meaning of this familiar household phrase by living was quite different from quoting it in conversation in Italy or New York. To describe these lessons and their slow, organic, chemical, and spiritual processes is prohibited to me. I can only write now about the superficialities of our life, and still hope that the most valuable lesson of all will reveal itself here somehow of its own accord. The lesson is said to be an old and hackneyed one but it was new to me: that love can finally overcome all the conditioning of the years gone by, and all the crystallizations of heredity and environment. This was a major discovery that did not reveal itself until its teaching was halfway accomplished and those who remember know that it took years for this instruction to alter the stubborn inflexible habits, for love to reshape the iron and the stone, and for consciousness to add one iota to its proud imagined scope.

The pages I must write, as well as the ones I must not write, are all about this miracle. It seems to me I have to let others know there is a true and possible change of being that can take place, and that I have passed the latter part of my life in this work of change. If I who was nobody for so long, a zombie wandering empty upon the earth, could come to life, who cannot? My empty memories must have shown what life had done to me, my recorded thoughts, reactions, and motivations and how they were, and what they were (underneath the mask of the *persona*) are not so different, I fancy, from many other typical products of our time. It is for those desperate and frightened people I am trying to write now as it was for them I wrote before. Revelations of the hidden distortions, the cripple under the veils of civilization, the mind breaking under its strain, and the heart atrophying in its insulation—those were the intimate memories of my life until I came to Taos where I was offered and accepted a spiritual therapy that was cleansing, one that provided a difficult and painful method of curing me of my epoch and that finally rewarded me with a sense of reality.

Chapter Thirty-one

THE MORNING we started on our journey up to Blue Lake, was one of those days that seem dark with sunshine. There is a sunniness so deep and so mellow it is like a cloak. The big trees on either side of the Pueblo road hung their branches heavily dark and still and their shadows were profound, with thick gold splashing through. Deep July, deep summer day in July, with the green grass black in the shade and sparkling with dew in the open places!

Tony and the other Indians brought horses down from the Pueblo and our departure made a disturbance in the quiet street, the sound of voices and laughter breaking on the air while the packs were tied on, and everyone's saddle and stirrups being adjusted. The long line of us, as we started off in a clatter, was varied, for we wore the queerest collection of clothes—just whatever we happened to have.

Mary and Gabrielle Young-Hunter were with us and Miriam and Herbert Stockton were staying in Taos and went along, too. In fact, perhaps it was their party and we joined it—the details are gone from my memory. I think Maurice stayed at home for he was hurrying to finish the head of Albidia so he could leave.

One thing I must admit I do remember, though, and that is the picture of Elizabeth riding a little horse that looked like a burro, with her white Greek draperies and that wide-brimmed haymaker's hat on her head. Her animal kept pace with ours very nicely, for though we took off up the road at

a brave canter like an attacking army, no sooner did we turn
off at the graveyard than we slowed and just eased along,
walking our horses most of the time.

At Prado we turned from the road into the wide Indian
pastureland that stretched for miles of short-cropped turf all
the way to the mountains.

It was lovely to ride on, firm and yet soft to the horses'
hooves, and easy on the eyes, out there in the wide, treeless
space. The good moist green was under us and about us, and
it swept on up to the sky, so there was no glare to make us
wince. We had the feeling of a vast parkland to play in and
explore, for nature here was kind. It was like moving in a
fairy story, to amble over this interminable green velvet lawn
where short-stemmed flowers, red and white, yellow and violet, pricked through the thick, short blades.

Far and near the Indian horses, loose to wander in these
meadows, were dotted all about in groups, cropping the succulent grass and when we passed near any of them they would
interrupt their everlasting feeding to raise their heads and
stare at us with soft, surprised eyes as though we had disturbed
their dreams.

Tony and I rode together at the head of the column. It
seems to me we were a little party of twelve or fourteen, Indians and whites, but I was oblivious of all the others. They
did not exist for me. We didn't talk much. He sang, and the
other Indians behind us sang happy songs that were part of the
fine fresh morning. Sometimes he pointed out things that interested him, trails up on the mountainside in front of us
hardly visible to my unaccustomed eyes, old trails he had
known since he was a child; or he drew with outstretched
finger the passage of the little Lucero stream where it meandered across the distant country background on our left, out-

lined by the tufty cottonwoods and the red-stemmed willows that always follow water.

This landscape made me think of a painting by Constable with its thick, soft, faraway clumps of trees, and then I was impatient because I did not want to connect this new world with the old. I wanted it to be itself alone and not a part of any past I had ever known. I did not want to be reminded of old familiar things.

"We goin' to eat lunch over there on the Lucero Creek where it comes out the canyon," Tony told me. "Best water in the whole world. Star water called."

It took us all the morning to reach this place he had chosen, and when we got off our horses we felt it was plenty far enough to go, for we were not used to hours in the saddle.

The grassy banks of the ice-cold pale water were as untouched as though no one had ever been there before; no footprints, no vestige of humankind, marred that empty hermitage. Tall trees stood with their trunks plunging deep into the grass and white violets and wild strawberries were thick in the cool shade. Everything in this garden was composed like poetry, and romantic like poetry may be.

"Shakespearean," I thought, and then quickly dismissed the analogy. Was one to be forever reminded of something else and never to experience anything in itself at first-hand? My mind seemed to me a waste-basket of the world, full of scraps that I wanted to throw away and couldn't. I longed for an immersion in some strong solution that would wipe out forever the world I had known so I could savor, as though it were all there was to savor, this life of natural beauty and clarity that had never been strained into Art or Literature.

It had begun to appear to me that there had always been a barrier between oneself and direct experience; the barrier of other people's awarenesses and perceptions translated into words or paint or music, and forever confronting one, never leaving one free to know anything for oneself, or to discover the true essence in anything.

No—everything in the world outside had been distilled into art, defined by ruthless, restless, wordmongers, or other artists in transformation, and they had used it all up. I did not want that old world any more. I knew unless I found a new fare I would admit *actum est* and give up.

Tony said, "Now we rest and eat lunch." He unpacked the saddlebags, and the other Indians took the saddles off the horses and led them a short distance down the stream where they could graze in the shade, and soon we were drinking hot coffee and munching our sandwiches.

"You people always eatin' sandwiches!" exclaimed Tony, with a smile around our circle. He was holding a pronged green branch with a piece of meat speared on it over the little fire.

"Why? Don't you like sandwiches?" someone asked.

"No. I don't like that cold, wet food. No. I like hot food. 'Course I like bread: like fruit . . . but sandwiches seem kinda dead. Think so?" he asked me.

Well . . .

"How you like to have some deer meat?" Juan Concha inquired, slyly giggling. Being a close friend of Tony's he was often with us and he was Eliseo's father. Everything made him laugh. He was always gurgling and haw-hawing deep and low in his throat. "Deer meat!"

"Wonderful!" murmured Tony, reverently, staring up the mountainside that rose like a wall beside us.

The Indians all instantly fell into their own soft speech together, a language that was a blending of outdoor sounds, like running water and the wind in the trees, but that was particularly musical from the kindness in it, often falling into tenderness that was very caressing to the ear. There always seemed to be this loving kindness in them, not sentimental at all but the expression of the smooth concord of their lives.

We meant to reach Twining that night but about three o'clock the habitual afternoon shower descended upon us in such torrents that we were soaked through before we could untie our yellow slickers and slip them on. The rain was heavier near the mountains than down in the valley, and we were skirting the base of the Arroyo Secco range on our way to the Hondo Canyon. After a discussion with his friends, Tony told us we would not try and climb up to Twining that night, that we would stop and camp below the waterfall.

I was glad, for I had never seen it yet, though I had heard much about it from him. It was a stream that tumbled steeply down the side of the mountain and fell over the opening of an old cave. The cave had a bad name among these Indians who believed it was still used by witches, and that it had been used for terrible things in the faraway past before the memory of this tribe.

When Tony said we were going to camp there, I was surprised, because he had told me the Indians would never stay in it or near it at night, so I asked him why he chose that particular place, why we didn't go further on and make a camp at the mouth of the canyon we would be climbing in the morning.

He did not answer me, he just turned his horse right towards the cave that, from where we were, was hidden, I knew, behind a fold of the pine-clad slope. I obediently followed behind, though I was feeling mystified, and the others came on in Indian file. The ground was slick and slippery now and

2 2

the rain washed over our faces, but the air was all perfumed with the soaking wet pine, and sage, and wild flowers and ferns.

We crossed the Secco creek and it was brown and full from the rain, and then we started up towards the hidden waterfall. The horses slid and left long gashes in the sticky clay of the little trail we were on, so we had to go slowly, watching every step, but finally, after we wound our way up through a magical grove of symmetrical bright green, dripping Christmas trees, we came to an open place of emerald lawn where a brook was running deep through round, green grassy banks, the overflow of the waterfall that we could hear now wildly, continuously, thundering above us at this spot.

Tony turned in his saddle and announced: "We camp here." All unexpectedly, his face was a little stern and serious and he looked like a person compelled to some ordeal, though able to go through with it and even to smile while doing so, for as I looked at him somewhat anxiously, I suppose, he got off his horse and walked up to stand beside me, saying gently, "Come on. We got to stay here," in a tone of voice that assured me he would see me through it.

He put it in my mind that I was the cause of something that had changed his mood and that gave him some concern, but that he was going to stand by just the same. Perhaps in that moment I was given at last a complete feeling of security in someone outside myself, and that has never once failed me since that day, so, if I have succeeded in a measure in gaining confidence in myself, and a partial deliverance from evil, it dates from that hour below the waterfall. Of course, this took place in a flash of time and I was quickly down on the ground, and so were the others and the Indians were unpacking the loads and hobbling the horses.

Though they lighted fires to dry out the damp ground and chopped armfuls of pine branches and stripped the soft twigs from them to pile for us to sleep on, everything seemed wet forever and, as night came on, cold.

There was so much work to do no one spoke of the cave right above us waiting behind the trees, but when a lull came and we were all sitting around the fire, after a thin sunset that left us in the shadow while it lighted the great spread of the valley stretched out below like a green and gold carpet, I said:

"Can't we go up and see the waterfall? I can hear it plainer than ever now."

The Indians' dark faces all turned towards me, and they were perfectly inscrutable, their eyes veiled, but very watchful.

Tony said, "Just up there. You go on, see it if you want to."

"I want you to come with me," I urged, feeling hurt.

"Better you go alone," he replied, but he tempered this refusal with a beautiful, radiant, encouraging smile, and he got up and stretched his hand to pull me up, and went on:

"Come on. We wait you here. You better go and try—"

"No!" I interrupted him vehemently. "I don't want to go near it without you."

He seated himself again, and an Indian said something very low, something confidential, hidden from the rest of us not only by language but from our intuition as well.

"It feels spooky here," announced Elizabeth crisply, looking around the circle of faces.

"July full moon," Juan Concha told her, giggling. His voice sounded both explanatory and apologetic. Yes, just then the moon shot up with a leap from behind that far eastern hill over there where my new house stood with its back turned to the sage-brush desert that sloped up to the eastern range.

"I don't like the moon," I contributed in a conversational voice.

Tony had heard this from me before and he did not care for it. I actually felt him recede from me when I said things like that; his ebbs and flows were free and apparent to anyone who was noticing.

"I guess the moon your friend, ain't it?" asked Juan Concha meaningly.

"How do you mean?" I fear I was getting petulant!

"The sun, the moon, the stars, everybody's friend. You can't turn your back on the moon! Moon right there all the time! Someday you like him: wait and see. But he don't care."

The Indians began to sing in low voices and soon we grew drowsy and wanted to sleep. I asked Tony to put a heap of pine twigs under a tree away from the others, for I did not want to sleep in a row, and he took the old wagon sheet that the blankets had been rolled in and he hung it on the lower branches and let it fall to the ground so I had a small shelter inside it. As I bent to go in, he said in a low voice: "Sleep well. I be right here to help you."

It seemed I was going to need help, for soon I was racked with pain that shot through me like knives, and presently I had to get up and go outside. Tony was lying on the ground near by, wrapped in a blanket, and as I staggered out he sat bolt upright and silently watched me and let me go.

"I've got an awful pain," I whispered to him, as I picked my way past. I had to go some distance to get far from the camp but the moon was shining brightly so every step was plain to be seen.

Out there under the trees away from the others the world seemed very big and strong and as though going its own road. It was cold and clear and wet, the wind made a humming sound in the high tree-tops, a continual singing and sighing, and now the roar of the invisible waterfall was louder than before.

I felt I was battling in the night, for my bowels writhed in me and I was on the rack of a new pain that I had never had before. After a while I weakly made my way back to my bed and found Tony standing beside the flat red embers of our fire. His face was turned to the moon and he looked as though he had been praying.

"Come warm yourself," he said in a voice like a doctor. He did not make any move to help me. He just offered the fire as though that was all he could offer. I felt stricken, for he conveyed to me that I was all alone, and no one could cross over to where I was with my twisting pain and its surprise attack.

I lay down upon the fire-warmed earth and closed my eyes, but there was no rest for me for long. My body was a battlefield; all night I rambled weakly back and forth between the trees, my feet wet through, my clothes wet from the still dripping branches. All night I half heard the pounding waterfall and the sighing pines, and all night Tony replenished the fire and stared at the moon and seemed to be praying. He did nothing else. He sat on the far side of the fire so it was between us, and he let me go back and forth between the dark trees until it seemed I must have rejected everything in me, right to my vital organs.

I was weak when sunrise came and the other people woke and stirred about, coming over to the still burning fire, with sleepy eyes and foolish smiles as they always do in camp when they return from sleep to the everyday world and find themselves in company.

Tony was at the side of the stream washing his face and hands.

"I've been sick all night," I told them. "Such cramps!"

"Well, we'll make some coffee right away," and the comfortable everyday bustle began.

Tony came back with a branch of cedar in his hand and Juan Concha must have known his intention, for he unhooked the wagon sheet from the tree and brought it over to where I sat by the fire. Then Tony lighted the cedar and he let it blaze till half the green was afire before he blew it out, and it made a thick blue smoke. Juan Concha suspended the sheet over me like a little tent and Tony handed in the smoking branch, and it enveloped me in a cloud of perfume that saturated me through and through and was satisfying and what I wanted in some inexplicable way. There was strength and comfort and purification in the cedar perfume and I inhaled it deeply.

"Caught cold," I heard someone say outside. "This wet is so penetrating."

"Yes. We ought to have brought some brandy along. It's the best thing for dysentery."

"He goin' to be all right now," Tony's voice replied. "You see."

"Coffee! Coffee ready!" an Indian sang, and I pushed the sheet aside and poked my head out. Juan Concha giggled tenderly. "All well now?" he asked.

"Weak," I told him, feeling happy.

"That's nothin'. Weak! Some weakness good."

"Come on!" Tony called to me from the fire. He stood with his back to it, with his hands stretched out to the blaze behind him. His head was thrown back and he looked down towards me with his beautiful eyelids like hoods over his deep eyes. He was smiling and natural again. His smile was sometimes mysterious as though he knew things I didn't, a knowing smile, and sometimes it was purely kind and affectionate and comforting and so it was this morning.

I got up and went over near him and the hot coffee was wonderful and restoring.

All day as we slowly wound our way up the Hondo road, back and forth, over nine bridges, crossing the cold, rough stream again and again, I felt weak, and I could hardly hold myself upright on my horse, but Tony was solicitous and tried to make me forget myself by calling my attention to the red-winged birds that flitted into the shadows, or the brightly singing invisible birds in the higher branches. Once he dismounted and gathered a few huge mauve columbines and brought them to me and they were like large butterflies.

When we finally reached Twining at four o'clock, it was raining again and all I wanted on earth was to lie down.

The old white abandoned hotel was there, empty, and Tony and Juan Concha helped me into it while the others unpacked. They spread blankets on the floor and I lay down gratefully. Tony went out to look for Jack Bidwell but he was away that day.

I don't know how long I lay there. The others came in to see me once in a while, but I told them I was really all right, only very tired, and they left me to myself. There were fires to be made and cabins to choose for themselves, empty and windowless but dry, and then supper had to be cooked. The quiet, persistent rain made a soft, soothing whisper on the roof and I was comfortable enough.

Finally Tony and Juan Concha appeared, carrying a lighted lantern. Juan Concha knelt down beside me and offered me a tin cup, saying, "Here. Drink this. Help you."

"What is it?" I asked them, raising up on my elbow.

"Medicine Juan fix for you. Better drink," Tony told me.

I would do anything he told me to do, and I obediently took the cup from the gentle, solicitous figure bending over me and drained it. It was very hot and bitter. "What *is* it?" I sputtered.

"The medicine," Tony said gravely.

Peyote! Well!!

Tony arranged the blanket so it covered me up and then they, too, left me to myself. Immediately the Indian singing commenced out beside the fire.

The medicine ran through me, penetratingly. It acted like an organizing medium co-ordinating one part with another, so all the elements that were combined in me shifted like the particles in a kaleidoscope and fell into an orderly pattern. Beginning with the inmost central point in my own organism, the whole universe fell into place; I in the room and the room I was in, the old building containing the room, the cool wet night space where the building stood, and all the mountains standing out like sentries in their everlasting attitudes. So on and on into wider spaces farther than I could divine, where all the heavenly bodies were contented with the order of the plan, and system within system interlocked in grace. I was not separate and isolated any more. The magical drink had revealed the irresistible delight of spiritual composition; the regulated relationship of one to all and all to one.

Was it this, I wondered, something like this, that *artists* are perpetually trying to find and project upon their canvases? Was this what musicians imagine and try to formulate? Significant Form!

I laughed there alone in the dark, remembering the favorite phrase that had seemed so hackneyed for a long time and that I had never really understood. Significant form, I whispered; why, that means that all things are *really* related to each other.

These words had an enormous vitality and importance when I said them, more than they ever had afterwards when from time to time I approximately understood and realized their secret meaning after I relapsed into the usual dream-like state of everyday life.

The singing filled the night and I perceived its design which was written upon the darkness in color that made an intricate pictured pattern, not static like one that is painted but organic and moving like blood currents, and composed of a myriad of bright living cells. These cells were like minute flowers or crystals and they vibrated constantly in their rank and circumstance, no one of them falling out of place, for the order of the whole was held together by the interdependence of each infinitesimal spark. And I learned that there is no single equilibrium anywhere in existence, and that the meaning and essence of balance is that it depends upon neighboring organisms, one leaning upon the other, one touching another, holding together, reinforcing the whole, creating form and defeating chaos which is the hellish realm of unattached and unassimilated atoms.

A full realization of all this broke upon me in a new way not just apprehended as an idea but experienced in my body, so that oddly I felt that the singing and the pattern that it was composed of was also the description of my own organism and all other people's, and it was my blood that sang and my tissues that vibrated upon the ether, making a picture and a design. There was such a consolation in this discovery that I was strengthened and raised up, and I got to my feet and went out to the others.

The abandoned little village was all lighted and rosy, the flames of the big campfire ran high and showed up the farthest cabins with dim trees standing behind them, and there was a circle of people lying and sitting in the firelight.

The Indians sat upright, shoulder to shoulder, and their voices were perfectly in unison. They sang a phrase repeatedly, over and over until the waves of it spread rapidly out from them one after another and the surrounding night became filled with it. When it was packed and complete, they changed the phrase.

The waves of their living power ran out from them upon the vehicle of sound. They penetrated and passed through each listener, altering him a little, shaking old dead compactnesses of matter apart, awakening the paralyzed tissues. This kind of singing is mantric and has a magical influence. No one can lay himself open to it and not be imperceptibly altered by it. Few know and realize this, however; people constantly play in dangerously magnetic neighborhoods and never know what is happening to them.

I wrapped myself in my shawl and sat upon a log. Tony's eyes fell upon me across the blaze but they did not linger and he made no sign. I felt a vast peace all through me and a sense of secret knowledge.

Though I had just had a lesson in the invisible coherence of all human beings, it did not seem illogical that I felt entirely separated from the others out here. There was a new faculty of detachment from them dawning upon me, a different kind from the solitary, unbalanced attitude which was the only one I had ever known. It is difficult to define. There was the beginning of objectivity in it, a realization of our oneness and dependence upon all others, with, at the same time, the realization of the need for withdrawal, for independence, for non-identification with the mass. In a new dimension one might, nay must, realize that one is related to and identified with this universe and all its aspects, and yet that one must become more than that, more than a bright neighborly cell in the great organism. One must know that one is that cell, seeing it flash, and sensing the quiver and vibration of being, one must observe and keep the order of creation, always understanding one is a part of that scheme, but the step beyond is to know that one is also more than that, and in the strict detachment from organic life that characterizes the new-born observer, he watches himself functioning as a material cell, and by this detachment he draws the material to nourish the infant soul up out of the observed activity of the organism. How this flash of revelation worked out into fact and substance took twenty years of living to be proved a reality.

The Indians sang for many hours until one by one our party slipped away, but I sat sleepless all night and I felt fresh and made over when morning came.

That long, wakeful night was the most clarifying I had ever had, and the momentary glimpse of life I was given by an expansion of consciousness always remained with me, though it was often forgotten.

Just before dawn when I was lying down again in the bare room, Juan Concha returned and knelt beside me, and he said in the kind, gentle Indian way, "Come now! Drink again and you be well and strong." He put the cup to my lips and I drank the hot infusion obediently. Then he left me, and soon I heard the camp awakening outside, someone chopping wood, and low voices speaking together in the high, clear morning stillness. I had never had an awakening like that one. Though I had not actually slept, it was as though I had, as though I had always been asleep and was awake now for the first time.

The release from the troubled, senseless, nightmarish night my life had been, the relief at coming back to the reality of the bright, confident day, was overwhelming. I could feel my quivering nerves and my loud, frightened heart gradually compose themselves after a lifetime of concealed apprehension and alarm.

I lay there and gave myself up to the luxury of being at peace within the framework of a vast, beautiful creation. Safe. Nothing mattered. Knowing what I knew now, nothing mattered, everything was taken care of. I was taken care of, and what we saw about us was a mask for something else far more meaningful than anyone knew.

Little things happened, and plans changed and it was all significant, though no one knew what it meant. The setting was so full of splendor and majesty I wondered how we could bear it. How could we endure the sight of these great pine trees *growing,* living in growth, pulsating in their deep, green-springing, upward urge, vibrating through and through with life and making their low strong music? How support the shining sky and the torrential stream, knowing their relation to each other, perceiving their mysterious connection? No, not knowing it, being it, experiencing all that in oneself because one was not cut off from life any more.

So that from now on one would not look at life again and read it as one reads in a book, and learn its constituents as one learns lists; all this learning in the brain, and never in the blood was ended. One could really learn only by being, by awakening gradually to more and more consciousness, and consciousness is born and bred and developed in the whole body and not only in the mind where ideas about life isolate themselves and leave the heart and soul to lapse inert and fade away. Yet never to cease watching was imperative also; to be aware, to notice and observe, and to realize the form and color of all, the action and the result of action, letting the substance create the picture out of abstract consciousness, being always oneself the actor and at the same time the observer, without whom no picture can exist.

This new way of perception was speeding through me, informing every part with its message, while outside the business of life went on apparently as accidental and as unimportant as ever.

Breakfast was prepared, someone had caught cold in the night, Jack Bidwell arrived driven in a two-seated buggy by a Mexican and joined the group who were drinking coffee around the fire. Then horses were saddled, one of the Indian's guns could not be found, Mary's horse threw her and her back was hurt.

A cloud scurried across the sun, the rain began to fall again, and the others decided to give up going on higher to Blue Lake and to return to Taos, letting Mary drive back with the Mexican. All very strange and like the activity of ants, purposeful and mysterious.

Then Tony and I alone were climbing on horseback up the steep mountain to the ridge towering above us in the clouds.

For a long time the strangeness preoccupied me and we did not talk. This was a new world and I was so taken up with it, observing it and myself in it, seeing beauty in a new way that I could say nothing. Up and up we climbed past the pine forests, until we reached the soft, bare windswept summit, and it was narrow and empty, with both sides sloping steeply down. It was a long, undulating ridge and it was carpeted with a dry, furry growth that had no sap or juice. There was a strong, sweet perfume in the air and I saw that the vegetation, for all its aridity, was thickly studded with tiny flowers; they were deeply blue and breathing out a powerful scent that came to us on the gusty wandering wind of that high, empty place.

"Oh, lovely! Like forget-me-nots!" I exclaimed, and Tony got off his horse and plucked a few of these and gave them to me. They were like small stars and their stems were as dry as straw.

The clouds lifted and the sun came down on us, and I was surprised to find it almost white, for we were high up where the yellow is drained away. We ourselves, and our horses, and the earth and the shadows upon it, were colorless and combined into a black and white picture, and only the intense blue flowers held on to their color. Strange that as soon as I had been shown living color down below in Twining, I had left it and now I could see non-color just as plainly.

On and on we marched high above the world, which, when we looked down upon it on either side, seemed composed of wave after wave of mountain ranges like a stormy ocean and we on the high crest.

At midday the mountains were rising and dipping in broader meadowlands, and the space we crossed had widened. Here great flocks of sheep grazed and we came upon a shepherd cooking dinner in a black iron pot hung over a fire that was pale in the high noon.

We stopped with him and he fed us well, making hot tortillas on a heated stone and offering us the tender meat of his lamb stew. We hooked out our portions with sharpened sticks and ate it with salt and the sweet-tasting toasted bread.

Tony and he chatted in Spanish together about the flock and the pasture and the rain, and I understood what they said but I only listened and never spoke.

After lunch the men threw themselves face down upon the ground and slept while I sat and took account of myself. I

HARVEST   *by Ernest Knee*

felt invisible and yet a participant: the self and the non-self were on a journey together.

We went on in an hour, crossing up over peaks, then dipping down again. The sun pealed over the sky like a bell swinging and we heard it. Towards the end of the afternoon we came upon a forest of shining silver tree trunks; without branches, with no trace of color upon them or under them, they stood gleaming, lifeless, in the light of the pale sunshine. They were musical like trumpets and I stopped my horse in amazement. On all this strange journey I had not seen anything so wondrous as those tall silver tree trunks. Tony saw me staring at them and he smiled.

"Forest fire," he explained. "Nothing left but the tree trunks. The wind an' rain an' sun make them nice, like silver."

We went on. I thought, How I would like to have one of those trees! Could one be brought down to the new house? How far, far away out of the strangeness that seemed.

After a while we stood side by side upon a high peak and Tony was pointing downwards.

I looked and my heart stopped, for the face of the Lake gazed up at us. It was directly below, a pool of lambent burning blue. It smiled. It had life, it had conscious life. I knew it.

"Wonderful," Tony said in a low voice. "Blue Lake."

We wound down until we were beside it. It was sunset and the air was still as at sunrise and the Lake lay in the stillness.

We dismounted and sat beside the deep blue water for a while. The pine trees sloped steeply down all around its edge except at one end where it flowed out forever, down the long decline of the canyon, down the mountain, down the mountain, down the canyon, turning, twisting, persisting upon its course until it came to Taos Valley, crossed it, fell into the Rio Grande, and ran down to the Gulf of Mexico where In-

2 3

dians like these drink it, and it binds them further into one flesh and blood.

"I can see life whole," I said to Tony, beginning to talk again after the silent day.

"Yes," he answered.

"My voice sounds queer. It seems to be over there," I told him. "Does it sound over there or here to you?" I asked.

"That's all right. You here, you there, both. The medicine show you." He smiled reassuringly.

We mounted and went down into the world. It took hours and hours, for the horses were tired and it was twenty-two miles from the Lake to the Pueblo.

We reached it after midnight and it was all asleep and quiet, and Tony skirted the broken adobe wall around the village so as not to disturb anyone. But our horses' hooves made a clatter upon stones and in an instant two Indians came running up to us. They spoke in some excitement to Tony.

He calmed them and they slid away and we went on down the lane towards Taos that seemed thick and soft and perfumed with a summer unlike the one we had left behind us.

"What was the matter with them?" I asked Tony.

"Watching," he replied briefly.

"Watching what?" I persisted.

"Oh, watching for Mexicans an' Americans an' animals," he explained.

He left me at the gate of Manby's house and then vanished into the night with the two tired horses.

Chapter Thirty-two

WE HAD bought a little tepee to take to Blue Lake with us, and now I had Tony put it up in the garden for me. I liked to go out and lie upon the cool grass inside it and be alone.

Maurice was delayed in completing the head of Albidia. Soon it would be the first of August and he was not by any means ready to go, and we all seemed to be living in a period of suspension. Had it not been for the sweet, easy atmosphere and the reassurance of the work going on over there across the fields behind Manby's house, I would not have been as patient as I was, for I had not learned anything about patience yet.

Finally he was almost ready to leave Taos, though it would be some time after the first of August.

I had heard from Tony of a big Corn Dance that would be going on all day on the fourth of August in Santo Domingo Pueblo and I decided to drive down to it. I thought while Maurice was going away I would absent myself, for I had a tender, soft, sorry feeling about him now. Perhaps I never loved him naturally until now, with a gentle, upspringing affection, an unselfish comprehension of his difficulties, as one, as most people, would have for a dear friend, as I perhaps had never had for anyone. For even my friendship for Hutch had been self-seeking, clutching at comfort and reassurance. Now it seemed as though the human responses were coming of their own accord, and I could be fond and affectionate and regretful. But I could not say so to anyone yet. I was alive but

I did not know how to show it. The machinery of real human intercourse was rusty and out of repair. Since how long? Perhaps since childhood. Only with Tony could I act like a human being, spontaneous, unconscious, and real.

I moved in a vague silence most of the time, though I was not unhappy any more, and since I was not unhappy now, I ceased my old continuous carping and criticizing of others, that inner comment that had nearly always been going on, that sly and miserable, inward, forever dissatisfied picking upon everyone I encountered. They had been hard to bear, all the years of my one-sided perception! Worse for me, I imagine, than for the subjects of my penetrating searchlight. I had not so loved the world that I could give myself to it and so sanctify my brief lifetime here, and I had felt it was none of my fault that I had not been able to do so, and that people were as they were and that I saw them through and through, and could not stomach them. I think I was right, too. I had not chosen my heredity and my early environment that had so conditioned me that I was crippled and reduced to a limited intuitive capacity to look and look and look at partial portraits of life! Well—compensating for all the cut-offs I certainly had seen plenty if always through the glass darkly. Now what pleasure to see things beginning to shape differently!

Anyway, I had not the courage, feeling as I did, to see Maurice go away. I knew it was forever, and I knew to what world he was returning. I felt I had been delivered from it and that he was still condemned. I somehow knew that I would never have to pretend to be a part of that old world again and that the need to conform to that environment, as Brill had tried to teach me to do, was really not a necessary exercise. Perhaps some day I would try and show how it had appeared to me, but not until I had learned the secret of the cure for it, or completely seen another world that could take its place, in fact, not until I had learned to truly see.

Tony was working upon me continually and his influence upon me apparently came from the way he saw me, how he looked at me. From his eyes came the magnetic drag that pulled up the sleeping spirit out of the depths. As he saw me so I was slowly becoming; he saw me into being.

Poor Maurice. I was sorry he had to plunge back into all that old turmoil with his two black wax Indian heads, while I would be here in this happy place learning how to be human! I let the sadness bubble up and up in my heart but I could not show it to him and he never knew I felt it.

It was a small party that set out for the Corn Dance in our Ford touring car. Tony, Luis Castillano, Jack Young-Hunter, I, and Adolfo des Georges driving us, and the journey down and back comes back in scraps to me now.

When I recall the early morning in camp on our way to Domingo, I remember Tony and Luis warming themselves with their backs to the fire while I bathed and combed my hair inside the little tent, and I can see the air blue with the cedar boughs they burned to saturate themselves with. The blue smoke rose softly and slowly in the early sunlight and perfumed the air all about us. I remember, when I think of these early summer mornings, there were birds that sang wherever one wakened, at Manby's, or in camp; they were real songs, those in the dawn, and I will never forget them; there is no danger that I will, for I can hear them any morning in any summertime of my life. And later, when we were stuck in the deep sand that always covered the road over to Domingo

2 3 .

Pueblo, it is Tony I remember pushing the car, putting his weight against it and almost lifting it out of the deep ruts.

When we finally came to the Indian village it was dark evening and we made a camp outside and soon went to sleep, for we were tired from the struggle of our journey, and in the morning it was beautiful!

The sun was pouring down and taking the night chill from the air, and the sun and the air alone seemed to make life sufficiently rich. The sky reached down to the round horizon, from the darkest cobalt to a light turquoise blue where the hills, shaven clear of trees, made a rippling edge to the great earthen bowl that held us.

This was a very different neighborhood from the one I had grown used to. It was several thousand feet lower, and the Indians of this tribe were of quite another order of being. They were fiercer and more barbaric than the pastoral Taos Indians. They wore their hair tied in the back and had heavy fringes coming down below their eyebrows.

There were more than a thousand souls in this village and they composed one of the most conservative groups in the Southwest, keeping their customs securely. Probably the fact that no American town grew up at their gates helped them to preserve their integrity.

Santo Domingo lay at ease on the plain with the Rio Grande running beside it. The one-story mud houses are older than anyone living can know and the Spanish Church—standing apart and facing the village like a father before his family— is comparatively modern, with its sixteenth-century date.

The village lies in three long streets and a Kiva, or sacred dwelling for communal meetings and religious ceremonials, waits at each end. The houses are white-washed inside; on the outside they are so exactly the color of the soil that they are only distinguishable by the inky black shadows that they cast.

Even in summer there is hardly any green anywhere; this life is all red and magenta and blue and orange against a pink and tawny background. But sometimes a green of the sharpest emerald color cuts through the hot shades of an Indian dress.

This morning was very still: The tempo *molto largo*.

We could hear the ponies in the near-by corrals and a cock or two was crowing. Some woman was grinding corn between two stones, a group of young men were singing low with heads close together, and the blue smoke rose from a dozen chimneys against the pink brown earth. The sun poured and poured down until it penetrated every damp and dreary place. There are no bad smells in this land, there are no ugly sounds here, there are no awkward ways of life. All is serene, and ennobled by the sun.

Fifteen miles away we saw two Indians moving like sticks across the hills, and we heard a woman laugh a mile away. A thousand souls were at ease here. There is sun—air—color—beauty—in space and time.

"Lord, we have done as thou hast commanded, and yet there is room."

All of a sudden a hundred white pigeons were circling around and around over the Pueblo.

We went into the houses with their white walls and heavy-beamed ceilings. The beds were mattresses around the walls, and were covered with bright blankets in the daytime. The most biting magenta and vermilion blankets and scarfs hung on a rope across one end, and the saddles were polished and hung on posts. Near the end of the room there was a picture of a bleeding Christ—and next it was a painted triumphant sun symbol.

Everywhere there were Indians leaning against the sun-soaked walls. They were wrapped in striped blankets and had red handkerchiefs tying back their black hair and they saluted us gravely.

Then came a row of six men, singing. They walked in a rhythmical beat up one street and down the next and up the last and they sang, announcing to all that the Corn Dance would begin soon. They passed from sun to shade and sun to shade; sometimes they were against the turquoise sky—black-haired, red-skinned and flames seemed to pass with them. In the shadow they were black like Spanish painted things.

The people gathered on their roofs, a long line of color against the burning blue; the sun shone in their eyes and they covered their mouths with their blankets, sitting and standing im-movable.

Soon we heard the great drum throbbing. This is the most exciting sound ever heard. It is like hearing the sun beat. It goes right through one in waves—heating one. All around was the dark immobile race, waiting while the drum beat the sun through them in waves of hot sound. These waves make a living vessel to contain the dancers—they hold the dancers in living walls—pulsating but motionless.

Then a hundred men were beating out the dance; it is a dance of the sun energy converted into a man form. Millions of feathers and bells and shells fly and ring on hundreds of men, each man is followed by a sober woman with downcast eyes waving small branches of pine rhythmically, and their feet caress the earth or stamp fiercely.

They sang and sang and turned and bent; the sun-beats of the drum supported and carried them; they were not separate from each other or from the sun. They were all one, and the earthen houses and silent watchers were one with them.

The hours went on; the sun climbed into the blue. It was

DANCING BOY   by Ernest Knee

noon. The pigeons circled around again. It seemed to us that we were losing our identity, that we were becoming one with the sound and the sun-beats. The movement of sound had become one with the movement of our breathing—and we floated in it. We were living in rhythm—we were rhythm. There was no more you or me, or hot or cold, or dark or light. There was only the sun-beat.

The Spanish bell in the church tower sounded suddenly with shivering agitation. We looked up from the bottom of our bowl and saw two Indian youths pummeling the bell with leather mallets. So it was noon. The sun had reached the limit of its climbing, and the dancers slowed down, and gradually the waves of sound and heat diminished, letting it easily die and the dancers left, trotting; the people disappeared into their houses. They would eat and rest now.

Only the sun was left in the village street—only the black shadows and the burning sun. The sun behind the sun has retired; the life of the sun would rest now.

In the afternoon we climbed the hill until we reached the tableland, up the narrow trail we went till we came to the great plains above our bowl. Here we could see for miles and miles. Here we could see how happy Santo Domingo was— lying in the bowl resting. No movement came from it save the blue chimney smoke. We lay on the hot earth of the hill and rested too. The dancers had beaten out our latent sun life —we flowed with them in a hundred million sun waves; they had danced for us until we were empty of our sun-stored life; they had danced us and all the watchers weary. We were empty now. We would be filled again if we lay in the sun on the hill and let it fill us with a fresh abundance. So we became refreshed and renewed and gathered a new energy; so the women can let life pour through them as they become beaten into the dance on the waves of sunlight; so the men remain strong and fierce—always filled with the sun life.

In the evening the warm moon streamed upon the Pueblo as we went down the street whispering. Everyone spoke low. Lights shone out of all the houses, for groups of dancers visited every house.

We followed the feathered dancers: the leader squatted on the ground and beat the drum while seven young men moved together as one and sang a strong song. The babies were asleep in perfect security and all the people gleamed and glowed like coals in the light from the open fire—they were hot and glowing and happy.

Soon it was finished and we followed them out to the next house.

But in the street we saw a group of black naked bodies shining like ebony in the moonshine. These were warriors with emerald green helmets and turquoise jewels and their naked arms and legs were bound with branches of pine. They were painted black and carried notched clubs. They were very fierce, for they had evoked in themselves the sleeping madness and cruelty of men. They were panting from their own darkness and wildness—they issued forth from their inner fastnesses as they sang and danced the war rhythm; they were letting loose all the buried life of hate. As they went from house to house, they left a new trail behind them and on this trail floated out old days and old antagonisms. The air smoldered and grew heavy—eyes were gleaming now, the brows were scowling.

Then came three jokers. Three half-nude boys in masks were singing now in the heavy air. They were imitating the Mexican traders and soon everyone laughed and rocked with amusement. The air cleared. All became very gay and light again. "Noch, noch!" ("Again, again!") everybody begged and they repeated their imitation again and again.

Happy! Happy!

"Let us stay outside in the moonlight, Tony."

"Yes, we sit here."

So we sat together on the plaster wall of the porch and watched the coming and going. To north and south and east and west drums beat and groups of singers chanted the life of the people to the people. The singers and the listeners were one—it was in common.

The moon cut the streets into black angles where silent men moved up and down. Though the night air was cold, it was intensely alive. Here was real living.

All around the pointed hills leapt up to join the moon and the light was so intense that purple triangles upon them marked their deep indentations.

The moon reached its center now and it had come to the place we saw the sun twelve hours ago so it was time to rest again. Tony pointed to the centered moon.

"You sleepy?"

"Yes. Now we sleep."

Again the streets were empty and the lights went out one by one.

We moved away in the sandy road and our shadows moved black ahead of us and we went to our camp and soon everyone slept.

Chapter Thirty-three

ON THE way home from Domingo, we turned off towards the mountain range upon our left and visited Cochiti Pueblo. It lay at the foot of the big mountains that looked, from the high road, heavily piled one upon another.

For some reason or other, these Indians seemed to have mixed more with the Mexican blood than the other groups I had seen. At the same time and maybe because of that, they had bits of carved furniture in their houses and old carved doors and corbels in the buildings which were quite lacking among the pure Indian tribes.

The car had had a great struggle in the drifted sand, and with high centers in many places and it began to sound wrong on our way out of Santa Fe, and grew worse and worse as we went along. Presently Adolfo said that he couldn't make it go any farther until he got something mended. We were near San Juan Pueblo and he turned in there.

By the side of an old stream which was their *acequia*, we made a little camp. Adolfo tinkered with the mysterious machine until he had partially repaired it, but he said he thought he had better go up to Taos alone and get it really mended. He or Tony, I forget who, suggested that we take the little Denver and Rio Grande train near by at Buckman or Chamita the next day, and then we could be met at Taos Junction station with the restored car.

So he rattled away and there we were left under some big cottonwood trees beside the running ditch. But it was calm in the valley with the ranges on both sides of us turning dark while their peaks were still rosy, and the branches of the heavy green trees hung silent and still. We had our camp supper to cook: coffee, cans of beans, little sausages, and the loaves of Indian bread that had been given us, and Tony lighted a fire and filled the coffee pot.

He said, "I guess we go over and see what's goin' on in the Pueblo. Want to come, Jack?" They wandered off and I got busy with the tin cans. We slept that night in the greatest peace with the vast mountains sheltering the quiet desert between them.

Soon after sunrise I was up before the others and standing in the cold water, bathing. It was so good to be down to the essentials of living and to find them as delicious as they were. In all my days I had never lived like this. I was loath to leave the pleasant refreshing water, so I collected the garments I had worn during these last days and I scrubbed them with my cake of soap, standing in midstream in the brown clear ripple, with my gingham skirts turned up and pinned at the back.

I splashed and whacked the wet clothes together and wrung them out. I got wet and liked it. When I turned to wade out, I saw Tony sitting on the bank, laughing. This made me feel how much friendliness there was in the morning; the early sunshine, the fresh cool water, the freedom and ease and Tony laughing in such a kindly amusement. I have never yet seen the mean, malicious laughter of the world upon his face, never anything but the jovial laughter the gods used to show mankind.

It took an extra day for Adolfo to get Oscar Davis to mend the broken parts and then Oscar drove over to meet us at Taos Junction on a late afternoon. The wagon road down one side of the Rio Grande Canyon and up the other was a caution; it was narrow, with a sharp precipice on the side and I was scared, but we made it all right.

We reached the plaza and Jack got out. Then Manby's, and I got out. There was a strange silence and emptiness to face in the house, although there were people inside there. Tony said, "I goin' home now but I come down tomorrow to see how the work goin' on."

Oscar started the car again and drove him up the road in the gathering dusk and I turned in at our gate.

Now I knew that I must really face life. My heart was beating anxiously when I woke up the next morning and I had an apprehensive feeling when I turned into the heavy shade of the curving lane to go over to my own place.

Tony was sitting under a tree, waiting for me halfway over and as I came along, I saw him pondering, as though in a deep meditation. He sat on the ground, leaning against the trunk of the tree, his knees drawn up and his hands clasped upon them.

I reached him and dropped beside him.

"Maurice is gone," I said.

He nodded, but answered nothing.

"Tony, I'm worried," I began uneasily.

"Worried about what?" He looked full at me to search my face. There was a kind, helpful look in his eyes, as though he would do all he could for me.

"About that *peyote*. It frightens me. What do we know about it? I know now that it seems to magnify something in one's mind, and to make everything stronger, colors, sounds, tastes . . . but I sort of feel we should be able to do that by some power in ourselves and not through any outside thing. How do you feel about it, really?"

"Sure. The Peyote is a big power. Why that frighten you?"

"Well—it's about consciousness. Anything that tampers with consciousness always frightens me—consciousness is all we have —just as it is. We have some faculties in us that, maybe, can increase our consciousness if we would learn how to use them. Then there are the things outside us to increase it or to change it or diminish it, like drink, and drugs, and kinds of love affairs. But somehow I feel we make a big unnatural mistake to influence our consciousness from anything outside like those things. Don't you see? *Peyote* seems to be one of those things. That frightens me. I mean it frightens me to think that you would go away from me in your consciousness and I could not follow you or know where you are. Do you understand what I mean?"

"Sure I understand. Then what?" he persisted, trying to help me get it all out.

"Tony! You know if we come together now there's no turning back. Do you feel that?"

"Yes." He nodded. "I know this not play. This forever."

"I mean, I know it is like going across a deep gulf on a bridge that goes with me, is gone when I reach you. I will not be able to return because you will make all of my own kind of life unreal for me. It has always been more or less unreal—you will make it impossible."

"I give you a new life, a new world—a true one, I think."

"Oh, *yes!* I know that—but don't you see? Because it will be true and what I want, I am afraid of the *peyote*. I am afraid the *peyote* will make it unreal, make you seem unreal if you are using it. If I come together with you, won't you give up the *peyote*?" I begged, terribly in earnest.

"I guess you not makin' a bargain with me," he replied as though announcing a fact. "No. We not makin' a trade to-

2 4

gether. I always goin' to do things because that help you, make
you happy, make you feel life good. You goin' to do the way
I want because you want to make the life good. No need to
bargain, us!"

Well, this was making me feel a little ashamed now. Why
could I not take a big, broad view of things as he always did
—trust him? I knew I could trust him. Why did I not act
upon my trust?

He went on after a silent moment.

"It's not important, that Peyote. I mean it's not important
to use it. One must know it is a big thing God put here in
the world, but one doesn't have to use it. Better not to use
it than not use it right. Ever'thing must be used right. I have
seen that. Trouble. Danger. But you not be worried. Ever'thing
goin' to be all right. You see."

He rose and pulled me to my feet.

"We go see the new room now," he said. "That be nice?"

In the few days' absence there was a difference to be found
over there.

The wall was up so high that now the beams must be laid
across them and the roof would be started. The roof! Everyone here felt it to be the most significant part of a house, and
it took the longest time of all the building to do, for it had
to have first the beams, then the ceiling of the fitted saplings,
then the layer of sweet-clover or sage to spread wet mud upon,
four inches deep.

An air space came next, and after that the joists, of two-
by-four pieces of lumber; upon these the rough boards of the
roof, sloping one inch to a foot, and again the mud, mud,
mud! Around the top of the house, to hide the slope, a little
wall must be built to make the house look as level as a box.

In the case of our big room, we need not have gone to all

this roof-work, for almost immediately we went on to build two bedrooms and an open sleeping porch on top of it. This would be the second time a second story and sleeping porch of adobe would be seen in Taos. The Harwoods had the first one.

I spent the day at the house, going home at noon to fetch some lunch and to see John for a few moments. He seemed occupied with his own concerns and I went quickly back to the place that was coming to feel like a home.

When Tony walked home with me at five o'clock, he stopped in the garden beside the tent which was already set up again under the trees.

The day had been smooth and full of certainty, and the reassurance I had learned to draw for myself from the poise of the Indians was deep in me. They could always drive away the peculiar nervousness and anxiety that waited beneath the surface ready to lay assault upon my composure. It is true they had great direct problems to face, problems connected with the welfare of their crops, their children, their land, and their religion. They had always had an uncertain tenure of peace since the Spaniards had first broken their ancient adaptation to life. But they did not go about ridden by fears and worries; they were free in their souls. When a difficulty came they took issue with it but they never anticipated it. They lived in the here and now, giving little energy to past or future. They were not neurotic. The word is out at last. The Indians were not neurotic, for they had not lost their vision of creation. They had not any phrase about life in their language, like ours when we speak of "the creation *myth*"! They were too healthy for words like that. Now I had come to the place where one life ends and another may begin. The old mythical life could end at last. I looked up at Tony where he stood so serious, sure, and strong. For the first time in my life I had discovered I could trust someone always and that I could be trustworthy to someone always and that this would be true in spite of anything we could do!

He bent a firm, gentle look down upon me and held out his hand, and I took it.

"I comin' here to this tepee tonight," he said, "when darkness here. That be right?"

"Yes, Tony," I said, "that will be right."

And it was right.

Index

335